HOUSEHOLD SERVANTS IN
EARLY MODERN ENGLAND

Manchester University Press

Figure 1 Susan Gill, maidservant to the Beale family, by Charles Beale II (1680s) (British Museum)

HOUSEHOLD SERVANTS IN
EARLY MODERN ENGLAND

R. C. RICHARDSON

Manchester University Press
Manchester and New York
distributed in the United States exclusively by Palgrave Macmillan

Published by Manchester University Press
Oxford Road, Manchester M13 9NR, UK
and Room 400, 175 Fifth Avenue, New York, NY 10010, USA
www.manchesteruniversitypress.co.uk

Distributed in the United States exclusively by
Palgrave Macmillan, 175 Fifth Avenue, New York,
NY 10010, USA

Distributed in Canada exclusively by
UBC Press, University of British Columbia, 2029 West Mall,
Vancouver, BC, Canada V6T 1Z2

British Library Cataloguing-in-Publication Data
A catalogue record for this book is available from the British Library

Library of Congress Cataloging-in-Publication Data applied for

ISBN 978 0 7190 6894 2 hardback

ISBN 978 0 7190 6895 9 paperback

First published 2010

Typeset in 10/12pt Minion
by Graphicraft Limited, Hong Kong
Printed in Great Britain
by TJ International Ltd, Padstow

꞊

CONTENTS

℘

ILLUSTRATIONS

℮

PREFACE

This book has been a long time in the making, much longer, certainly, than first expected. Its origins date back to 1997 when during a visiting professorship at Southern Oregon University to fulfil part of my remit I chose to give a public lecture on 'Servants and Service in Shakespeare's England', one of a number of such presentations delivered under the auspices of the Center for Shakespeare Studies. More research on the subject followed and a much revised treatment of the same topic was presented as my inaugural lecture later that same year as Professor of History at what is now the University of Winchester. My research has continued since then and successive preliminary instalments of it have been published on both sides of the Atlantic.[1]

All this has coincided with an unmistakable growth of interest in house-hold servants in the past, not just in the academic community but in the public at large. It is one obvious expression of the democratisation of history that servants, for so long ignored or hidden from view, should now be capturing the popular imagination. August bodies like the National Trust are belatedly attuning themselves to the changing times. In 1999 that organisation issued a book entitled *The Country House Servant*, and the properties for which it is responsible now go out of their way to parade rather than conceal the service quarters which made possible the day-to-day functioning of elite houses; Charlecote, Erddig, Petworth and Uppark are just four which spring to mind. Even the National Portrait Gallery – once exclusively the showplace for celebrities – in 2003 staged a major exhibition on servants in art and produced a handsome illus-trated book to accompany it.[2] In the last decade also several films dealing with household servants have been released, *The Remains of the Day* (1993), *Her Majesty Mrs Brown* (1997) – a film which no doubt encour-aged the opening up of the servant quarters at Queen Victoria and Prince

Albert's Osborne House on the Isle of Wight to public view – and *Gosford Park* (2002) are notable examples. The television series on *The Servants* (2003) was another landmark. DVDs of the earlier *Upstairs, Downstairs* series (1971–75) are still on sale. Remarkably, at least seven new books on servants and servant-keeping have been published since 2004, one of them – Alison Light's excellent study of *Mrs Woolf and the Servants* (2007) – performing the unlikely feat of establishing a link between the Bloomsbury set and their hard-working, indispensable but much-complained-of domestics. How things have changed from what they were only fifty-odd years ago when J. Jean Hecht's *The Domestic Servant Class in Eighteenth Century England* (1956) stood, almost apologetically, in lonely isolation! There is a heavy irony in observing that household servants in England, the unsung, frequently downtrodden workhorses of the past, are fast becoming a 'fashionable' subject.

What is offered here takes full account of the earlier historiography of the subject and provides a socio-cultural history of servants and service in England in the period extending roughly from the mid-sixteenth century to the mid-eighteenth. (Occasionally, to emphasise a point or contrast, the treatment moves outside these chronological limits). The book depicts service as a vertical feature of English society, extending from top to bottom. It brings individual servants' life histories into prominence and examines relationships between servants themselves and between servants and their employers. The contents page makes clear that this is chiefly a thematic treatment of the subject, though the themes themselves are chronologically handled, and changes over time (such as gender balance) are addressed. So, too, are differences between servants and servant-keeping in London and the provinces; the 'servant problem', discussed at some length in chapter 8, for example, was over-whelmingly perceived to be a metropolitan phenomenon. Not a monograph – its coverage is far too broad for that – *Household Servants in Early Modern England* is nonetheless a survey firmly grounded in the author's own research and brings together in a single volume of manageable proportions innumerable local and personal histories. Its treats a subject which by its very nature cannot be self-contained and so throws light on a great many features of the workings of early modern English society and economy and the climate of ideas in which they functioned.

PREFACE

NOTES

1 For example, 'Social engineering in early modern England: masters, servants and the godly discipline', *Clio*, 33:2 (2004), 163–87; 'Making room for servants', *Literature & History*, 3rd ser., 16:1 (2007), 96–102; 'The "servant problem", social class and literary representation in eighteenth-century England', in S. Barker and Jo Gill (eds.), *Literature as History. Essays in Honour of Peter Widdowson* (London, 2010), pp. 106–17.

2 Giles Waterfield *et al.*, *Below Stairs. 400 Years of Servants' Portraits* (London, 2003).

ॐ

ACKNOWLEDGEMENTS

As with all research projects this one has led me to incur and recognise many debts. I am grateful to the librarians and manuscript curators at the Huntington Library, San Marino, California, the Hampshire County Record Office and the British Library, where much of my research over the last ten years has been conducted. Parts of the book have been tried out in a number of public lectures and research seminar papers where I profited from the resultant discussion. My debts to particular individuals are almost too numerous to catalogue. Stephen Reno and Alan Armstrong at Southern Oregon University made possible and encouraged my work there during my extended visiting professorship in the 1990s. Joan Thirsk, as always, was unstintingly helpful. So, in different ways, were two other former teachers of mine, the late Babette and Rupert Evans of the University of Leicester. Elisabeth Arbuckle of the University of Puerto Rico read and commented on some of my findings. Myron Yeager and the late Betsy Truax of Chapman University, Orange, California, were always willing to discuss and help. Sara Jayne Steen, Irene Collins and Martial Rose have shown a keen interest in the development of the project. Visits to the Huntington have always been made even more pleasurable by the good company and shared interests of Paul Hardacre, Mary Robertson and Barbara Donagan. Yale University Library kindly provided me with a photocopy of the only known surviving copy of an eighteenth-century servants' manual. I benefited enormously from the doctoral thesis of Jane Holmes, a former Winchester student ('Domestic Service in Yorkshire, 1650–1780', D.Phil. thesis, University of York, 1989). Good, long-standing friends like Michael Martin have always been ready to provide encouragement and to share in the excitements of research. I learned much from talking with Gladys Trickle, a long since retired household servant who worked for the last private owner of one of my favourite country houses, Hinton Ampner, a few miles from Winchester. Dongyoung Kim, whose computer wizardry more than compensates for my own ineptitude in that department, has willingly provided assistance in reformatting my draft chapters. First Alison Whittle and then Emma Brennan, my editors at Manchester University Press, have combined encouragement with patience as delays in completion occurred. Research for the project, which had no neat boundaries, no self-contained unitary collections of source materials and which took me in so many different directions and in out-of-the-way places, stubbornly resisted the tight schedule originally imposed on it. But I owed it to the household servants recalled in this study, who had it instilled in them that their 'calling' would not countenance a task left undone, that the book just had to be finished. And so, at last, it is.

I am grateful to the British Library, the Hampshire Record Office, and the Huntington Library, California, for permission to quote from manuscripts in their holdings. Acknowledgements for the illustrations are given on p. vi above.

R.C.R.

NOTE ON THE TEXT

Dates are given throughout following the modern practice of designating each new year as starting on 1 January. Spelling in all quotations, but not in titles, has been modernised. Money values are expressed in pre-decimal currency – pounds, shillings and pence.

1

*

STUDYING HOUSEHOLD SERVANTS

> The history of domestic service in England has yet to be written . . .
> Historians have usually been too little concerned with them. The material
> for their study is scattered and difficult to assess; even the word 'servant'
> is not easy to define . . . Yet the investigation is well worth making. Too
> many persons have gained their livelihood in this way for the subject to
> be ignored by the social historian.

So wrote Dorothy Marshall over sixty years ago in a pioneering brief
sketch of *The English Domestic Servant in History* (London, 1949), which
identified some of the changing trends in household service over a 300
year period, the conditions under which servants worked, their position
under the law, and the way they were treated by their employers and by
society. For the reasons stated in the quotation above the bibliographical
note with which this twenty-five-page overview concluded was necessarily
scanty. A few references to printed primary sources such as the diary
of Samuel Pepys, some of Daniel Defoe's writings, Beresford's 1930s
edition of James Woodforde's long-running and methodically kept
Diary of a Country Parson, and to novels by Samuel Richardson, Henry
Fielding and Charles Dickens were given pride of place. Hardly any recent
secondary sources were mentioned, however, since they were simply not
there to be cited. The classic early twentieth-century history of female
employment – Alice Clark's *Working Life of Women in the Seventeenth
Century* (London, 1919) – held off from offering much on household
service, and the promised companion volume in which this subject
might have been treated never appeared. In default of anything else
on the early modern period Marshall included a rather unenthusiastic
reference to the then recent publication *The English Abigail* (London, 1946)
by Dorothy Margaret Stuart. This book, however, as even the most
cursory examination reveals, was little more than a series of entertaining

vignettes of individual maidservants from different times, written by a non-professional historian. 'This is not a history of domestic service in England,' its author accurately confessed. 'It is nothing so ambitious – or so controversial. Such a history, heavy with ethics and stiff with economics, will no doubt be written some day, but not by the present author.'[1]

Dorothy Marshall (1900–94) herself, despite a remarkably long career, did not go on to write a full-length study of the subject she had opened up in her Historical Association pamphlet of 1949. Her first book, *The English Poor in the Eighteenth Century* (London, 1926, repr. 1969), indeed, had offered very little on pauper servants, the only aspect of the topic which would have come within its purview, though she partly compensated for this in an article on 'The domestic servants of the eighteenth century' which came out in 1929. Her later books took her in many other different directions.[2]

In fact it was an American historian, Harvard-trained J. Jean Hecht (born in 1915), who stands out as the first key figure in the historiography of household service in England. His two publications of 1954 and 1956 represented the earliest full-length treatment of the subject. The first contribution was a long essay, 'Continental and colonial servants in eighteenth-century England', published under the auspices of the university at which he was then teaching (Smith College Studies in History, 40, Northampton, MA, 1954). It was an examination of the ways in which European domestics – French, Italians, Germans and Swiss were the largest groups – entered a growing number of wealthy English households as maids, cooks, valets and footmen, adding an exotic touch, which harmonised perfectly with the eighteenth-century Enlightenment. French servants predominated, partly a consequence initially of the French Protestant diaspora associated with the revocation of the Edict of Nantes. Hecht examined the uneven welcome they received in England from both contemporary commentators and native-born servants. A similar mixed reception awaited the even more exotic human imports – negroes and Indians – who later came in as novelty by-products of the expansion of the slave trade and the British Empire.

Hecht avoided going over the same ground in his full-length book *The Domestic Servant Class in Eighteenth Century England* (a revised version of his 1948 Harvard doctoral thesis), which appeared two years later; the foreigners, after all, could be said to have comprised a discrete group. Like his earlier work Hecht's book was qualitative rather than quantitative in approach. Meaningful statistics, he argued, even those which on the face of it could be reconstructed from the returns for the Servant

Tax from the 1770s, were quite impossible. The eight pages which Hecht devoted to wage rates, for example, were based on individual cases only, which exhibited considerable variations even for the same occupation at the same date. Rather noticeably Hecht's principal sources – newspapers, diaries, sermons, tracts, sermons, diaries, autobiographies, plays – were heavily weighted towards London. Contrasts and comparisons with the provinces, though occasionally attempted, were not pursued systematically. Generally speaking, too, servants here were looked at through the eyes of their masters and of commentators from a higher social rank. Moreover Hecht's was chiefly a static picture; changes were inadequately pursued and depicted. Sometimes his suggestions and hypotheses were less than convincing. For example, was the satire of Swift's *Directions* or Townley's *High Life below Stairs* really directed at servants, as he appeared to believe, or chiefly at their employers?

Nonetheless Hecht's pioneering work had, and still retains, many merits. Placed within the context of the time when it appeared it was self-evidently a notable venture into social history though it was chiefly a 'top-down' view of its subject. It ranged widely across a broad area of subject matter – demand and supply, internal household hierarchies, master–servant relations, conditions and rewards of service – and took tentative steps towards recognising the importance of servants as cultural intermediaries and as agents of social change. Hecht had a good eye for detail and telling quotations, and his text was constantly lit up with personal histories and anecdotes concerning particular servants and particular situations. He posited some interesting connections or further developed some first made by contemporary commentators. The likely link between the decline of small farms and the scarcity of good servants and the association between the spread of tea-drinking and the expansion of servant-keeping are just two examples. He was honest in admitting that he had not explored certain aspects of his subject – Methodism's impact on servants, for instance, and the alleged criminality of servants as an occupational group. But the central paradox of the book, surely, was that having clearly depicted the essentially plural and diverse character of household service in this period the author opted for a title for his study which registered a single *class* of servants, though that 'class' was never really defined.[3] In this as in other respects his landmark study was chiefly descriptive rather than argumentative.

Hecht's work on servants, published in the 1950s, remained for a very long time in comparatively lonely isolation. 'History from below', excitedly advanced from the following decade by Christopher Hill, E. P.

Thompson, E. J. Hobsbawm and others, largely bypassed servants and was drawn rather to noisier and more dramatic subjects – the popular activists of the English Revolution and the later embattled domestic textile workers and rural labourers of the Industrialising Age – and in general to the social history of men rather than women. And when servants did start to attract more attention it was those in the nineteenth century and later who found their historians. With her book on *The Rise and Fall of the Victorian Servant*, first published in 1975, Pamela Horn launched herself into a sequence of books on the subject.

A direct successor to Hecht's book was a long time in coming. Bridget Hill's study of *Servants. English Domestics of the Eighteenth Century* did not appear until 1996, though she had devoted a chapter to the subject in one of her earlier books.[4] In the interval between her book and Hecht's, which she rightly held up as a landmark study defining the field, servants had continued to be a neglected subject. Largely a series of essays dealing with different aspects of the subject, Hill's book – as its title indicated – focused chiefly on the eighteenth century, the same period addressed earlier by Hecht. The solitary illustration – Hogarth's warmly sensitive group portrait of his own servants – which was chosen to adorn the dust jacket further underlined the period focus. But Hill's book contained occasional backward glances to the previous century (the special preserve of her husband Christopher) and much forward looking to the nineteenth century. At times, in fact, period hopping produced some loss of clarity.

A literary scholar by training, Bridget Hill made sure that literature dealing with servants was freely drawn into the discussion. Richardson's *Pamela* had a chapter to itself. Defoe, Charlotte Bronte and Flora Thompson were quoted. Chapter 11 was devoted to 'literate and literary servants in eighteenth-century fact and fiction'. Some chapters had a very specific focus. The rare autobiography (though a product of the nineteenth century) of a servant maid – Mary Ashford's *Life of a Licensed Victualler's Daughter, written by Herself* (London, 1844) – was allocated a whole chapter and carefully mined for all that it could reveal about attitudes to service, the economics of the occupation, servant mobility (Ashford had twelve employers in seventeen years), promotion prospects and servant marriage. The Lancashire diaries of the eighteenth-century Roman Catholic country squire Nicholas Blundell were systematically quarried in chapter 8 in the course of an examination of patterns of servant employment, recruitment, wages, length of service, family religion, household management and employer–servant relations.

Hill's study, no less than Hecht's, was a qualitative, not quantitative, examination of its subject but in the later book the author was careful to avoid even the suggestion that servants constituted a distinct 'class'. They were too varied, regionally and socially, for that to be the case. Hill, like Hecht, conducted her research almost entirely in printed sources but the finished result in this case was far less London-centred than the earlier book. Clergymen masters – who often wrote a great deal about servants in their diaries – were very visible in Hill's study. Diaries of all kinds, in fact, occupied a prominent place in her research. (Regrettably, however, Hill's book came out the year before the publication of Gertrude Savile's extraordinarily revealing diaries, which have been considerably utilised at various points in the present study.)[5] Nonetheless, Hill revisited some of the same ground over which her predecessor travelled. The vexed subject of vails and other perks was covered here, for instance, as it was in Hecht's book, and the gathering opposition to these practices charted; Scotland led the way. Unsurprisingly Hill's book offered more than Hecht's on women and their sexual vulnerability in the household. This author's most original contributions were those chapters dealing with the employment of kinsfolk as servants and with pauper servants, the usually unpaid lowest of the low in the servant hierarchy. Though, like Hecht, Hill was far more comfortable with handling details than trends, there was a clearer sense here than in the earlier book of the elasticity of the term 'servant' and the very broad spectrum of employment that it covered. In the last analysis Hill's book is undoubtedly useful and exploratory, though not particularly incisive. Description too often appears to outweigh source interrogation and argument. The author was on the whole too deferential to Hecht, too content to let his book and its findings stand unchallenged, and to offer her own study chiefly as a supplement to his.

Conceptually and methodologically timid and somewhat old-fashioned was Tim Meldrum's general verdict on Bridget Hill's book when his own very differently conceived study of *Domestic Service and Gender, 1660–1750* was published in 2000. For Meldrum many of Hill's assertions about the nature of household service outran her evidence and she was, in his view, far too willing to back-project anachronistically into the eighteenth-century findings and theories which had more currency in the succeeding period:

> When Hill asserts that servants were 'often virtually cut off from contact with the world outside' with little eighteenth-century evidence to support so bleak a portrait, she appears to have adopted an aspect of

late nineteenth-century historiography and dragged it, mute and pliant, backwards one hundred years.[6]

Hill was also, in Meldrum's view, insufficiently attentive to the wider implications of gender for a subject that was inseparably bound up with it. As a result her book had a 'dated' feel to it. Other studies, he contended, focusing on youth and life cycle, potentially had more application to a rethinking of household service and its place in society, even though in the event these had chosen to offer more on the subject of apprenticeship. Based on his 1996 Ph.D. thesis, and concentrating on the 'undeniably exceptional environment' of London, Meldrum's book displayed an author much more at ease than his predecessors in the field with statistics and much more willing to engage with theory (post-structuralism, for instance), to test its validity, and in some cases (as with the 'threshold' and 'privacy' models) to reject or advise caution in using such concepts. He was also much more cautious than most in generalising about 'domestic ideology' and about treating the intrinsically varied middle ranks of the capital as a homogeneous 'class'. Nor was there much to be gained, Meldrum wisely emphasised, in generalising about servants' work as though it was an undif-ferentiated experience. The drudgery which some in this occupational cat-egory undoubtedly had to endure contrasted markedly with the decorative idleness of many liveried servants in large aristocratic households.[7]

Ultimately, Meldrum in this book repeatedly attempted to come to terms with the varied 'lived realities' of London households and their servants. What employers and servants had to say about their dealings with each other and about their shared and separate spaces, he argued, always needed to be carefully considered. In this important respect Meldrum's principal source – depositions of evidence in the London con-sistory court – came into its own, though he recognised that the very young and the very poor were much less likely to be called as credible witnesses and that much of the testimony provided in the court setting would necessarily tend to be negative in its nature. Words were not uttered and heard casually in dialogue between masters and servants and between neighbours in this period, as the very large number of cases relating to slander and defamation of 'reputation' amply reveals. Meldrum insisted, in contrast to those who in the past had taken a top-down view of the subject, that servants' *interactions* with those around them, employers included, always needed to be carefully weighed and interrogated. 'Domestic servants were not simply victims,' he declared. 'To reduce them to life-cycle pawns is both jaundiced and one-dimensional.' What servants actually experienced in different kinds of household could vary markedly. 'Those historians who have tried to pass definitive judgement on domestic servants,' Meldrum concluded, 'risk building walls around the diversity found in the chapters here.' Even when cursed with employment in the worst setting, servants, after all, unlike apprentices, could change master with relative ease, certainly in London, where there was an apparently insatiable market for workers of this kind.[8]

Within four years of the appearance of Meldrum's book in 2000 another valuable contribution to the growing literature of this subject had been published – Pamela Horn's *Flunkies and Scullions. Life below Stairs in Georgian England* (Stroud, 2004). Less argumentative and combative than Meldrum's book, and aimed more squarely, like all Horn's books, at the general reader, this study nonetheless rested on firm research foundations and was geographically broader in its range than Meldrum's study, which had confined itself to London. By the time Meldrum's and Horn's books appeared household servants unmistakably were becoming more and more noticed. The prolonged period of neglect of which writers like Marshall, Hecht and Hill had earlier complained was over and literary scholars as well as historians were now contributing to this growing field of study. Mark Thompson Burnett's *Masters and Servants in English Renaissance Drama and Culture* (London, 1997) was pathfinding. Linda Anderson's *A Place in the Story. Servants and Service in Shakespeare's Plays* (Newark, DE, 2005) and Judith Weil's *Service and Dependency in Shakespeare's Plays* (Cambridge, 2005) were important and insightful additions to the rapidly extending list of literature-inspired secondary sources. In the same year (2005) the *Shakespearean International Yearbook* devoted a special issue to 'Shakespeare and the Bonds of Service'. (See pp. 24–7.) Moreover, servants were being investigated not only as a subject in their own right but integrated into historians' treatment of other areas of social history. Household servants, servants in husbandry and apprentices had a secure place in Peter Laslett's survey of *The World we have Lost* (London, 1965, 1983). Ann Kussmaul's *Servants in Husbandry in Early Modern England* (Oxford, 1981) provided a valuable reminder that there was often no absolute dividing line between those employed on farms and in dairies and those who worked in the household setting; multi-tasking was commonplace. In rural households servants whose normal work routines was indoors were conscripted as extra hands at harvest time just as at busy times in the social calendar estate workers could be co-opted as temporary, and clumsy, additional staff in the hall, kitchen, or dining room.

The great burgeoning of interest in women's history, of course, could not fail to have an impact on historians' understanding of an occupation which became increasingly feminised in the course of the early modern period. Anne Laurence's *Women in England, 1500–1760* (New York, 1994) and Olwen Hufton's weighty and insightful tome on *The Prospect before Her. A History of Women in Western Europe, 1500–1800* (London, 1995) led the way. Sara Mendelson and Patricia Crawford's *Women in Early Modern England, 1550–1720* (Oxford, 1998) and Pamela Sharpe's edited collection on *Women's Work. The English Experience, 1650–1914* (London, 1998) followed. The growing amount of attention devoted to the history of the family unit was another historiographical trend which directly related to household servants. Lawrence Stone's controversial blockbuster on *The Family, Sex and Marriage in England, 1500–1800* (London, 1977) followed by his trilogy on marital problems and divorce had much to offer on servants and servant-keeping and all the ways, clandestine as well as contractual, in which servant lives intersected with those of their masters and mistresses.[9] Ralph Houlbrooke's volume on *The English Family, 1450–1700* (London, 1984) was joined in due course by other revealing studies such as Naiomi Tadmor's *Family and Friends in Eighteenth-Century England* (Cambridge, 2001), all of which stressed the integral position of servants within family structures. Studies of individual elite families in the seventeenth and eighteenth centuries shed light on servant-keeping and servants in particular household settings in different parts of the country. Miriam Slater's *Family Life in the Seventeenth Century. The Verneys of Claydon House* (London, 1984), Jacqueline Eales's *Puritans and Roundheads. The Harleys of Brampton Bryan and the Outbreak of the English Civil War* (Cambridge, 1990) and D. P. Mortlock's, *Aristocratic Splendour. Money and the World of Thomas Coke, Earl of Leicester* (Stroud, 2007) were three significant examples. A household of a different kind, including the servants within it, had been earlier examined in Alan Macfarlane's *The Family Life of Ralph Josselin, A Seventeenth-Century Clergyman* (Cambridge, 1970).

Recent studies of unmarried women – Bridget Hill's *Women Alone. Spinsters in England, 1600–1850* (New Haven, CT, and London, 2001) and Amy M. Froide's *Never Married. Singlewomen in Early Modern England* (Oxford, 2005) – necessarily paid some attention to the employment and work routines of maidservants. So did Lynn Botelho and Pat Thane's edited volume on *Women and Ageing in British Society since 1500* (Harlow, 2001). The growing number of studies of sexuality have sometimes highlighted the experiences of both vulnerable and ambitious household servants.

G. R. Quaife's *Wanton Wenches and Wayward Lives* (London, 1979) and Martin Ingram's *Church Courts, Sex and Marriage in England, 1570–1640* (Cambridge, 1987) were pioneering ventures in this field. Margaret R. Somerville's *Sex and Subjection. Attitudes to Women in Early Modern Society* (London, 1995), Anthony Fletcher's *Gender, Sex and Subordination in England, 1500–1800* (New Haven, CT, and London, 1995), and Laura Gowing's compelling explorations of *Domestic Dangers. Women, Words and Sex in Early Modern London* (Oxford, 1996) and *Common Bodies. Women, Touch and Power in Seventeenth-Century England* (New Haven, CT, and London, 2003) all made important contributions to the uncovering of servant sexuality and other hidden aspects of their lives. Bernard Capp's highly original book *When Gossips Meet. Women, Family and Neighbourhood in Early Modern England* (Oxford, 2003) examined women's strategies – including those of maidservants – to negotiate the constraints placed upon them in a male-dominated society and their partial success in defining their own separate cultural worlds. Individual maidservants – Agnes Bowker, Mercy Gould, Rose Arnold *et al.* – figured equally prominently in the different women's spheres and life stories probed in detail in David Cressy's *Travesties and Transgressions in Tudor and Stuart England* (Oxford, 2000).

That all but seven of the twenty-four books mentioned in the previous paragraphs were published after 1990 is a sure indicator of the growing interest in the place of servants in early modern English society. In addition many more books on servants and servant-keeping in the post-1750 period took their place alongside them, one of them at least – a densely detailed case study of master–servant relations in the industrialising West Riding of Yorkshire – overlapping with the time span considered here. The fascinating domestic saga of A. J. Munby's late nineteenth-century secret relationship and marriage with the maid-of-all-work Hannah Cullick has been uncovered and carefully explored. Bruce Robbins surveyed the representation of domestic staff in nineteenth-century British writing in his book *The Servant's Hand. English Fiction from Below* (Durham, NC, 1993). On the other side of the early modern period some revealing work has also been done on late medieval upper households and their servants.[10]

Modern editions of some important primary sources have been published. E. P. Thompson and Marian Sugden brought out a timely reprint of *The Thresher's Labour, by Stephen Duck* and *The Woman's Labour, by Mary Collier* (London, 1989). Peter Quenell's modern edition of the *Memoirs of an Eighteenth-Century Footman* by John MacDonald appeared in 1985. Ann Haly and Pamela Horn published a new reprint of *The Complete Servant, by Samuel and Sarah Adams* (Lewes, 1989). Dorothy Wise edited the revealing *Diary of William Tayler, Footman, 1837* (London, 1962, 1998).[11]

At the same time a growing number of studies have appeared dealing with servants and servant-keeping in other countries, most of them written by historians based in the United States. Sarah Maza's *Servants and Masters in Old Regime France* (Princeton, NJ, 1983) and Cissie Fairchilds's *Domestic Enemies. Servants and their Masters in Old Regime France* (Baltimore, MD, 1984) were two complementary investigations which decisively opened up the subject for that country.[12] (See pp. 220–1.) Servant-keeping in Italy came under review in Dennis Romano's *Housecraft and Statecraft. Domestic Service in Renaissance Venice, 1400–1600* (Baltimore, MD, 1996). Outside Europe Gary P. Leupp took up the subject of *Servants, Shophands and Laborers in the Cities of Tokugawa, Japan* (Princeton, NJ, 1992). Books such as David Galenson's *White Servitude in Colonial America. An Economic Analysis* (Cambridge, 1981), Sharon V. Salinger's *'To serve well and faithfully'. Labor and Indentured Servants in Pennsylvania, 1682–1800* (Cambridge, 1987) and L. W. Turner's posthumously published *'A good master well served'. Masters and Servants in Colonial Massachusetts* (New York, 1998) underlined the importance of all kinds of servants to the economic development of the American colonies and the special significance of indentured service within that context. *Maître et serviteur dans le monde anglo-américain aux XVII et XVIII siècles* (Rouen, 1986) was unusual both in blending an examination of aspects of service in the Old World with that of the New and in its interdisciplinary approach.[13]

For boldness of intention and breadth of coverage other publications in this field would be exceedingly hard pressed to rival Antoinette Fauve-Chamoux's edited symposium on *Domestic Service and the Formation of European Identity. Understanding the Globalization of Domestic Work, Sixteenth to Twenty-first Centuries* (Berne, 2004). The book derived from an EU-funded project set up in 1996 which enlisted a team of sociologists as well as historians based chiefly on the European mainland. The geographical coverage of the essays in this volume coincided with the academic homes of its providers; single chapters only were devoted to household service in America, India, Japan and Turkey. An extraordinarily wide range of sources was deployed, though the absence of literary scholars from the project team led to an obvious conceptual limitation and to a notable void in the findings. The result of all this effort, it has to be said, was ultimately less impressive than the intentions. Highly miscellaneous contents clearly prevented the editor from welding them together into an effectively unified whole, a problem exacerbated by the fact that some, at least, of the contributors strayed from their brief. Others tended to recycle what was already fairly well known. Inept translations added unintended humour. The absence of an index impeded cross-referencing. Sadly, the central aim, proclaimed in the title, of connecting household service with 'the formation of European identity' remained elusive.

The sources available for studying household service have certainly become more widely known and tapped than in the 1950s when Hecht was researching his pioneering study. But we must accept that it is almost always more difficult to gain access to the lives and experience of *ordinary* people in the past, since, inevitably, they left fewer traces behind. It must also be recognised that there is a gender imbalance in the surviving records; it is always even more challenging to track maidservants and mistresses than their menfolk. Even in a full-length book wholly devoted to a careful West Riding of Yorkshire case study of the relations between a single master (the Rev. John Murgatroyd) and an individual female servant (Phoebe Beatson) the servant maid still remained in the shadows. Most of what is known about Phoebe was derived from information and comments provided by the caring elderly clergyman who employed her; the religion of the servant, for instance, was inferred to be very largely an extension of her master's.

Nonetheless early modern servants can be investigated and partially resurrected by painstakingly piecing together material drawn from an extensive variety of source material and rigorously interrogating it. Public records relating to the operation of the law in its various branches and to the administration of parishes, towns, cities and counties necessarily touch on employers and servants, and sometimes bring them into temporary prominence, since they both fell within their respective remits. Literary evidence of all kinds offers insights into, and representations of, service and servants in this period. There was a great outpouring of sermons, manuals and devotional literature relating to household management in which ideals of godly masters and godly servants were held up in the national interest for imitation by others. Promotional literature publicising the struggling young colonies in America sometimes specifically targeted badly needed servants in order to induce them to join the migration. Proverbs – always securely anchored in the social conditions of the day which generated them – relating to master–servant relations abounded in the sixteenth and seventeenth centuries. 'England is the paradise of women, the hell of horses, and the purgatory of servants,' said one of them, written down for the first time in 1591. 'Masters love services and not the servants,' declared another in 1616. 'A master of straw eats a servant of steel' was a proverb with a very pointed message dating from 1640 and uttered amid a deepening political crisis which erupted into civil war barely two years later. 'He that has one servant has two, he that has two has but one and a half, and he that has three has none at all' was a jaundiced, world-weary proverb first retailed in 1658.[14]

Drama and other imaginative literature of this period depicted servants of many kinds and in many roles – not surprisingly, since they were a ubiquitous presence in the society for which these media catered and for which they were commonly a major social concern. (See pp. 21–35.) At least one play in the eighteenth century – James Townley's *High Life below Stairs* (1759) – placed servants and the domestic quarters in which they lived and worked at the very centre of the action. Samuel Richardson's epistolary novel *Pamela* (1740) was on the same distinctively new wavelength in having a maidservant as its pivotal central character. Daniel Defoe and Jonathan Swift devoted whole works to denouncing and satirising the many glaring shortcomings of household servants and, sometimes, their masters. (See pp. 46–7, 180–4, 186–90.)

Household servants necessarily figure in the family papers of elite families. Information about household organisation, contracts and wages can be found there in abundance; some of these records, indeed, are not simply a factual record but judgemental in that they provide ratings of the quality of servants' work and, often, specific reasons for dismissal. (See p. 176.) Even more frank comments about servant performance can be found in employers' letters and diaries. Samuel Pepys provides a classic case study of this kind from the seventeenth century. (See pp. 75, 117, 227.) Unexpectedly Virginia Woolf, as a 2007 publication has abundantly revealed, is a no less expressive witness on this subject from the twentieth century.[15]

Probate records, by contrast, provide many examples of grateful employers rewarding faithful servants in their wills. (See pp. 39–40, 79.) Other employers, in addition, wrote or commissioned epitaphs on loyal individual family retainers. (See pp. 12–13, 117–19.) Whole volumes of them, indeed, have been published. J. W. Streeten's *Epitaphia, or, A Collection of Memorials inscribed to the Memory of Good and Faithful Servants* (London, 1826) ran to 300 pages. Later in the century, however, A. J. Munby, mesmerised by the attractions of all kinds of female manual labour, produced an enlarged edition which more than doubled the number of Streeten's examples and systematised its listing (*Faithful Servants, being Epitaphs and Obituaries recording their Names and Services*, London, 1898).

> Perhaps it is no longer possible to arouse whether in masters or in servants [Munby declared in his preface] a sense of the fact that all honest service, and chiefly all domestic service, is worthy of respect and honour. But that need not prevent one from recording the respect and honour that were once paid to it.

Some such servants became immortalised in art, either simply because they were on hand to be used as models by portrait painters like Mary and Charles Beale II (mother and son) in the late seventeenth and early eighteenth centuries or William Hogarth who were also employers or, as with epitaphs and bequests in wills, because this was deliberately judged an appropriate way of rewarding and celebrating them. Charles Beale II's portrait drawing dating from the 1680s of Susan Gill, one of his family's young maidservants, forms the frontispiece illustration of this book. John Riley's portrait of Bridget Holmes, a humble ninety-six-year-old servant in the royal household (1686) – her unenviable chief responsibility was to empty chamber pots – was produced in the same decade. Hogarth's affectionate 1750s group portrait of his own domestic staff (three young women, two men and a boy) is reproduced here (figure 2). Fashionable painters of the second half of the eighteenth century – Gainsborough, Reynolds, Romney, Stubbs and Zoffany – all depicted servants in their art; in Stubbs's case, it is true, the servants were there simply as appendages to horses. At Erdigg, near Wrexham, from the late eighteenth century the Yorke family commissioned a whole gallery of portraits of their indoor and outdoor servants.[16]

In a class of its own is the emblematic painting of 'The trusty servant' (figure 3) which hangs in Winchester College. Dating back, it would seem, to 1579 and first painted by John Hoskyns, a Winchester scholar, the picture was reworked at least seven times in the succeeding 150 years, so that the figure depicted in the version which survives is dressed in a way which does not recall the habit of an Elizabethan menial. The accompanying verse underlined for extra emphasis the features of the servant depicted in the allegorical painting:

A trusty servant's portrait would you see
This emblematic figure well survey.
The porker's snout, not nice in diet, shows
The padlock shut, no secrets he'll disclose.

Figure 2 The heads of six of his servants, by William Hogarth,
c. 1750–55 (Tate Gallery)

Patient, the ass, his master's rage will hear.
Swiftness in errand, the stag's feet declare.
Loaded his left hand, apt to labour saith.
The vest, his neatness; open hand, his faith.
Girt with his sword; his shield upon his arm,
Himself and master he'll protect from harm.

Despite the double explication, in art and verse, certain ambiguities remain, as Mark Thornton Burnett has indicated. There are hints of defiance, perhaps even menace, in the painting. It is implied that, given half a chance, the stag-footed servant would run away. The padlocked mouth suggests that, without it, he would freely and dangerously gossip and inflict harm on his employers; this servant is 'trusty' only through imposed restraints. The tone of the painting is generally condescending and could easily have been resented by those thus depicted. No wonder that some men, at least, spoke up for servants. William Basse's *Sword and Buckler, or, The Servingman's Defence* (London, 1602) was one such example.

Figure 3 'The trusty servant' (Winchester College)

But in these times, alas poor serving men,
How cheap are we grown into.
With what enforcing taxes now and then
This envious world doth our estates pursue.
How poor, alas, we are ordained to be.
How ill regarded in our poverty.[17]

The present book utilises the whole range of the different kinds of sources outlined above but in its coverage does not set out to compete with the grandiose ambitions of Fauve-Chamoux's project. Much more modestly and realistically the geographical coverage here is chiefly confined to England, though evidence from Scotland, the European mainland and elsewhere is occasionally drawn into the discussion by way of comparison. Much is said here about London, the main hub of servant-keeping, as of so much else, though most certainly not (as in Meldrum's book) to the exclusion of the provinces. Different local histories are highlighted here, including those of Bath and other fashionable spas and watering places which required mini-armies of servants to make them function, even though a book of this type, attempting to look at the whole picture, cannot confine itself to a single locality. Drama and other forms of literature add substantially to the discussion by foregrounding prevailing attitudes to household service – and sometimes fears and phobias – among the employing classes from whom these writers were drawn and for whom in turn they catered. This study, therefore, is a socio-cultural history of its subject. Chronologically the survey extends chiefly from the mid-sixteenth century to the mid-eighteenth, though from time to time, to underscore a point about continuities or differences, the treatment moves outside these boundaries. The final chapter, in fact, depends on this for its rationale and attempts to offer a succinct assessment of the place of the early modern experience of household service in England within its broader context in order to highlight its distinctive features. Though nowhere near as ambitious in its breadth as the Fauve-Chamoux volume, *Household Servants in Early Modern England*, clearly, still has a challenging agenda.

The structure and presentation of the findings here blend thematic and chronological approaches. Individual chapters are devoted to particular aspects of household service. Within them the specific topics under discussion are generally dealt with chronologically. Since household service rested on contractual relations between employer and employed, each chapter presents its findings in relation to both parties and to the different expectations and experiences which they brought to bear; both masters and men and mistresses and maids are present alongside each other throughout the whole discussion. This book also recognises that servant-keeping was a vertical, not horizontal, feature of English society in this period. Pauper servants find a place in these pages, as do the often ornamental, self-preening upper servants of elite households.

The structure of the book is designed to follow a logical sequence, though, necessarily at times, since no aspect of this subject is discrete and free-standing, there is some unavoidable overlap. Appropriately the book begins with an examination of the most frequently encountered representations of household servants offered to the public, those present in drama – outsiders' depictions, derived chiefly from the experience and standpoint of those who *employed* servants though ones which still strove to allow servants' own voices to be heard. To balance this there follows in chapter 3 a discussion of household servants' self-representations, contained in court-case depositions and other legal records and in the autobiographical or quasi-autobiographical writings (both verse and prose) of a growing number of servant authors. Uniquely this kind of evidence allows the historian to enter into servants' own life stories, their estimates both of their own role and of their employers, their life style and conditions of work, their difficulties and their reflections on their social station. This book in part, therefore, is an attempt at 'history from below' and resists accepting the view from the top as anything other than partial.

Two chapters follow (4 and 5) on 'Employing and serving' and on 'Housing, diet, dress, welfare, education and recreation'. These consider in some detail a whole range of issues relating to the recruitment and employment of household servants, the changing gender balance of the occupation, pay, perks and by-employments, conditions of service, the sexual vulnerability of maidservants, servant mobility, servant marriage and employers' attitudes to it, educational opportunities, and the treatment of servants in sickness and old age. Chapter 5 partly raises questions about how much bargaining power servants could possess and how and under what circumstances they chose and were able to exert it. Chapter 6 moves on to assess the great outpouring of religious writing extolling the need for, and benefits of, godly households; anxiety-induced social engineering, it is argued here, often inspired it. The next chapter, on 'Order and disorder in the household', follows naturally and demonstrates that the godly ideal was often contradicted by very different and uncomfortable realities. Perceptions of the steady worsening of these realities by employers and commentators in the eighteenth century gave rise to an abundant literature on the 'servant problem' which is discussed in chapter 8. A chapter on the complex interaction of servants and the law follows. In what ways did the law frame, and impinge on, servants' lives, and how successfully were they able to avail themselves of it on their own behalf, are among the questions considered here. Chapter 10 ends the book with a final stock-taking of the findings presented and with an attempt to place the early modern experience of household service within a longer and broader chronological and geographical frame. What was distinctive about the experience and terms of employing and serving in the early modern period? Was the English experience of household service significantly different from that of other countries? Definitive answers to those questions, like so many others related to this subject, are unlikely to be found, but the questions still need to be posed. A history which simply describes and does not interrogate its materials and findings, after all, is a missed opportunity. It would also be a mistake to treat household service as a discrete, self-contained topic of study. Above all, this is a book about social and economic relations, about some of the ways in which early modern English society operated and the cultural and moral climate which surrounded and conditioned it.

NOTES

1 Marshall, *English Domestic Servant*, p. 1. Marshall's pamphlet was published by the Historical Association; Stuart, *English Abigail*, p. v.

2 *Economica*, 9 (1929). Marshall's other writings included *English People in the Eighteenth Century* (London, 1956), *Dr Johnson's London* (London, 1968), *Industrial England, 1776–1851* (London, 1973) and *Eighteenth-Century England* (2nd edn. London, 1974). She also wrote biographies of John Wesley, George Canning, Lord Melbourne, Fanny Kemble and Queen Victoria. Dorothy Marshall's autobiography, covering her early life, was published posthumously: *The Making of a Twentieth-Century Woman. A Memoir* (London, 2003).

3 When Hecht's book was reprinted in 1981 (by the Hyperion Press, Westport, CT) the word 'class' was quietly dropped from the title. Little is known of Hecht beyond his authorship of the two studies of servants mentioned above. After his time at Smith College he held university posts at St John's University and Columbia University in New York. As well as reviewing books in his field Hecht served as General Editor of an eight-volume Cambridge University Press series of bibliographical handbooks published in the 1960s and 1970s under the auspices of the Conference on British Studies, an organisation of which he was a co-founder.

4 This was in her study of *Women, Work and Sexual Politics in Eighteenth-Century England* (Oxford, 1989), pp. 125–47.

5 A. Saville (ed.), *Secret Comment. The Diaries of Gertrude Savile, 1721–1757*, Thoroton Society, 41 (1997). Bridget Hill had no such excuse for not spotting this invaluable source when researching her later book *Women Alone. Spinsters in England, 1660–1850* (New Haven, CT, and London, 2001).

6 Meldrum, *Domestic Service and Gender*, p. 72. Meldrum, like a number of others, was also critical of many of the assertions about family life, domestic privacy, spatial zoning and the chronology attached to them in the work of Lawrence Stone.

7 Ilana K. Ben-Amos, *Adolescence and Youth in Early Modern England* (New Haven, CT, and London, 1994) and P. Griffiths, *Youth and Authority: Formative Experiences in England, 1560–1640* (Oxford, 1996); Meldrum, *Domestic Service and Gender*, p. 73. Chapter 5 (pp. 128–82) in Meldrum's book surveys the variety of servants' 'work' and its meanings.

8 Meldrum, *Domestic Service and Gender*, pp. 124, 207.

9 Stone, *The Road to Divorce. England, 1530–1987* (Oxford, 1990), Stone, *Uncertain Unions. Marriage in England, 1660–1753* (Oxford, 1992), Stone, *Broken Lives. Separation and Divorce in England, 1660–1837* (Oxford, 1993). Stone's findings and socio-cultural chronologies are now much contested. See Helen Berry and Elizabeth Foyster (eds.), *The Family in Early Modern England* (Cambridge, 2007).

10 This was Carolyn Steedman's *Master and Servant. Love and Labour in the English Industrial Age* (Cambridge, 2007). Other notable studies of servants in the nineteenth and twentieth centuries have included Pamela Horn's *Life below Stairs in the Twentieth Century* (Stroud, 2001). Pamela Sambrook published two general books on household servants, *The Country House Servant* (Stroud, 1999) and *Keeping their Place. Domestic Service in the Country House* (Stroud, 2005) as well as a monograph on servant-keeping in north-west England, *A Country House at Work. Three Centuries of Dunham Massey* (London, 2003). E. S. Turner's *What the Butler Saw. Two Hundred and Fifty Years of the Servant Problem* (London, 1962, 2001) offered a very readable popular survey. D. Hudson, *Munby. Man of two Worlds* (London, 1972); *The Diaries of Hannah Cullwick, Victorian Maidservant*, ed. Liz Stanley (London, 1984). On the medieval period see, for example, Kate Mertes, *The English Noble Household, 1250–1660* (Oxford, 1988), Anne Curry and Elizabeth Matthew (eds.), *Concepts and Patterns of Service in the later Middle Ages* (Woodbridge, 2000) and Marjorie K. McIntosh, *Working Women in English Society, 1300–1620* (Cambridge, 2005).

11 Mrs Beeton's *Book of Household Management* (1861) has been many times reprinted. *The Footman's Directory and Butler's Rembrancer* (1823) was reprinted in 1998. Modern reprints of *The Duties of Servants* (1894) and *The Servantless Household* (1913) appeared in 1993 and 2002 respectively.

12 Representations of servants in French drama were covered in W. Hawley's *Servant Roles in French Comedy of the Seventeenth Century* (Austin, TX, 1948) and J. Emelina's *Les Valets et les Servantes dans le Théâtre Comique en France de 1610 à 1700* (Cannes and Grenoble, 1975).

13 Less novel but still notable was the attention paid here to the representations of servants in the plays of Jonson and Etherege.

14 M. P. Tilley (ed.), *A Dictionary of Proverbs in England in the Sixteenth and Seventeenth Centuries* (Ann Arbor, MI, 1950).
15 Alison Light, *Mrs Wolf and the Servants. The Hidden Heart of Domestic Service* (London, 2007).
16 See *The Excellent Mrs Mary Beale* (exhibition catalogue, London 1975); Bridget Holmes's portrait is reproduced in G. Waterfield *et al.*, *Below Stairs. Four Hundred Years of Servants' Portraits* (London, 2003), p. 68. The same book, issued in connection with an excellent exhibition at the National Portrait Gallery, includes reproductions of works by some of the other painters referred to, including Gainsborough's famous portrait of Ignatius Sancho (p. 146); M. Waterson, *The Servants' Hall. A Domestic History of Erdigg* (London, 1980). For comparative purposes Elizabeth O'Leary, *At Beck and Call. The Representation of Domestic Servants in Nineteenth-Century American Painting* (Washington, DC, 1996) is instructive.
17 M. T. Burnett, 'The "trusty servant": a sixteenth-century emblem', *Emblematica*, 6:2 (1992), 237–54. In the village of Minstead, in the New Forest, not far from Winchester, there is a pub of this name with a pictorial sign offering a rendering of the same portrait; William Basse, *Sword and Buckler, or, The Servingman's Defence* (London, 1602), stanza 9.

2

ℓ

THE INSTABILITIES
OF REPRESENTATION:
HOUSEHOLD SERVANTS IN
EARLY MODERN DRAMA

O good old man; how well in thee appears
The constant service of the antique world
When service sweat for duty, not for meed!
(Shakespeare, *As you like it*, *c.* 1600, Act II, scene 3)

Madam, like all other fashions it wears out, and so [spleen] descends to
their servants; though in a great many of us I believe it proceeds from some
melancholy particles in the blood occasioned by the stagnation of wages.
(Farquar, *The Beaux' Stratagem*, 1707, Act III, scene 3)

Shakespeare, as J. R. Marriott's *English History in Shakespeare* (1918) long
since attempted to show, was once commonly looked to as a source of
information about the English past; he was the people's historian as well
as the national bard. Similarly, popular images of servants in the early
modern period have often derived most insistently from Shakespeare's
plays and other drama of the early modern period, in which they are such
a staple element. Firmly anchored in the social and cultural world which
produced it, and catering for a society in which servants were ubiquitous,
drama in this period is indeed a kind of running commentary on the
system of service and its social ramifications. Drama devoted more space
than any other genre of writing at this time to master–servant relations.
A play like *The Tempest* (1611), for example, is layered with representations of the different kinds and language of service associated with Ariel,
Caliban, Gonzalo, Stephano and Trinculo; Ferdinand and Miranda
also, though neither servants nor servile, both choose to serve. Without
a single exception all of Shakespeare's plays contain servants, the only
occupational category to be so represented. Sometimes they stand out

quantitatively in a single play; four of the twelve named characters in
Two Gentlemen of Verona (1594) are servants. In *The Taming of the Shrew*
(1594) virtually no one remains untouched by the experience and challenges of service and serving. In many cases, it is true, servants in
plays of this period are simply supernumeraries; they form part of the
human landscape of the action chiefly carried forward by their social
superiors or political leaders. Some of these servants may not even be
identified by name in the plays in which they figure, their speaking parts
may at times be perfunctory and minimal, and their dramatic impact
almost negligible; they come across sometimes as faceless, passive human
furniture. But this is far from invariably true. Many of the servant characters in early modern drama are highly defined, credible individuals.
They have clear dramatic functions; they are not mere appendages to
their employers. Shakespeare's *Timon of Athens* (1605–08) starkly contrasts the failings of the master who gives his name to the play with the
unswerving loyalty and charity of Flavius, his faithful and long-suffering
steward. The self-serving, scheming, malign, inhuman Iago is central to
the unfolding plot of *Othello* (1604) and is the figure who calculatingly
manipulates his general's tragic fall. No one is allowed to stand in his
way; the stage becomes strewn with his targeted victims. Service and
servants are defining and enabling features of *The Winter's Tale* (1610–11),
a play which contains in Paulina arguably the most perfect embodiment
of service in the early modern dramatic canon. Old Adam, however, in
As you like it (*c.* 1600), though undeniably a less pivotal figure, stands
out as one of Shakespeare's most telling examples of servanthood and
its challenges.

He is the loyal family retainer in Sir Rowland's household who stays on
after his old master's death to face the very different, chillingly unconge-
nial, climate which sets in under his elder son and successor. (A recent
modern-dress production of the play in Ashland, Oregon, depicted the
transformed household as a brutal inter-war American meat market!)
Devalued as an 'old dog' by his new master Old Adam links his fortunes,
literally, with Orlando, the younger son, and puts at his disposal the
substantial lifetime's savings he has hoarded while in household service
as insurance against want in his final, declining years.[1] His declaration of
undying loyalty and Orlando's response are justly famous and highlight
significant features of the ways in which old-style service based on
paternalism and dependence was giving way in Shakespeare's day to the
harsher, more impersonal, economics of the market place.

Adam. I have five hundred crowns,
   The thrifty hire I sav'd under your father
   Which I did store to be my foster-nurse
   When service should in my old limbs lie lame
   And unregarded age in corners thrown . . .
       Let me be your servant . . .
   I'll do the service of a younger man
   In all your business and necessities.

Orlando. O good old man; how well in thee appears
   The constant service of the antique world
   When service sweat for duty, not for meed!
   Thou art not for the fashion of these times
   Where none will sweat but for promotion;
   And having that, do choke the service up
   Even with the having; it is not so with thee . . .

Adam. Master, go on; and I will follow thee
   To the last gasp, with truth and loyalty,
   From seventeen years till now almost fourscore
   Here lived I, but now live here no more.
   At seventeen years many their fortunes seek
   But at fourscore it is too late a week;
   Yet fortune cannot recompense me better
   Than to die well, and not my master's debtor.[2]

It is a language of service which strikes no chord with Old Adam's new, hard-nosed, master for whom commercial dealings, expediency and the needs of the moment are all that matter. Both the past and long service are, for him, irrelevant. It was a cultural change in the nature of service lamented by the author (perhaps Gervase Markham) of *A Health to the Gentlemenly Profession of Servingmen* (1598).

Servants in drama provide links – sometimes literally as messengers – between different theatres of action. Their presence extends the social and linguistic range of the plays. Similarly, they provide egalitarian moments in the drama, not least since from time to time they appropriate wit, an elite plaything. They provide incisive, frank and sometimes irreverent commentary on, and dramatic echoes of, the main action. They confide in and make appeals to the audience and are frequently confided in by other characters to become allies. The porter in Shakespeare's *Macbeth* is probably unique in having the stage to himself for such a relatively long, uninterrupted length of time. Humour is provided both by them and at their expense. They exhibit the hierarchical workings of society. How many of Shakespeare's servants are given orders by those who are not their actual employers but who are simply exerting the natural mastery bestowed by rank? Servants can be exploited and enlisted, as in Thomas Kyd's *The Spanish Tragedy* (1592) to do dark deeds.[3] Honest servants collide with evil masters in Thomas Heywood's *A Woman killed with Kindness* (1603) and *A Yorkshire Tragedy* (1607–08). Service and reward are pivotal to Webster's *The Duchess of Malfi* (c. 1616), and in Middleton and Rowley's *The Changeling* (1622) De Flores's erotic ambitions and humiliations are tellingly juxtaposed. Servant characters dominate subplots, they facilitate the movement of the main plot and not infrequently become direct agents in the action – in a sense, therefore, makers of history in their own right. It is not surprising that the subject of servants in drama is belatedly attracting a great deal of scholarly attention.

In a number of respects Mark Thompson Burnett's book *Masters and Servants in English Renaissance Drama and Culture. Authority and Obedience* (1997) pointed the way in an attempt at a genuinely interdisciplinary study drawing on a range of both familiar and unfamiliar plays. 'The theatre,' he declared, 'discharged a range of functions, both permitting a critical undercurrent to express itself and providing a forum within which contemporary anxieties were granted their most forceful and enduring statement.' Examining the dramatic functions of servant characters in these plays led him to recognise how pivotal these could sometimes be. In *The Changeling*, for example, 'the social order has a servant to thank for its reformation'.[4] Other writers have followed suit in giving centre stage to servants in drama. No fewer than three such studies appeared in the course of 2005 alone: Vol. 5 of *The Shakespearean International Yearbook*, Linda Anderson's *A Place in the Story. Servants and Service in Shakespeare's Plays* and Judith Weil's *Service and Dependency in Shakespeare's Plays*.

The first of these was partly devoted to a weighty special section on 'Shakespeare and the bonds of service' edited by Michael Neill, who also contributed. David Schalkwyk opened with a thoughtful and stimulating re-reading of the culture of service depicted in Shakespeare's *The Taming of the Shrew* (1594) and *All's well that ends well* (1595–1603). Here, as elsewhere in Shakespeare, the coexistence was displayed of older, quasi-feudal forms of service and their newer, more commercial, wage-centred successor. Schalkwyk underscored the potentially subversive trading of places which master and servant Lucentio and Tranio engage in and compared it with the way in which the rebellion of the 'upstart' servant Grumio was quickly defused by rendering him little more than a clown. The braggart Paroles in *All's well*, by contrast, came close to embodying that hated phenomenon of the Tudor Age, a masterless man. Autolycus in *Winter's Tale* was most certainly one of their number. David Evett took *King John* (1596) as his case study, making the obvious point in doing so that the 'Histories' frequently get overlooked in discussions of Shakespeare's treatment of service.[5] It is courtly service, of course, which figures in *King John*, especially in the persons of Philip Falconbridge and Hubert de Burgh. These are faithful, willing servants, even though faithfulness is shown to be a difficult path to follow in this troubled reign. Michelle M. Dowd and Mark Thornton Burnett take us back to more well trodden dramatic territory in their respective treatments of *Twelfth Night* (1601–02) and *King Lear* (1606), though they have many new insights to offer.

Against a background of unidentified contingents of attendants and musicians service figures prominently in *Twelfth Night* and its sexual power games. Viola's version of service, made possible by her cross-dressing, seemingly comes closest to the feudal model; she is not – and does not need to be – driven by economics, since being a servant is for her merely a facilitating disguise and not her regular profession. Viola, however, interacts with four 'authentic' servants in the play, all of them in the household of the countess Olivia and positioned in a clearly defined, though contested, hierarchy. Malvolio, the steward, is the chief of them. He superintends, keeps – or attempts to keep – order in, and audits, the household, and is obviously trusted and valued by Olivia. Anderson often tends to overlook this and gives Malvolio a consistently bad press; to her he is an incompetent, rude and arrogant bully. His social origins are never precisely revealed in the play but his social ambitions, his puritanism, and the attitude of others towards him, would all tend to place him in the middle ranks. Maria, described as Olivia's serving woman, occupies a key place in the play and in modern discussions of Shakespeare's servants. She may well be socially superior to Malvolio, though she ranks below him in office in the household. There is a social as well as moral tension between them. She is clearly at ease in genteel society, is well educated, accomplished and witty. She is the one who initiates the plot against Malvolio. In this as in other respects there is always a threatening side (actual or potential) to her independence. She is the one at the end of the play who appears to be making concessions by marrying Sir Toby, Olivia's impoverished, hard drinking hanger-on of a relative, though in society's eyes marriage renders her 'safe'. Fabian comes lower down the hierarchy of Olivia's household, though not at its base. He takes orders, never gives them. He is conscripted into the plot against Malvolio, eventually confesses details of it, and takes no independent action of his own. Feste, the jester in Olivia's household, like all others of his kind in Shakespeare's plays, has an allotted role in her entourage and has a licence to say, more or less, what he likes. He has apparently uncontrollable energy and wit. He does some freelancing guest appearances at Orsino's court and is always cheekily on the lookout for supplementary income. Anderson describes Feste as 'the most frequently rewarded servant in Shakespeare's plays'. But he knows that if he oversteps the mark he will be disciplined.[6]

The conflict model representation of service in *King Lear* is well known and has received much comment. Burnett in the 'Shakespeare and the bonds of service' collection argues convincingly that '*King Lear* is constructed upon the basis of binary servant polarities'. It is unquestionably a bleak play in which moral blindness and social injustice stand side by side and the instabilities and contradictions of service are painfully exhibited. No play of this period exposes the raw nerves of service in a more telling way. Cordelia and Kent quickly fall from grace at the start of the action, their old-style loyal and unflatteringly honest service spurned. Kent, part feudal vassal, part Renaissance courtier, epitomises traditional values and standards. But he combines absolute devotion to Lear with absolute devotion to the truth. He alone in Act I, scene 1, has the courage to face up to Lear at the height of his raging and tell him that he has wronged Cordelia. Kent's dealings with Oswald, Goneril's hireling, bring the two opposites of loyal service and mere serviceableness into sharp contrast; Oswald is contemptuously branded as a mercenary. Lear's fool, clearly, is no ordinary servant and, though unnamed, he has a status which is quite different from Feste's in *Twelfth Night*. His role as a kind of refracting mirror image of Lear himself has been the subject of much discussion among scholars. But undoubtedly the starkest representation of servants and service in *King Lear* is in Act III, scene 7, where Cornwall's three unnamed servants react strongly to their master's punishment of Gloucester. The first of them uses a show of force to try to prevent the blinding from taking place.

> Hold your hand, my lord;
> I have serv'd you ever since I was a child;
> But better service have I never done you
> Than to bid you hold.

He dies in the attempt, having first mortally wounded Cornwall. The two other servants, not bold enough to openly defy Cornwall in the blinding but disgusted and outraged by what they have been forced to witness, afterwards disown their master and do all they can to help the blinded old man. *King Lear*, Burnett concludes, is a play in which the whole fabric of society and state is shaken; neither masters nor servants can shelter from the shock waves. Anderson reminds readers that the telling sequence in the play of servant resistance to Gloucester's blinding was deliberately omitted from the famous Brook/Schofield production to take away from the audience even a brief moment of moral reassurance.[7]

Shakespeare's servants, all these studies agree, are far more than stock characters and they are not treated patronisingly by the playwright, himself a licensed servant of sorts. Anderson is correct in underlining that Shakespeare's dramatic world and its service sector is predominantly peopled with more males than females, and with hardly any apprentices and servants in husbandry and no black servants. Domestic routines – insufficiently dramatic in their own right, no doubt – scarcely figure at all in the plays, which, as Anderson makes clear, depict both the ideal and the indignities of service and the interdependence of masters and servants. Antony and Cleopatra emerge as the two Shakespearean characters most dependent on servants and most exposed to the effects of servant desertions. Anderson underlines how so many of Shakespeare's servants claim and exert a kind of equality. Juliet's nurse, indeed, seems to go a stage further by almost tyrannising her employers; her garrulity is unstoppable. Sycophants among Shakespeare's servants are few in number; many of them, in fact, see through their masters and social betters and bluntly expose their failings. An absence of servants, as Anderson stresses, shows a lack of, or reduction in, power in their masters. A servantless Lear and an unattended Hamlet, different in most respects, at least share the common denominator of growing isolation. To be dispossessed of his own retinue of retainers is an unthinkingly deflating prospect for the recently abdicated King Lear. The ideology of service in Shakespeare's day, as Anderson's densely detailed book makes clear, was plural and full of cross-currents. The language of service was no less complex and pervasive, and bred a teeming progeny of metaphors.

Judith Weil's book covers some of the same ground as Anderson's but its methodology is less traditional. Theory – conspicuously absent from Anderson's book – raises its head here in the author's explorations of the dynamic interactions involving service in the criss-crossed early modern 'border country' in which they were situated. Service, says Weil, was 'a mobile and adaptive institution', a set of relationships, and servants are 'slippery people'.[8] In examining her subject Shakespeare's plays are *interrogated* here much more insistently than in Anderson's book as 'evidence of how [the playwright] tested and explored cultural attitudes towards service and dependency'.[9] Unlike Anderson, Weil draws heavily on the work of social historians in her treatment of the shift away from older, feudal forms of service and dependence towards more commercial, contractual relationships. She recognises that the long-lived survival of moralising literature about service in tracts, sermons and household manuals was a rearguard action against the growing tide rather than a literal description of real conditions. Much is made of Hamlet's resistance to both loyal and ingratiating servants, Polonius, Rosencrantz and Guildenstern in particular. Hamlet prizes Horatio's friendship precisely because of his steadfast independence. Like Hamlet, Coriolanus has a 'scornful view of underlings' and has an uneasy self-estimate of his own role as a 'public servant'.[10] He is distinctly uncomfortable in this 'border country'. Weil sees discomfort, too, but of other kinds, shown by servant characters in *The Taming of the Shrew, All's well, Winter's Tale* and *Othello* as they get drawn into the strained relations between husbands and wives and the repercussions which follow. But this author is surely right to say that servants are agents and not simply victims in such situations. It is a painful learning experience, based on her observation of others, for Katherine in *Taming of the Shrew* to grasp that outward subservience can be the key to harmony or even power.

Fewer plays are examined in detail in this book than in Anderson's and they are used more selectively to open up the twin related themes of service and dependency announced in the title. Both the fact and the consequences of the interdependence of master and servant are constant themes here. *Henry IV* Part 2 portrays the unrealistic ambitions of retainers hoping for instant gain when Hal becomes king. Enobarbus in *Antony and Cleopatra*, by contrast, is presented here as losing himself when he deserts Antony. Macbeth and his wife, says Weil in a telling phrase, 'become servile by enslaving others'.[11]

Though the representation of servants and service in the plays of Shakespeare and his contemporaries has become a major topic for study among modern scholars, drama from later decades of the seventeenth century is in some ways no less rewarding of study. The loyal Andrew, servant to the character who gives his name to Fletcher's *The Elder Brother* (1637) stands out as a very active contributor to discussion of his master's affairs, as a repository of common sense and as an adviser. He laments the fact that his young master is so wholly absorbed in his books that he fails to understand what is happening around him. He cannot bear to see him cheated out of his inheritance by his father and younger sibling and makes it his mission to ring every possible alarm bell to prevent this from happening.

Servant characters still have a place, though it is often a rather different, less sustained and, almost always, less central one, in Restoration comedies and the urbane, genteel, witty world of sexual politics which they depicted. Servants, like citizens, tend to be on the outside edge of this polite world – generally the setting is in London – though they are complicit in the stage action and facilitators of it from time to time. They are confidants, shrewd observers and critics of marriages of convenience, fashions, manners and polite society's empty rituals, targets of their employers' and others' cruel wit and bad temper. They are go-betweens, double dealers, disillusioned hangers-on who parody the gentility of their betters.[12]

It is rare in these plays to find an employer who does not simply take servants for granted and who, for better or worse, is conscious of the mutual dependence of master and man. But Aphra Behn's *The Rover* (1671) contains frank exchanges between the serving maid Moretta and her mistress, Angellica, on love and infatuation.[13] Servant characters – Dufoy, Jenny and Letitia – talk as equals with their employers and their associates in Sir George Etherege's *Love in a Tub* (1664), and it is the besotted Dufoy's predicament in Act IV, scene 6, which gives the play its curious title.[14] Lady Cockwood in Etherege's *She would if she could* (1668) has a recurring, uncomfortable, awareness of employer–servant interdependence, not least in respect of her own servingwoman, Mrs Sentry.

> I am still so pester'd with my woman I dare not go without her; on my conscience she's very sincere but it is not good to trust our reputations too much to the frailty of a servant.
>
> (Act I, scene 2)
>
> . . . A lady cannot be too jealous of her servants' love in this faithless and inconstant age.
>
> (Act IV, scene 1)
>
> . . . A lady's honour is not safe that keeps a servant so subject to corruption. I will turn her out of my service for this.
>
> (Act V, scene 1)

she says at different points in the play before concluding, after an exhausting succession of near escapes, that the relative safety and dullness of the countryside are preferable to the dangerous minefield of London life.[15]

Though hardly painted in an admiring light the mistress and her perception of the employer–servant relationship stand out most clearly in this play. And so it is also in Etherege's *The Man of Mode* (1676). Dorimant bemoans the low standard of his footmen to Handy, his valet, a man always willing to speak his mind:

> *Dorimant.* Will they ever lie snoring abed till noon?
> *Handy.* 'Tis all one, Sir. If they're up you indulge 'em so they're ever poaching after whores all the morning.
> *Dorimant.* Take notice henceforward who's wanting in his duty; the next clap he gets he shall rot for an example.

Sir Fopling has a different problem – servants' names. 'Trott, Trott, Trott!' he exclaims in horror when given the name of a footman. 'There's nothing so barbarous as the names of our English servants.' The bemused offender is promptly renamed 'Hampshire', his native county, to the general satisfaction of those present, who applaud the simple but effective remedial action. (David Postles's work on the use of servants' names has found that servants were commonly referred to only by a contraction of their christian name. Servants having little standing in society, their names could be regarded as legitimate playthings by their employers, those in public office and others of higher rank. The way in which servants were listed in burial registers – often as mere appendages of their employers – suggests that parish officers thought it not worth their trouble to find out more about them.)[16]

William Wycherley (1640?–1716) displayed few illusions about servants in his play *The Country Wife* (1676). To spread the word about Horner's pretended impotence far and wide in London Quack assures him that he has passed on the sensitive information about his sexual condition in the strictest confidence to servant maids:

> I have told all the chambermaids, waiting-women, tire-women, and old women of my acquaintance; nay and whispered as a secret to 'em, and to the whisperers of Whitehall; so that you need not doubt 'twill spread . . .
> (Act I, scene 1)

For sexual gossip and frank, down-to-earth views on making the burdens of marriage bearable, maidservants, indeed, had no equal. Lucy, Alithea's maid, is always lecturing her mistress on these matters:

> The woman that marries to love better will be as much mistaken as the wencher that marries to live better. No, madam, marrying to increase love is like gaming to become rich. Alas, you only lose what little stock you had before.

And what fate could be worse for a young wife than to be confined to her husband's country estate?

> The country, I find, is as terrible to our young English ladies as a monastery to those abroad; and, on my virginity, I think they would rather marry a London jailer than a high sheriff of a county since neither can stir from his employment. Formerly women of wit married fools for a great estate, a fine seat, or the like. But now 'tis for a pretty seat only in Lincoln's Inn Fields, St James's Fields, or the Pall Mall.
>
> (Act IV, scene 1)[17]

The fashionable characters in his *The Way of the World* (1700) by William Congreve (1670–1729) certainly do not mince words when passing judgement on their servants, or on those who appear no better than servants. Witwoud gives up Petulant as a lost cause, for 'he never speaks truth at all . . . He will lie like a chambermaid or woman of quality's porter. Now that is a fault' (Act I, scene 6). Written off by polite society, Petulant consoles himself with the favours of a maidservant. Lady Wishfort's dissatisfaction with her servants probably remains unsurpassed in Restoration comedy. Peg, her unfortunate chambermaid, is variously denounced as 'fool', 'changeling', 'puppet' and 'thing' (Act III, scene 1), while her lady's maid, Foible, once highly valued, falls from grace with a resounding crash when she betrays her mistress to gain a husband conveniently provided for her, and endowed with a livelihood, by Mirabell:

> Out of my house, out of my house, thou viper, thou serpent, that I have fostered; thou bosom traitress that I raised from nothing . . . This exceeds all precedent. I am brought to fine uses, to become a botcher of second-hand marriages between Abigails and Andrews.
>
> (Act V, scene 1)[18]

Sir Wilfull Witwoud, an ill-at-ease novice in London, for his part can only marvel at the high turnover of servants employed in elite households:

> *Wilfull.* How long hast thou lived with the lady, fellow?
> *Footman.* A week, sir; longer than anybody in the house except my lady's woman.
> *Wilfull.* Why then, belike thou dost not know thy lady if thou see'st her, ha, friend?
> *Footman.* Why truly, sir, I cannot safely swear to her face in a morning, before she is dressed. 'Tis like I may give a shrewd guess at it by this time.
>
> (Act III, scene 14)[19]

Though there are fewer of them, such servants as there are function in telling and active ways in the drama of Sir John Vanbrugh (1664–1726). Herein lies the most paradoxical feature of this playwright. Vanbrugh, of course, was chiefly famous as a leading architect – Castle Howard and Blenheim were his most notable commissions – and in this capacity he succeeded, by innovatively constructing passageways, back staircases and separate living quarters, in making servants an almost invisible component of country house living. On the other hand in his plays on a number of occasions servant characters, far from being out of sight, share the stage with their masters and debate with them on an equal footing. In his play *The Confederacy* (1705) we have a maidservant cynically defending her mistress to her weary master:

> Look you, sir, pray you take things right. I know madam does fret you a little now and then, that's true; but in the Fund she is the softest, sweetest, gentlest lady breathing. Let her but live entirely to her own fancy and she'll never say a word to you from morning to night.

In *The Country House* (1715), a reworking of a French original, he has a master and his servant conducting as equals a reasoned discourse on the advantages and disadvantages of maintaining an establishment in the countryside.[20]

Vanbrugh's much more well known play *The Relapse* (1696) presents Sir Tunbelly Clumsy hastily marshalling his inept servants to receive important guests, and two principal servant characters are provided with distinct roles of their own. Miss Hoyden's nurse is one of them and she functions in the play chiefly as a contributor to the comic action but also as a demonstration of the fact that servants are easily bribed (Act IV, scene 1). The other, who has a more active presence, is Lory, manservant to the financially stretched young Fashion. As in *The Country House* master and man in this play also stand side by side as they exchange forthright views, in this case about Fashion's future options and possible exit points from his unenviable economic position. An army career – Fashion's first preference – is quickly dismissed by the more realistic manservant: such a move will neither pay off his debts nor cover his expenses. The only way out of the present crisis, Lory insists, is by Fashion's appealing to his elder brother, Lord Foppington, and 'like a trout tickle him' with all the flattery that he can muster. Flattery, after all, though distasteful and an affront to conscience, is a small price to pay if it staves off starvation. Without it, Lory pronounces, 'you must be content to pick a hungry bone' (Act I, scene 3). By extension, of course, that would also be Lory's own lot, a fate he cannot under any circum-stances contemplate.[21]

The Recruiting Officer (1706) by George Farquar (1678–1707) does not have servants and servant-keeping at its heart but it does offer some revealing throwaway remarks from Melinda on what servant maids might expect from a young unmarried mistress:

> I must not lose the pleasure of chiding [she declares] when I please. Women must discharge their vapours somewhere, and before we get husbands our servants must expect to bear with 'em.'

Farquar's *The Beaux' Stratagem* (1707) is more expansive on the subject of master–servant relations, with different perspectives being brought into play by Scrub (Squire Sullen's servant), Cherry (an innkeeper's daughter) and Francis Archer (a gentleman of broken fortune masquerading as a servant of Thomas Aimwell). Scrub is all too aware of the necessity of discretion for one of his kind. 'Had I not learned the knack of holding my tongue I had never lived so long in a great family.' But it is a corrupt world, even in provincial Lichfield, where the play is set. Archer is advised by Cherry that to succeed in love 'he must bribe the chambermaid that betrays him and court the footman that laughs at him' (Act II, scene 2). Archer's disguise enables him to span both polite and plebeian society. As a servant familiar with the fashionable world of London he is well placed to hold forth, satirically, on conditions of employment:

> I remember the good days [he tells Scrub] when we could dun our masters for our wages, and if they refused to pay, we could have a warrant to carry 'em before a Justice. But now if we talk of eating, they have a warrant for us and carry us before three Justices.

But he knows a good post from a bad one, which kinds of families to avoid and how to lessen his work load:

> My memory is too weak for the load of messages that the ladies lay upon their servants in London . . . I take care never to come into a married family. The commands of the master and mistress are always so contrary that 'tis impossible to please both.

And he has an intriguing theory about the sociology of illness:

> *Mrs Sullen.* I thought that distemper [spleen] had been only proper to people of quality.
> *Archer.* Madam, like all other fashions it wears out, and so descends to their servants; though in a great many of us I believe it proceeds from

some melancholy particles in the blood occasioned by the stagnation of wages.[22]

But that his role playing as a servant is no more than a temporary expedient and source of humour is made clear when Cherry's offer to him of marriage and a £2,000 dowry is easily dismissed as demeaning. Hard pressed financially though he is, marriage to a servant is out of the question:

> Let me see – two thousand pounds. If the wench would promise to die when the money was spent, egad one would marry her. But the fortune may go off in a year or two, and the wife may live Lord knows how long. Then, an innkeeper's daughter, ay that's the devil. There my pride brings me off.[23]

Young Marlow in *She Stoops to Conquer* (1776), admittedly not contemplating marriage with a social inferior, is notably at ease in the company of maidservants, whereas with ladies of his own class he is awkward and tongue-tied.

A similar hard-headed attitude to marriage, but coming from the direction of the servant, appears in *The Intriguing Chambermaid* (1734), a reworking of a French comedy by Henry Fielding (1707–54). Here we have Lettice, the chambermaid, defending her mistress against her aunt's machinations to get her married to Oldcastle, her elderly, ugly but wealthy admirer. To save her mistress from such a dreadful fate she expresses her guarded willingness to marry him herself:

> for I think you could not have the conscience to live a year or a year and a half at most. And I think a good plentiful jointure would make amends for one's enduring you as long as that, provided we live in separate parts of the house and one had a good handsome groom of the chambers to attend one.[24]

James Townley's farce *High Life below Stairs* (1759), wholly given over to servant life and shenanigans in a London gentleman's household, is considered elsewhere in this study. (See pp. 68, 85, 161–2.) David Garrick's *The Lying Valet* (1741) has a mistress, Melissa, reflecting on the dangers involved in allowing servants to get too close. 'We discover our weaknesses to our servants, make them our confidants, put 'em upon an equality with us and so they become our advisers.' The same author's *Bon Ton, or, High Life above Stairs* (1776) was a sequel of sorts to Townley's farce and capitalised on the continued success of the earlier play. Here Sir John Trotley, dyed-in-the-wool provincial, reluctantly finds himself adrift in London and is constantly uncomfortable amid its loose morals and corrupting effect on honest servants, like his own Davy, coming in to the capital. Always previously reliable and obedient, Davy now takes his cue from other London servants, staying out late, getting drunk, changing his hairstyle and ignoring orders from his master, who rapidly becomes in his eyes 'an old out of fashioned codger':

> I wish that I was to live here all my days [says the liberated, intoxicated Davy]. This is life indeed. [In London] a servant lives up to his eyes in clover. They have wages and board wages and nothing to do but to grow fat and saucy. They are as happy as their master. They play for ever at cards, swear like emperors, drink like fishes, and go a-wenching with as much ease and tranquillity as if they were going to a sermon.

All that Sir John can do is helplessly lament the fall from grace of his formerly faithful retainer. 'Here's an imp of the devil! He is undone and will poison the whole country . . . Servants don't do as they are bid in London.'[25] Oliver Goldsmith's Squire Hardcastle's rustic household as depicted in *She Stoops to Conquer* (1773), with its inept, impromptu trained, ill-at-ease servants easily mistaken by young Marlow for staff at a badly run inn, might well be a representation of the kind of domestic setting from which Sir John Trotley comes. There are echoes here, too, of Petruchio's disordered, chaotic household earlier depicted in Shakespeare's *Taming of the Shrew* at the beginning of the previous century. Some servant stock types in drama and dramatic situations involving servants went on being recycled and embellished even as playwrights knowingly catered in other respects for their changing audiences. Dramatists' representations of servants, indeed, had a remarkable longevity in the early modern period. Very much later J. M. Barrie's play *The Admirable Crichton* (1902) placed a servant character at the centre of the action. But for today's audiences, too, representations of very different settings of service and servants still have a capacity to resonate forcefully, as successful television series and films such as *Upstairs, Downstairs*, *The Remains of the Day*, *Her Majesty Mrs Brown* and *Gosford Park* have shown.

NOTES

1 The practice followed the standard advice offered in instruction manuals. That Old Adam had steadily accumulated his wages over a long period occasions no surprise, nor, given the absence of any defined 'retiring age', does the fact that the old man was still in employment at eighty.

2 *As you like it*, Act II, scene 3.

3 Pendringano is employed to murder Balthazar's servant and is then expediently betrayed to ensure his own execution.

4 Burnett, *Masters and Servants*, pp. 186, 109.

5 David Schalkwyk's book *Shakespeare, Love and Service* (Cambridge, 2008) unfortunately appeared too late to be used in the present study. David Evett provides a fuller discussion of this and other aspects of his subject in his book *Discourses of Service in Shakespeare's England* (Basingstoke, 2005). Judith Weil makes a similar point about the neglect of service as a topic in the Sonnets. *Shakespearean International Yearbook*, pp. 86–102.

6 Anderson, *Place in the Story*, p. 46. As a character always on the lookout for perks Mistress Quickly in *Merry Wives* must come a close second to Feste.

7 Burnett, in *Shakespearean International Yearbook*, pp. 71, 82–3; Anderson, *Place in the Story*, p. 307.

8 Weil, *Service and Dependency*, p. 1. The phrase 'border country', of course, is taken from Raymond Williams, *The Country and the City* (London, 1985), p. 197.

9 Weil, *Service and Dependency*, p. 1.

10 *Ibid.*, p. 33.

11 *Ibid.*, p. 129.

12 Susan J. Owen (ed.), *A Companion to Restoration Drama* (London, 2001), Susan J. Owen, *Perspectives on Restoration Drama* (London, 2002) and D. Hughes, *English Drama, 1660–1700* (Oxford, 1996, 2002) are recent overviews of the subject. See also J. Loftis, R. Southern, Marion Jones and A. H. Scouten, *The Revels History of Drama in English*, V, *1660–1750* (London, 1976).

13 F. M. Link (ed.), *Aphra Behn, The Rover* (Lincoln, NE, 1967), Act II, scenes 1 and 2.

14 H. F. B. Brett-Smith (ed.), *Dramatic Works of Sir George Etherege* (2 vols., Oxford, 1927), I, pp. 58–60.

15 *Ibid.*, II, pp. 112, 143, 171–2, 178. On Etherege see Barbara A. Kachur, *Etherege and Wycherley* (Basingstoke, 2004).

16 Etherege, *Love in a Tub*, pp. 190, 242; D. A. Postles, *Social Proprieties. Social Relations in Early Modern England, 1500–1680* (Washington, DC, 2006), pp. 9–10, 49, 51.

17 Wycherley, *Country Wife*, in E. Gosse (ed.), *Restoration Plays from Dryden to Farquar* (London, 1912, 1925), pp. 85, 124–5. On Wycherley see Kachur, *Etherege and Wycherley*, passim.

18 Gosse, *Restoration Plays*, pp. 176, 192–3, 221–2. D. Thomas, *William Congreve* (London, 1992) provides a brief introduction to the playwright's work and the late seventeenth-century context. A Dutch play of 1682 by Thomas Asselijn featuring a truculent servant was much criticised when first staged for setting such a bad example of the type. Bertha Mook, *The Dutch Family in the Seventeenth and Eighteenth Centuries. An Exploratory/Descriptive Study*, Ottawa, 1977, p. 147.

19 Congreve, *Way of the World*, p. 202.
20 Cited in M. S. Dawson, *Gentility and the Comic Theatre of late Stuart London* (Cambridge, 2005), p. 75; B. Dobrée and G. Webb (eds.), *The Complete Works of Sir John Vanbrugh* (London, 1927), II, p. 215. See also G. M. Berkowitz, *Sir John Vanbrugh and the End of Restoration Comedy* (Amsterdam, 1981), K. Downes, *Sir John Vanbrugh. A Biography* (London, 1987), and F. McCormick, *Sir John Vanbrugh. The Playwright as Architect* (University Park, PA, 1991). Much later Arthur Murphy's now long-forgotten play *All in the Wrong* (Cork, 1762) has the servant Robert doing his best to soothe the mutual jealousies of his master and mistress.
21 *The Relapse*, ed. C. A. Zimansky (London, 1970), pp. 16, 17, 23.
22 Farquar, *Recruiting Officer*, Act IV, scene 2, in W. Archer (ed.), *George Farquar. Plays* (London, 1949), p. 309; *Beaux' Strategem*, Act III, scene 3, in Gosse, *Restoration Plays*, pp. 339, 330, 339, 341–2.
23 Farquar, *Beaux' Stratagem*, Act II, scene 2, in Gosse, *Restoration Plays*, p. 332.
24 Fielding, *Intriguing Chambermaid*, p. 10 of 1790 edition.
25 Quoted in Holmes, 'Domestic Service in Yorkshire', p. 274; Garrick, *Lying Valet*, pp. 13, 29, 28. Garrick (1717–79) was pre-eminent among the actor managers of his day.

3

SELF-REPRESENTATIONS OF SERVANTS

I will be a servingman and wait upon a gentleman and then I shall go a hawking and hunting and have my delight as gentlemen hath. I shall have two new coats a year, I will have my suits of hose, my hats with feathers and be all in the bravery after the new fashion . . .
(J. Fit John, *A Diamonde most Precious, worthy to be marked, instructing all Maysters and Servants how they ought to lead their lives*, London, 1577, sig. Bii)

The life of a gentleman's servant is something like that of a bird shut up in a cage. The bird is well housed and well fed but it is deprived of liberty, and liberty is the dearest and sweetest object of all Englishmen. Therefore I would rather be like the sparrow or lark having less housing and feeding and rather more liberty . . .
(*Diary of William Tayler, Footman*, 1837, ed. Dorothy Wise, London, 1962, 1998, p. 79)

At a time when the rage of writing has seized the old and the young, when the cook warbles her lyrics in the kitchen and the thresher vociferates his heroics in the barn . . . it may seem very unnecessary to draw any more from their proper occupations by affording new opportunities of literary fame.
(Samuel Johnson, *The Idler*, 2, 22 April 1758)

The plays – multivocal by definition – discussed in the previous chapter bring into prominence perceptions and images of servants and servant-keeping which figured in seventeenth and eighteenth-century English life. Such depictions have had a lasting impact. Servants had a place in many other kinds of contemporary literature as well, in sermons, tracts, treatises, domestic manuals, satires, travellers' accounts and all the rest, which offered a predominantly top-down view of their world. And it is this range of contemporary perspectives which have informed much of what we know, or think we know, about servants in early modern England. It needs to be remembered, however, that contemporary images and assessments of early modern servants – visual as well as written – were generally filtered through 'observers', 'outsiders', servants' employers, their social betters, many of them clergymen. Servants were idealised, praised or denounced according to external standards and judgements which derived from outside the inner world of service. Servants' own voices were less frequently audible, since, unsurprisingly, they left fewer direct traces behind in the records. But they are there to track down and, once found, their self-representations – both those unwittingly expressed and those intentionally fashioned and articulated in print – are far more numerous than might have been expected and far more varied in provenance and in kind.

There are a number of surviving letters from servants, sometimes in connection with requests for testimonials and sometimes registering complaints. The Verney family archive contains almost 600 letters from servants dating from 1692 to 1717.[1] Another employer, the Rev. Richard Lardner, found himself in 1745 on the receiving end of a blunt resignation letter from an irate servant:

> I see there is no such thing as pleasing you . . . and though I can't please you I don't doubt I shall please other people very well. I never had the uneasiness anywhere as I have here and I hope never shall again . . . When I am at fault I desire to be told of it but not to be told of other people's. Betty is too good a servant for you. You never had a better nor will have again . . .[2]

The incessant letter-writing which formed the basis of Samuel Richardson's *Pamela*, however, apparently had no recorded counterpart in reality.

Additionally, servants, and not only upper servants, in some cases made wills. Jane Whittle's work on East Anglia in the early modern period discovered sixteen servants' wills, indicating modest possession of land and livestock in some cases. Eleven made bequests to masters and masters' children. In eight cases there were also bequests to fellow servants. The will of Margaret Parke, housekeeper to Bryan Salvin, Esq., of Croxdale, County Durham, made in 1734, revealed her to be a fairly wealthy woman. In addition to bequests to her sister and other relatives Parke left £100 to Mrs Jane Haggerston, her former employer, and gifts to each of the children of her present master, who was appointed her sole executor. Clearly a devout Roman Catholic, Parke made bequests to a number of priests serving in the Newcastle area, and to the English nunnery at Pont-Oise, and she set up a fund which would pay for masses to be said for her soul.[3] William Stoddard, coachman to the same Salvin family in County Durham, who died in 1750, was considerably less prosperous than Parke but left a variety of money gifts to friends and relatives as well as a silver watch and other prized possessions.[4] George Cooke, steward at Dunham Massey, Cheshire, died a relatively wealthy man in 1791, with land and tenements of his own; he was a landlord in his own right. He left substantial bequests to his immediate family and a number of legacies to his employer, the Earl of Stamford, and his children 'as token of the many favours they have been pleased to confer on me'. His own personal servant, Hannah Leather, received the considerable sum of £100, and all the Dunham household staff were provided with legacies of two guineas apiece. No one, it seems, was forgotten.[5]

Servant voices were raised, more frequently and at greater length, in depositions in both civil and ecclesiastical law cases where servants figured either as contenders or as witnesses. A 1581 Wiltshire case involved William Yoonges, a servant who had boasted of his sexual exploits with one Joan Wootton. But he became seriously ill and was stricken with pangs of conscience for his misdeeds. 'I do burn and shall burn in Hell,' he said, 'for my wicked dealing with that wicked woman.'[6] A seventeenth-century Somerset maidservant resisting the advances of a would-be suitor declared, 'No truly you shall not lie with me till we be married for you see how many do falsify their promises. For my part I am but a servant and if your friends should not consent to our marriage we are undone.' A Surrey maidservant, Millicent Corick, complained to the local magistrates in 1703 that she was 'as great a slave as any in Turkey', being constantly overworked and beaten by her master and mistress.[7] In a notorious 1715 divorce case centred on a mistress, Diana Dormer, convicted of committing adultery with one of her menservants, Thomas Jones, the footman in question, had bragged to another that 'his prick was his plough'.[8] Elizabeth Bussell, maidservant to Samuel Firmin, button seller, of St Clement's Danes, lodged a grievance against him and his father-in-law to the magistrates in 1750 for 'their base and unkind treatment' in beating and ravishing her.[9] The same magistrates' bench in 1764 heard the sad story of Dorcas Edmunds, another maidservant, delivered of a bastard child. The father was named as John Brown, a gentleman's servant, 'the said Brown, as she heard say, left England to go to the West Indies and that he is since dead'.[10]

Some servants, sentenced to death for a capital offence such as infanticide, arson or murder, left dying speeches behind which were published as tracts by the clergy who officiated in their last hours and at their execution. The extraordinary story of Anne Green, hanged at Oxford in 1651 but who miraculously came back to life, is in a class of its own. (See pp. 206–8.) Sarah Malcolm, a London maidservant implicated in a case of robbery and murder, provided a full confession when she was executed in 1733. The unhappy case of another London servant, nineteen-year-old Matthew Henderson, was placed on record after his execution in 1746. But such publications, expressly designed as a warning to others to avoid a similar fate, often have a formulaic quality and bear the strong imprint of their 'editors' (often clergymen) and of the Ordinary of Newgate. Servants' own words in such cases were invariably filtered through the didactic agency of another.[11]

Examples of servants' self-representation in literary form are not numerous, though there are rather more of them than might at first be expected. Both verse and prose are included in the surviving texts. Some are intensely personal and stem from intimate familiarity with particular workplaces and work routines; they are chiefly autobiographical. Others are much more conventional and general in their discourse. Some of these servant authors spoke only for themselves while others were spokespersons for their occupational group. Unsurprisingly, since servants themselves were not homogeneous socially and ideologically, both conservative and radical opinions were indulged in print. Some servant authors published entirely on their own account and at their own charge; Mary Collier was such a one. Other writings by servants were 'packaged', mediated or 'corrected' in some way by editors, patrons and publishers. Some of these writings were penned by those who continued in service and never stood outside the work experience they were recalling. Other writers – like Robert Dodsley – had left service behind by the time they wrote about their earlier experiences. Some of these retrospectives – the classic example is that by Samuel and Sarah Adams in the early nineteenth century – were composed when the elderly authors were living in comfortable, self-satisfied retirement and were setting themselves up as an authority on the subject of service. Such differences, obviously, had a bearing on both the substance and stance of the different texts. In no sense can the self-representations of servants considered in this chapter be considered a uniform genre. The different circumstances surrounding their composition and publication, and the different purposes they were intended to serve, all have to be taken into account in interrogating and evaluating them. But simply by virtue of their authorship all these writings occupy a very special status and each demands careful, specific and appropriate consideration.

A *Letter sent by the Maydens of London* (1567) is a case in point. This was an anonymous response to another publication of the same year, Edward Hake's *The Merry Meeting of Maydens in London*, which offered some glimpses of the lives of maidservants employed in the capital. The pamphlet rejoinder may or may not have actually been composed by servants themselves – it is impossible to be certain – but its internal variations in style appear to suggest multiple authorship and the text as a whole certainly displayed some inside knowledge of the servants' world and of servants' social and legal position. This pamphlet, though always respectful to mistresses, consistently defended maidservants' right to decent working conditions, some leisure time, a period of notice before dismissal, and a free choice of their own husband. If maidservants were regimented and deprived of their rightful liberties in the ways which had been called for by Hake's tract then the inevitable result, the rejoinder insisted, would be an acute, paralysing servant shortage in London. Mistresses were pointedly reminded here that – elderly, obese and domestically inept as some of them were – they were in so many ways completely dependent on their maids. How could they possibly manage without their household servants? 'We are to you very eyes, heads, feet, and altogether.'[12]

Whereas the female authorship of the 1567 maidservants' pamphlet cannot be absolutely authenticated there is no doubt about that of *A Sweet Nosegay* (London, 1573). One poem in the miscellaneous collection penned by Isabella Whitney (d. 1573) dealt in a strikingly personal way with the long, regular routines of household service and with servants' duties. Little is known of Whitney, though she was probably raised in London and came from the 'middling sort' of people rather than from the elite. This social fact makes it even more unusual that Whitney enjoys the distinction of being the first named female author of a published book of secular verse. Internal evidence in her poems indicates that she herself had been in service as a lady's maid, that she was single, and that she had two younger sisters, also in service, to whom the advice in the poem was addressed.[13]

Hard work, vigilance, self-denial and godliness are the principal virtues rehearsed in this distinctively framed piece of advice literature. What is unique about this early example of the genre is that it is based on a servant's own direct, intimately unique, experience of the workplace, unlike virtually all the others, which rested on top-down moralising. It has a knowledgeable attentiveness to detail and to practicalities absent in the others which address 'work' as a largely undifferentiated activity. It is full of gentle reminders about all the many different tasks that claim a servant's attention and which should not be left undone:

Your master's gone to bed,
Your mistress is at rest,
Their daughters all with haste about
To get themselves undressed.
See that all their plate be safe
And that no spoon do lack;
See doors and windows bolted fast
For fear of any wrack.
Then help if need there be
To do some household thing;
If not, to bed, referring you
Unto the heavenly King,
Forgetting not to pray
As I before you taught
And giving thanks for all that He
Hath ever for you wrought.

Isabella Whitney projects rare direct servant testimony from the sixteenth century; hers is an inner voice from the world of work in its setting in Protestant households. The Civil Wars in the next century brought new challenges, much destabilising, but also new openings for both menservants and maidservants as they, like others in the lower ranks, became increasingly politicised and swept up in the rapidly moving flow of events. The breakdown of traditional authority and controls and the temporary weakening of the family as a social unit affected servants as it did others. Humble women, too, found their political and religious voice, participated in street protests, petitioning, played their part in defending besieged or vulnerable cities or sites like Bristol, Basing House, Corfe Castle and London, and found a congenial temporary home in some of the radical religious sects. (See pp. 153, 155.) *The Maids Petition . . . presented Tuesday 9 August 1647*, 'the year of England's freedom and liberty', is a telling example of its type. Claiming to come from 'the universal sisterhood' of maidservants and other unmarried young women in the capital, the petition asked for a day's holiday every month, the same allowance recently granted to apprentices. Since 'incessant drudgery', the infliction of their 'surly madams', was their lot, occasional respite from it was their due.[14]

The identity of those responsible for writing this tract, like so many involving multiple authorship, cannot be precisely established, nor can its gendered origins be absolutely vouched for. No such difficulties attend the reader of *The Gentlewoman's Companion, or, A Guide to the Female Sex* (London, 1673). Its author was the twice married Hannah

Woolley, or Wolley (1622?–74?), who earlier in her life had built up several years' personal experience of household service (as a governess) and who published a number of works on household management and cookery in her periods of widowhood. (Her first husband, a schoolmaster, died in 1661, her second – Francis Challiner – in 1669.) Governesses in some ways occupied an unenviably intermediary position in larger households, usually looked down upon by their employers and often distrusted by other servants on account of their separate routines and different lifestyle. Woolley may well have been recalling her own unhappy, isolated experience in service when she offered forthright advice to young mistresses to be more sensitive and considerate in their dealings with their household staff.

> Pride and imperiousness in a great person breeds scorn and contempt in the heart and tongue even of the meanest peasant. If God hath blessed you with birth and fortune above others be sure your virtue shine with greater lustre than others . . .[15]

All servants, she advised, should be treated fairly and without favouritism or anger. They should receive encouragement, be given an appropriate work load, an adequate diet, and should have access both to household religion and to services in church. Faithful, conscientious servants should be left in no doubt that their work was properly recognised and valued.

Woolley's book, an unauthorised publication, according to the *Oxford DNB*, provided knowledgeable guidance for all the different kinds of female servant to be found in medium-sized and larger households, though its perspective, in line with this author's own background, is quasi-distanced from those she was addressing. A lady's maid, she declared, should take care not to give herself too many airs and graces. A housekeeper needed to be 'grave and solid' to demonstrate fitness 'to govern a family' and be 'the first up and last in bed to prevent junketing.' A chambermaid in an elite household should be:

> always diligent, answering not again when reproached but with pacifying words, loving and courteous to your fellow servants, not giggling or idling out your time nor wantoning in the society of men.

A hasty marriage to another servant would destroy any chance of later becoming a mistress on her own account. A chambermaid in a more modest household was advised to be 'neat in your habit, modest in your carriage, silent . . . , willing to please and neat handed about what you have to do'. Gaudy dress, which merely cheapened the wearer, ought to be avoided. Nursery maids ought to recognise the heavy responsibilities that were theirs.

> Be not churlish or dogged [to the children under your care] but merry and pleasant and contrive and invent pretty pastimes agreeable to their age. Keep their linen and other things always mended and suffer them not to run too fast to decay. Do not show a partiality in your love to any of them for that dejects the rest. Be careful to hear them read if it be imposed upon you and be not too hasty with them. Have a special care how you behave yourself before them neither speaking nor acting misbecomingly lest your bad example prove the subject of their imitation.

Cook-maids should cultivate the skills their office required and be modest in demeanour and appearance as befitted their rank. 'Lay not all your wages on your back but lay up something against sickness and a hundred other casualties. Assure yourself it is more commendable for one of your profession to go decent and clean than gaudily fine.' The greasy, smutty work of under cook-maids required them to make extra efforts to keep themselves clean and resist the lusts of forceful male servants. No maid, however low her self-esteem, was safe. 'Hungry dogs will eat dirty puddings.' Clearly, Hannah Woolley, though she had service experience in her background, had never been a cook-maid herself! Her own, more elevated, position in a household hierarchy, which informed what she later write about service, had been quite different.[16]

It is a far cry even from this relatively lofty advice given to greasy cook-maids to Robert Dodsley (1704–64). Dodsley was best known in his own day as an author, playwright, bookseller and publisher (of Pope, Gray's *Elegy*, Voltaire's *Louis XIV*, Dr Johnson's *Dictionary* and the *Annual Register*). But he came from relatively humble stock – his father was a schoolmaster in Mansfield, Nottinghamshire – and, after a false start in the stocking weaving trade, he spent ten years or so in household service, first in the Midlands and then in London as footman to Charles Dartiquenave and Jane Lowther, daughter of John, Viscount Lonsdale, among others.[17] Both these employers assisted Dodsley in launching himself into print with publications which expressly capitalised on his own (sometimes galling) personal experience of service. 'One would be tempted to think that some gentlemen conclude when a man becomes a servant he ought no longer to look upon himself as a human creature but relinquish his passions and retain no sense of anger or resentment even upon the most provoking insults.' *Servitude. A Poem* (1729) and *The*

Muse in Livery, or, The Footman's Miscellany (1732) and his play *The Toy Shop* (London, 1735) were the results. In the play Dodsley satirised the vanities of the age, which included mistresses' preference for the well-being of lapdogs over the welfare of servants. A lapdog's death from catching a chill is blamed on a maidservant's negligence. 'O the careless, wicked wretch,' says the lady informed of this domestic tragedy. 'I would have had her tried for murder at least.'[18]

Certainly no radical – the successful author by this time had moved into polite society and had an eye on social advancement – Dodsley offered a blend of homespun philosophy and practical advice on the mutual benefits of household service, the interdependence of master and men, and how best to make the system work harmoniously. Recognising 'the irksomeness of service', Dodsley advised masters to show restraint and humanity in their dealings with those under their charge, 'to distinguish between the deserving and undeserving', to *encourage* servants, to avoid 'a haughty imperiousness of manner' and 'to command nothing but what is just and reasonable'.[19]

The poem which followed was aimed chiefly at fellow servants. In the text the footman author invariably identified himself with their number and wrote in the first person plural as their spokesman when rehearsing the necessary qualities in servants of honesty, obedience, diligence, submission and discretion.

> Purchas'd by annual wages, clothes and meat,
> Theirs is our time, our hands, our head, our feet.
> We think, design and act at their command
> And, as their pleasure varies, walk or stand.
> Whilst we receive the covenanted hire
> Active obedience justly they require.
> If we dislike and think it too severe
> We're free to leave and seek a place elsewhere.[20]

Moving on to another master, as Dodsley and so many others recognised, was one of the servant's ultimate weapons, and one that was usually to hand, certainly in eighteenth-century London.

In the course of all this Dodsley offered a sideswipe at Defoe's *Everybody's Business is Nobody's Business*. Sidney Lee's claim (rehearsed in the original version of the *DNB*) that the prose introduction to Dodsley's poem may actually have been written by Defoe himself seems intrinsically unlikely. Dodsley's text clearly provided an 'insider's' view of service, unlike Defoe's, and its message and tone are quite different from those of the author of *The Great Law of Subordination*. Dodsley's postscript, which describes Defoe's pamphlet as 'stuft with nothing in the world but opprobrious railings and spiteful invectives against the pride, laziness and dishonesty of gentlemen's servants', seems much more like genuine criticism from one whose own personal experience of service qualified him to know better. It does not ring true as tongue-in-cheek self-advertising from an artfully concealed Defoe.[21]

Dodsley's *The Muse in Livery* (1732) went over some of the same ground, it included an appreciative epistle to Stephen Duck, the thresher poet, 'A sketch of the miseries of poverty', a pictorial frontispiece depicting education as the route to happiness and virtue, and some pointed satire directed at fellow servants and their noisy criticisms of their masters when they gathered together. (The 'appropriation' of satire by servants and ex-servants was a recurring social statement in its own right which will be commented on in connection with some of the other eighteenth-century writers discussed here.)

> Whilst oaths and peals of laughter meet [declared Dodsley]
> And he who's loudest is the greatest wit.
> But here amongst us the chief trade is
> To rail against our lords and ladies,
> To aggravate their smallest failings
> T'expose their faults with saucy railings . . .[22]

In the much later *The Economy of Human Life* (1750) Dodsley, by now a well established businessman and more removed from his earlier years in service, offered more obviously pious platitudes about the advantages of servant life and the honour that came from fidelity to a master. Retrospectives on service from former servants much divorced in time from their actual work experience in that field often lost their cutting edge.

Mary Collier's *The Woman's Labour* (1739) was a landmark publication of altogether different origin, standing completely outside the long advice literature tradition, and came from an author who belonged unambiguously to the lower ranks of English society and whose stance was consistently, even defiantly, plebeian. Collier (1688?–1762) lived out her days in the border country between Sussex and Hampshire; born in Midhurst, she died in straitened circumstances not many miles away in Alton, Hampshire. Her parents were labouring folk and Collier, after her mother's early death, lived with and cared for her father until he sickened and died in the 1720s. Mary Collier, who remained a spinster, had long first-hand experience of service, mainly in the Petersfield area of Hampshire just over the county border from Sussex, eking out a living as a charwoman doing laundry work, brewing and other household cleaning chores. In her sixties she relocated to the Alton area to become housekeeper to a local farmer, moving into the market town itself in 1758 when she became too old and infirm to continue in regular employment. 'I have retired to a garret (the poor poet's fate) in Alton where I am endeavouring to pass the relict of my days in piety, purity, and a good old maid.' Unlike Dodsley, who quitted service as he made a name for himself and prospered, Mary Collier's remained an inner voice of household service always in tune with its pressing realities.[23]

Such early education as she received was from her parents but it was evidently enough to give her a lifelong taste for reading and a flair for writing. She clearly rejoiced in her far from basic literacy. 'My recreation was reading,' she wrote in a brief autobiographical preface to her published verse. 'I bought and borrowed many books. Any foolish history highly delighted me. But as I grew older I read Speed and Baker's chronicles, Foxe's *Acts and Monuments*, Josephus and others.'[24] Mary Collier's poems are her only claim to modest fame and are chiefly remarkable as self-reflections on her own working life combined with some general observations (and warnings) on the world of work. This was a woman whose feet remained firmly on the ground. She had no illusions. Only wine 'makes servants think they have their liberty,' she declared.[25]

The Woman's Labour, her first poem, published at her own expense in 1739, was intended as a riposte to Stephen Duck (1705–56), the labourer/poet patronised by Queen Caroline and applauded by Robert Dodsley. His early poem *The Thresher's Labour* had been completed by 1730 and was subsequently published.[26] Duck was one of the first eighteenth-century writers to dignify manual work as a fit subject for verse but his male-centredness and his dismissive comments on the lesser tasks undertaken at harvest time by 'prattling females, armed with rake and prong' stung Collier into making a poetic defence of her sex and of the often unrecognised importance of women's economic roles. 'On our abject state you throw your scorn,' she cried, 'and women wrong your verses to adorn.' Women worked as hard as men, she declared – even harder, perhaps, if proper account were taken of their combined labour in home and workplace:

> So many things for our attendance call
> Had we ten hands we could employ them all.

Surely, she insisted, women field workers had a right to talk to each other to help pass the time?

... none but Turks that I could ever find
Have mutes to serve them, or did e'er deny
Their slaves, at work, to chat it merrily?
... The only privilege our sex enjoy.

A proto-feminism surfaced in Collier's writing; she asserted the equality of women workers and their rights as Englishwomen. Work, gender, class and nation-building were the recurring themes in Collier's poems, insists Moira Ferguson, a modern commentator. 'Without women, men can't be at all,' Collier stated emphatically in one of her poems. Women had no cause whatever to be apologetic about their roles.[27] That said, Collier's later dealings with Stephen Duck showed her to be a generous controversialist, and she penned on his death an elegy to 'the muses' darling ... immortal Duck' which she included in her collected poems. Her published verse, perhaps not surprisingly, given the man's world in which it appeared, attracted more male than female subscribers.[28]

Having challenged Stephen Duck on his home ground of agricultural labour, Collier moved on to deal with her own kinds of domestic employment, a subject on which she could speak with particular authority and with a certain pride; simply writing about it in the way she did staked a claim for its importance. Washday, as she made clear, in big houses required much care as well as physical effort, since fine fabrics were so delicate, 'fashions which our forefathers never knew'. Scouring pewter and kitchen equipment was hard work, too, and brewing involved a great deal of lifting and carrying. 'Alas! our labours never know an end.' Her discourse on labour might suggest – though how likely it is must remain a conjecture – that Collier had some familiarity with Mandeville's *Fable of the Bees* (1723). Her view of servant–employer relations, however, was understandably more strident than his, or for that matter Robert Dodsley's and Stephen Duck's. The author of *The Thresher's Labour* was quickly tamed by the polite society which had absorbed and educated him and extended him patronage. (Duck was one of the chief plebeian poets celebrated in Robert Southey's *Lives of the Uneducated Poets*.) With Collier there is a clear sense that relentless routines of household cleaning – 'trumpery brought in to complete our slavery' – were unnecessarily heaped by unthinking or indifferent mistresses on their exploited maidservants:

So the industrious bees do hourly strive
To bring their loads of honey to the hive.
Their sordid owners always reap the gains
And poorly recompense their toil and pains.[29]

Unlike Duck, Collier found no influential patron, which helps explain why, in stark contrast to the erstwhile thresher poet, she kept her authentically proletarian muse. She was not coaxed into developing a new, and more refined, 'voice'. But the oddity of her status as the 'washerwoman poet' – others had to vouch for the authenticity of her published work to dispel public scepticism – enabled her to achieve some limited fame and support in her own locality and a modest supplement to her regular income. Her poems were reprinted (with some biographical notes) in 1762 and again (long after her death) in 1820. From today's very different perspective her early nineteenth-century editor missed the point completely by claiming that Collier's verse 'must be a convincing proof to every reader that that had her genius been cultivated she would have ranked with the greatest poets of this kingdom'.[30] Stephen Duck's sad fate – first being publicly paraded as a plebeian phenomenon, then his enforced absorption into polite society and, finally, the imposed drudgery of churning out banal neoclassical verse on demand – demonstrated the stifling, disorienting, destructive effects of 'cultivation' which Collier was spared. Duck's probable suicide was a tragic end to an uprooted life.

Collier overlapped chronologically with another poet – Mary Leapor (1722–46) whose background had something in common with her own. Leapor, Northamptonshire-born and bred, was the daughter of an estate gardener and later self-employed nurseryman from Marston St Lawrence. At different points in her life she assisted and cared for her father but additionally she had experience as a housemaid and kitchenmaid in gentry households and was all too familiar with the ceaseless daily round of women's labour. As in Collier's case these highly focused memories of work routines in household service became permanently etched into her mind and coloured her view of gender and employer–servant relations.

> A wife in bondage or neglected maid,
> Despised if ugly; if she's fair betrayed . . .
> Yet, with ten thousand follies to her charge,
> Unhappy woman's but a slave at large.[31]

She turned her domestic service experience to good use in depicting a kitchen scene in one of her poems, 'Crumble Hall' (based on Weston Hall or Edgcote House, near Brackley, Northamptonshire) which formed part of her posthumously published collected verse (1751):

> The sav'ry kitchen much attention calls.
> Westphalia hams adorn the sable walls.

The fires blaze; the greasy pavements fry
And steaming odours from the kettles fly.

Like Collier Leapor here celebrated the centrality, energy, dignity and
skill of labour; never has curd tart making and even dishwashing received
such a fulsome description!

> But now her dish kettle began
> To boil and blubber with the foaming bran.
> The greasy apron round her hips she ties
> And to each plate the scalding clout applies.
> The purging bath each glowing dish refines
> And once again the polish'd pewter shines.[32]

Domestic details of this kind rather than anything about the finer points
of the architecture, furnishings and polite social routines of the great house
became the main focus of Leapor's writing. She dwelt on the kinds of things,
the domestic 'nether world', usually omitted from top-down accounts
but in a more general sense offered what was unmistakably a servant's
eye view of the whole experience of country house living. To her the library
in the house was a wonderland overflowing with rich treasures of
literature; evidently to the master of the house it was chiefly a place where
he could sleep undisturbed. Fine china and tapestries received no more
attention from her than spiders' webs in out-of-reach places or mice
scampering with impunity in dark passageways. She said more about
servants and their own domestic drama than about masters and mistresses.
A portrait hanging in the hall was likened to 'a milk wench'. '"Crumble
Hall",' says Donna Landry in a telling phrase, is an 'anti-country house
poem.' It is:

> that rare artifact: a class-conscious plebeian country house poem that
> undeniably mocks and seeks to demystify the values of the gentry whose
> social power in large part depends upon the deference – and the con-
> tinued exploitable subservience – of servants and labourers. Leapor's
> poem opens up long-closed doors and back stairways, lets light into the
> servants' hall, shakes things up in a literary genre that traditionally works
> by assuring us that the world is best organized according to ancient
> custom and ceremony.[33]

There was a radical edge to Leapor's writing which Landry highlights.
But as a writer Leapor, generally speaking, cultivated a style – under the
influence of two female patrons, Susanna Jennens and Bridget Freemantle
– which was often too reminiscent of Pope (whom she greatly admired

and whose death in 1745 she lamented) to have the consistently authentic proletarian touch of Collier's less consciously artful performance. In any event pastoral subjects, not household work, were this short-lived poet's usual preference and the chief reason why for a time her work found favour in London as well as in her own locality.[34] Similar to Leapor in some ways was Ann Yearsley, Wiltshire milkmaid, whose poems were published through the promoting efforts of Hannah More and Elizabeth Montague, a heavyhanded and condescending patronage which the rustic author quickly resented and publicly criticised.

Another serving-maid poet of the late eighteenth century was Elizabeth Hands (*fl.* 1789). Nothing in her verse, it is true, expressed her work experience directly – her longwinded biblical epic on 'The Death of Amnon' was her major work – but in some of her shorter poems she offered some finely tuned, delicious satire dealing with polite society mistresses and their disdain for versifying maidservants incautiously moving out of their lowly sphere.

'A servant write verses!' says Madam Du Bloom.
'Pray, what is the subject? – a mop or a broom?'
'He, he he,' says Miss Flounce; 'I suppose we shall see
"An Ode to a Dish-clout"– what else can it be?'
. . .
'For my part, I think,' says old Lady Marr-joy,
'A servant might find herself other employ.
Was she mine I'd employ her as long as 'twas light
And send her to bed without candle at night.'
. . .
'What ideas can such low-bred creatures conceive,'
Says Mrs Nowaring, and laught in her sleeve.
Says old Miss Prudella, 'If servants can tell
How to write to their mothers to say they are well
And read of a Sunday *The Duty of Man* –
Which is more, I believe, than one-half of them can –
I think 'tis much *properer* they should rest there
Than be reaching at things so much out of their sphere.'

Specifically Hands went on to satirise a dismissive response to her own verse:

Had she wrote a receipt to've instructed you how
To warm a cold breast of veal, like a ragout,
Or to make cowslip wine that would pass for champagne
It might have been useful again and again.[35]

Satire was a bold appropriation in Elizabeth Hands's verse, as it was in other servant writers too, and was a weapon snatched from the grasp of those above her in the social scale only to be hurled back defiantly in their direction. Similar satire of the responses of others to plebeian writing also figured in Mary Leapor's 'An Epistle to Artemisia' and was almost as striking as that found in Hands's work. It pointedly mocked those who had first derided the labouring muse.

> *Parthenia* cries, 'Why, Mira, you are dull
> And ever musing till you crack your skull,
> Still poking o'er – what d'ye call – your Muse.
> But pr'y thee, Mira, when dost clean thy shoes?'
> Then comes *Sophronia*, like a barb'rous Turk.
> 'You thoughtless baggage, when d'ye mind your work?
> Still o'er a table leans your bending neck.
> Your head will grow prepost'rous like a Peck.
> Go ply your needle: you might earn your bread,
> Or who must feed you when your father's dead?'
> She sobbing answers, 'Sure, I need not come
> To you for lectures. I have store at home.
> What can I do?'
>   'Not scribble.'
>   'But I will.'
> 'Then get thee packing and be awkward still.'[36]

The *Grub Street Journal*, weary of the new democratisation of poetry, had wished out loud in 1731 that plebeian poets should speedily return to their proper calling and submit to 'an absolute restraint never more to write a line of verse'. The grudging comments contained in the letter from Hannah More to Mrs Montague on the literary efforts of her wilful former protégé, Ann Yearsley, easily bear comparison with this verdict. 'I hope she is convinced that the making of verses is not the greatest business of human life; and that, as a wife and mother, she has duties to fill, the smallest of which is of more value than the finest verses she can write.' The *Monthly Review* gave Yearsley's historical drama *Earl Godwin* a hostile reception in 1791.'When milkwomen write tragedies is it possible to refrain from a little vulgar wonderment?'[37]

Later examples of literary self-representation by servant authors by and large were of a different kind from most of those discussed above. Anne Barker's *The Complete Servant Maid* (*c.* 1770) had little in common with the work of Mary Collier, Anne Leapor and Elizabeth Hands, though it, too, came from an author with inside knowledge of housework and its demands. But it was first-hand experience of a particular kind. Barker took pains to inform her readers that she had 'for many years discharged the office of housekeeper in the most respectable families'; she herself, therefore, had never known at first hand the unrelenting and unpleasant routines of household drudgery. Barker's little book in the last analysis lacked a deep-rooted autobiographical dimension; it belonged chiefly to the long lineage of advice literature. Barker addressed servant maids directly and gave the benefit of her long experience in recommending the qualities needed in service – honesty, integrity, humility, modesty, cleanliness, equanimity. But although Barker, unlike Collier and some others, was not chiefly a poet, she enlivened her prose by framing it, at the beginning and end, with simple, mechanical rhyming verse. She began:

> Be honest and trusted, be prudent and praised,
> Be mild to be pleasing – and meek to be raised;
> For the servant whose diligence strikes envy dumb
> Shall in place be admired – and a mistress become . . .

And ended, satisfied that she had said what was needed:

> with care [keep] our precepts in your mind
> Be honest, active, diligent and kind.
> Then your employers will your deeds approve,
> Your friends applaud – your fellow servants love.[38]

On the face of it Oliver Grey's *An Apology for the Servants* (1760), like Barker's, is another insider's view of the world of service and its many challenges. Provoked by the endless pontificating going on around him about the 'servant problem', Grey's *Apology*, written by 'an old servant' in defence of his class, blended autobiographical insights with general reflections. Most immediately Grey's pamphlet was occasioned by the first performances in 1759 at the Theatre Royal, Drury Lane, of James Townley's farce *High Life below Stairs*, a witty and hard-hitting exposure of the pitfalls of servant-keeping. Grey's life in service, he informed his readers, began at the age of fifteen and at the time of writing (when he was sixty) he had served fourteen masters in all, hardly any of them caring or 'godly' in any recognised sense. When Grey was fifty-five one of them, a London merchant and insurer, who had invested his servants' savings and paid them 5 per cent annual interest, was bankrupted. He fled the country, leaving his household staff financially ruined and jobless.[39] Facts like these, Grey argued, surely put the so-called 'servant problem' in its proper perspective. The causes of the 'problem' in this case were plain for all to see. Blinkered and hypocritical masters carefully avoided self-criticism and blame and were all too ready to condemn servants, often for the same faults they themselves regularly committed. Card-playing, for example, was routinely denounced by them as a servant vice

> Why do horrid consequences attend the greasy kitchen cards any more than the spruce pack in the parlour? [Grey retaliated] . . . If the master plays only for amusement why not the servant? If he [the master] plays for more than he can afford how can he have the face to condemn his servant?

Faced with a life of unremitting, thankless toil and inconsiderate treatment from most masters, servants needed, and were entitled to, at least some relaxation.[40]

Deeply conscious that vails were a heated and much resented topic of the day, Grey spent some time in his pamphlet in defence of this indispensable (in his view) supplement to servants' meagre wages. Opposition to vails came chiefly, Grey opined, from the spongers, the hangers-on, who imposed themselves on the hospitality of friends and relations of the servants' masters. To servants themselves vails represented a legitimate recompense for the extra services (additional to their regular work load) which hordes of household guests arrogantly demanded and received. Without this extra income how could servants possibly provide for their old age? (On vails see pp. 87–9.)

> Who will take an old servant? Nobody. If he has saved nothing to support himself he must crawl to the workhouse. If he has got a little matter together his lot will not be quite so bad and he may end his days with an old she-mate in a sorry alehouse or a petty chandler's shop.[41]

In this, as in other respects, both the statements contained in, and the tone of, Grey's *Apology* appear to ring true. But 'Oliver Grey', apparently, was a pseudonym for James Townley (1714–78), clergyman, schoolmaster, friend of David Garrick and playwright whose *High Life below Stairs* was all the rage in 1759 and continued to be a popular offering in the theatres until well into the nineteenth century.[42]

But even if Grey was Townley's *alter ego* the sentiments expressed in *An Apology* gave credible voice to servants' own views and feelings. An endnote added by Townley to the eighth reprint of his play in 1759 aimed to put an end to controversies surrounding its authorship by laying claim both to *High Life* which was being attributed to Garrick (the actor manager who presented it at Drury Lane) and to the *Apology* and argued that, appearances notwithstanding, they shared much common ground. The servants depicted in the play were merely 'the instruments for conveying the satire', not the object of it. It was masters' mismanagement, not servant misrule, which ultimately was being held up to censure and ridicule. This subtext of the play, then, became the main drift of the pamphlet.

More examples of servants' own writings appeared in the late eighteenth and early nineteenth centuries, a reflection of rising literacy rates, the expansion of Sunday schools and, most fundamentally, the increased number of household servants. John MacDonald's *Travels in Various Parts of Europe, Asia and Africa* (1790) was one such autobiography, though its racy text was edited by another hand 'for the purpose of correcting and improving his style'.[43] MacDonald, a valet, who spent much of his life in service in Scotland and in London, was born in 1741. His father, a Jacobite, died in the bloodbath at Culloden, so the young John had painful first-hand experience of the brutal oppression, disruptions, poverty and insecurity which followed. His first steps in education were guided by other servants in the large Hamilton household, which he joined as a very junior member. 'I thought if once I could read the Bible I should not go to Hell.'[44] But he received some formal schooling through the good offices of his sympathetic master and mistress, who also gave him shirts, stockings and neckcloths. As he grew up John MacDonald had frequent changes of employment (including a period of service with James Coutts, the banker) and he offered some frank comments not just on individual masters but on different *kinds* of employer and what might be expected from them. MacDonald acquired, and gloried in, the reputation of being a ladies' man. He fathered several bastards, finally marrying the mother of one of them, and settled down in Spain.[45]

The History of Charles Jones, Footman, written by Himself (1797) appeared in the same decade as MacDonald's autobiography but projected a man who was made of sterner stuff – not surprisingly, since it found a place in the evangelical series of Cheap Repository Tracts. Born in Somerset, Charles was grounded in godliness by his pious mother, and entered service at the age of fourteen with a parson as his master and the clergyman's peevish wife as his mistress. Trials and tribulations constantly faced the young Charles, and he looked back with shame in recounting them in this overtly moralising text. (The moralising was indeed so heavyhanded that doubts arise as to whether Jones may have been a fictional creation invented to serve the purposes of an author of the Hannah More fraternity or of the evangelical publishing house which issued this tract-length piece.) Gossiping, gambling, loitering and lying were just some of the early vices to which Jones confessed. That his own employer was just and god-fearing made these sins all the more hideous; other servants, very differently placed, simply took their cue from reprobate masters:

> A servant is to do what is right [insisted the reclaimed Jones], let his master do what he will. If a master swears and gets drunk and talks at table with indecency or against God and religion, to God he must account for it ... But his example will not excuse our crimes.[46]

Translated to a larger household and a more lucrative position in London the now godly Charles Jones had to confront not only the snares of the capital but the taunts of fellow servants in the household in which he served. In London, he reflected, so many honest servants 'forfeit their integrity, their peace of mind, their health, their character, their souls'. First denounced by other servants in his master's household as 'parson', 'prig' and 'hypocrite', Jones persevered and eventually won their respect. To his master he showed unflagging honesty and devotion. He took no commission or poundage from tradesmen and owned up to the mistake when his master had once overpaid him. When offered a higher wage in another establishment the loyal Jones declined and stayed where he was.

> When you are once got into a good place stick to it like a leech [said Jones]. The rolling stone gets no moss. The more years you contrive to continue in one service the more you are respected by your master and the world. A good family considers an old servant as one of themselves and can no more see him want than a near relation. Whereas servants that are continually roving from place to place have no friend in distress, and seldom get a provision for old age.[47]

Loyalty, therefore, needed to be seen as not only a necessary feature of service in the short term but also a form of investment. Jones stayed on with his master and was promoted, first to butler and then to bailiff of the master's country estate; he married, and brought his aged mother to live with them. Jones's brother, by contrast, never satisfied with what he had, proved the victim of his own foolishness and improvidence, and was dismissed from service. He fell seriously ill and came to an early death.[48] No servant reader of this text can have been left in the slightest doubt about the moral of the autobiographical tale. Such, surely, was its intention.

Moralising was in fact rarely absent from any writing for – or, indeed, sometimes by – household servants in this period. It is certainly one of the ingredients of Samuel and Sarah Adams's *The Complete Servant*

(London, 1825), which though published outside the period covered by this book is still relevant here since it was based on long personal experience extending back to the 1770s. Time-honoured sentiments about service being divinely ordained were carefully rehearsed by these veteran servant authors. 'Some are rich, some are poor. Some are masters and others servants. Subordination indeed attaches to your rank in life but no disgrace. All men are servants in different degrees . . .'[49] Temperance, too, figured prominently among the virtues of servants which were applauded. Water was the best drink of all, the Adamses contended, and promoted both health and wealth. A variation of this – milk and water, not too rich and self-indulgent a drink – led to serenity of mind. Spirits, however, stimulated both moral and physical decline. Ill health attended them – dropsy, epilepsy, palsy, melancholy, madness and apoplexy – and they inspired swindling, perjury, burglary, murder and suicide. The drunkard's likely end was either transportation or the gallows.[50]

The Complete Servant, admittedly, was more than a mere repeat of the kind of moral tale which had been told since at least the sixteenth century. Its chief characteristic, as the authors proclaimed in their pre-face, was practical advice drawn from fifty years' first-hand personal experience of service. Samuel had started work as a footboy in 1770 and worked his way up through household hierarchies. Sarah, his wife, had progressed from maid-of-all-work to housekeeper of a large establishment. In their book the responsibilities and duties of servants were carefully set out and general precepts were blended with advice specific to particular household posts. It was 'career servants' they were primarily targeting.

> Be ever active [they said]. Let your whole mind be in your business. Think of what you have to do, of what must be done, and do it even before it is wanted and do not wait until you are ordered to do it. Never think any part of your business too trifling to be well done. Consider your business as a pleasurable amusement and you will make it so.[51]

Maintaining an 'unblemished character' was crucial for a servant, these authors insisted, 'for *very good* employers or *very good* servants seldom need apply to common Register Offices'. A long career in service, clearly, brought its own perspective on the subject. Samuel and Sarah Adams, though servants themselves, took a stance which at least approximated to that of employers and the top-down advice books.[52]

The Complete Servant had much in common with Barker's earlier *The Complete Servant Maid*, published in the decade in which the Adamses had started their long careers in household service. Both these books, which never called into question the justice of any aspect of the employer–servant relationship, stood far removed from the very different and more radical outlook on household service offered by Mary Collier, Mary Leapor and Elizabeth Hands. They lacked the uniquely personal, gentle touch of Isabella Whitney's verse. All these writings, without exception, however, were based squarely on inside knowledge of the servant's life – though Barker had familiarity only with the upper end of the servant hierarchy and the Adamses obviously rejoiced in reaching those dizzy heights as they composed their well ordered, distinctly utilitarian prose. All made high claims for the servant's work and its place in society. All demonstrated that household chores were a fit subject for the writer to address in prose or verse. But Collier offered the frankest account of the life and labours of a lower servant and unselfconsciously projected herself as one who had absolutely no illusions about the often thankless toil imposed by employers who had no real sense of the unreasonableness of some of their demands; hers was no hymn of praise about the innate dignity of labour. Oliver Grey, *alter ego* of the playwright James Townley, clearly glimpsed some of what the more consistently radical Collier saw all too clearly.

NOTES

1 Susan E. Whyman, *Sociability and Power. The Cultural Worlds of the Verneys* (Oxford, 1999), p. 204.

2 Lady Mary Jennings, *A Kentish Country House, or, The Records of Hall House, Hawkhurst* (Guildford, 1894), p. 73, quoted in Hecht, *Domestic Servant Class*, p. 78.

3 Sambrook, *Keeping their Place. Domestic Service in the Country House*, pp. 208–9.

4 *Ibid.*, pp. 203–4.

5 *Ibid.*, pp. 204–6.

6 Quoted in M. Ingram, 'The reform of popular culture: sex and marriage in early modern England', in B. Reay (ed.), *Popular Culture in Seventeenth-Century England* (London, 1985), p. 154.

7 Quoted in G. R. Quaife, *Wanton Wenches and Wayward Wives. Peasants and illicit Sex in early Seventeenth-Century England* (London, 1979), p. 71; quoted in Pamela Horn, *Flunkies and Scullions. Life below Stairs in Georgian England* (Stroud, 2004), p. 268.

8 Quoted in T. Hitchcock *et al.* (eds.), *Chronicling Poverty. The Voices and Strategies of the English Poor, 1640–1840* (London, 1997), p. 59.

9 T. Hitchcock and J. Black (eds.), *Chelsea Settlement and Bastardy Examinations, 1733–1766*, London Record Soc., 33 (1999), pp. 72–3.

10 *Ibid.*, 16 April 1764, p. 141.

11 *A True Copy of the Paper delivered the Night before her Execution by Sarah Malcolm* ... (London, 1733); T' .omas Broughton, *A Serious and Affectionate Warning to Servants* ... *occa ,oned by the Shameful and Untimely Death of Matthew Henderson* (Londr ,1, 1746); see J. A. Sharpe, '"Last dying speeches": religion, ideology and public execution in seventeenth-century England', *Past & Present*, 107 (1985), 144–67, P. Linebaugh, 'The Ordinary of Newgate and his *Account*', in J. S. Cockburn (ed.), *Crime in England, 1550–1800* (London, 1977), pp. 246–70, P. Linebaugh, *The London Hanged. Crime and Society in the Eighteenth Century* (London, 1991).

12 R. J. Fehrenbach, 'A letter sent by the maydens of London' (1567) in Kirby Farrell, Elizabeth H. Hageman and A. F. Kennedy (eds.), *Women in the Renaissance* (Amherst, MA, 1988), p. 38.

13 *Oxford Dictionary of National Biography*. See also Meredith Anne Skura, 'A garden of one's own: Isabella Whitney's revision of [Hugh] Plat's *Floures of Philosophie* (1572) in her *Sweet Nosegay* (1573)' in the same author's *Tudor Autobiography. Listening for Inwardness* (Chicago, 2008), pp. 149–67.

14 The Huntington Library has a copy of this rare tract, shelved at 300812. The tract continues with a review of some of the Civil War religious sects and ends with a plea for reconciliation between King and Parliament.

15 Hannah Woolley, *The Gentlewoman's Companion, or, A Guide to the Female Sex* (London, 1673), p. 28.

16 *Ibid.*, pp. 206, 207–8, 210–11, 209, 213, 214.

17 *Oxford DNB*.

18 *The Toy Shop*, p. 11.

19 Dodsley, *Servitude*, pp. 12, 6, 7, 11, 10.

20 *Ibid.*, p. 19.

21 *Ibid.*, p. 27.

22 *Muse in Livery*, pp. 20–1.

23 Collier, *Poems on Several Occasions* (Winchester, 1762), p. v.

24 *Ibid.*, p. v.

25 Collier, *Poems on Several Occasions*, p. 19.

26 On Duck see H. Gustav Klaus, *The Literature of Labour. Two Hundred Years of Working-class Writing* (Brighton, 1985), chapter 1, and W. J. Christmas, *The Lab'ring Muses. Work, Writing and the Social Order in English Plebeian Poetry, 1730–1830* (Newark, DE, 2001), chapter 2.

27 Ferguson, *Eighteenth-Century Women Poets. Nation, Class and Gender* (New York, 1993); 'The Three Wise Sentences from the first book of Esdras chapters 3 and 4', in *Poems* (1762), p. 23. See also Donna Landry, *The Muses of Resistance. Laboring Class Women's Poetry in Britain, 1739–1796* (Cambridge, 1990).

28 Landry, *Muses of Resistance*, p. 71.

29 Collier, *The Woman's Labour* (1739), reprinted in E. P. Thompson and Marian Sugden (eds.), *The Thresher's Labour, by Stephen Duck, and The Woman's Labour, by Mary Collier. Two Eighteenth-Century Poems* (London, 1989), pp. 16, 19, 22, 23, 24.
30 *Poems on Several Occasions* (1820), advertisement.
31 Leapor, 'An essay on woman', in R. Greene and Ann Messenger (eds.), *The Works of Mary Leapor* (Oxford, 2003), p. 186.
32 *Ibid.*, pp. 208, 210.
33 Landry, *Muses of Resistance*, pp. 110, 107.
34 Leapor's preference for the pastoral was later echoed by John Jones, a faithful upper servant whose poetry was published in the early nineteenth century thanks to the intervention of the Poet Laureate, Robert Southey. (John Jones, *Attempts in Verse*, London, 1831.) Very noticeably none of his verse addressed the subject of his daily work routines. On Leapor see R. Greene, *Mary Leapor. A Study in Eighteenth-Century Women's Poetry* (Oxford, 1993), Christmas, *Lab'ring Muses*, chapter 4, and Susan Staves, *A Literary History of Women's Writing in Britain, 1660–1789* (Cambridge, 2006), pp. 258–63. See Christmas, *Lab'ring Muses*, for a general discussion of the subject.
35 Elizabeth Hands, 'On the supposition of an advertisement in a morning paper of the publication of a volume of poems by a servant maid', in Hands, *'The Death of Amnon. A Poem', with an Appendix containing Pastorals and other Poetical Pieces* (Coventry, 1789). The second quotation is from Christmas, *Lab'ring Muses*, p. 231.
36 Lines 149–62, quoted in Landry, *Muses of Resistance*, pp. 102–3
37 Quoted in Klaus, *Literature of Labour*, p. 15; Ann Yearsley, *Poems on Various Subjects, 1787*, ed. J. Wordsworth (Oxford, 1994), p. xiii; *Monthly Review*, November 1791, p. 347, quoted in Ferguson, *Eighteenth-Century Women Poets*, p. 46.
38 Barker, *Complete Servant Maid*, preface, p. 48.
39 *Ibid.*, p. 15.
40 *Ibid.*, pp. 14, 20.
41 *Ibid.*, pp. 21, 22, 18–19.
42 The published text of the play was reprinted at least eight times in 1759 alone; clearly it was the talk of the town. The last reissue of Townley's play held in the British Library is dated 1865, more than a century after it was first performed. See pp. 21–37 for more on this and other plays depicting servant characters.
43 MacDonald, *Travels*, preface.
44 *Ibid.*, p. 42.
45 *Ibid.*, pp. 79, 130, 394.
46 Jones, *Attempts in Verse*, p. 6.
47 *Ibid.*, pp. 9, 14.
48 *Ibid.*, p. 15.

49 Adams and Adams, *Complete Servant*, p. 17.
50 *Ibid.*, p. 33.
51 *Ibid.*, p. 21.
52 *Ibid.*, p. 32. A lengthy appendix summarised the principal laws relating to masters and servants, and preliminary matter, addressed chiefly to employers, gave guidelines on the optimum correlation of household size and income and reasonable wage levels for the different classes of household servant.

4

𝒞

EMPLOYING AND SERVING

I am sure, be a man never so vertuous, unless he be a housekeeper no man will in the country resort unto him, or if he walk in the city without servants attending on him no man will put off his cap or do him reverence; how can such a man be honourable?
(Anon., *Cyvile and Uncyvile Life*, London, 1579, quoted in Anna Bryson, *From Courtesy to Civility. Changing Codes of Conduct in Early Modern England*, Oxford, 1998, p. 115)

Where every man is master the world goes to rack
(English proverb, 1616; M. P. Tilley, ed., *A Dictionary of the Proverbs of England in the Sixteenth and Seventeenth Centuries*, Ann Arbor, MI, 1950)

Let your servants be temperate, diligent and true . . . Converse not with the inferior servants of the family nor with any notoriously vicious . . . Take special heed of familiarity with them and suspect them of humouring your vices. For if they once serve you in base unworthy offices from that time they become your masters . . . A servant who dares speak truth to your distaste and will not assist or obey you in things dishonourable or wicked cherish and love.
(V. B. Heltzel, ed., 'Richard, Earl of Carbery's advice to his son', *Huntington Library Bulletin*, 11, 1937, 99, 102)

Good men make good servants. Profligate and extravagant masters corrupt the morals of the best servants.
(John Fielding, *The Universal Mentor*, Dublin, 1763, p. 191)

Employing household servants and working in this occupational category were two of the central defining features of early modern society. Around 40 per cent of households included servants, most of whom were young and unmarried. Sixty to seventy per cent of the fifteen to twenty-four age group worked as live-in servants. Only 2 per cent of household servants listed in the Ealing census of 1599 were over fifty. The median age of household servants born in the parish of Cardington, Bedfordshire, in 1782 was seventeen. It is a commonplace among social historians to recognise that household service was a life-cycle experience which often filled the gap between adolescence and marriage. Servants in husbandry and household staff who worked on a daily basis (laundresses, for example) and who lived in their own homes tended to have a different age structure from those servants who lived as well as worked in the employer's residence.[1] This was a labour-intensive society and one also that was characterised in its upper strata by eye-catching displays of conspicuous consumption in its many forms. Unsurprisingly, therefore, for both these reasons household servants formed a *vertical* feature of the social system, from top to bottom. Even the poorest of households often had a live-in servant to help with household chores, in many cases provided as a form of outdoor relief by parish guardians; it was a convenient and cheap method of assisting the aged and infirm. Geographically the largest concentration of servants (perhaps 25 per cent of the nation's total), as might be expected, was found in London, with the fashionable districts inevitably far outstripping the poorer parishes of the East End in the numbers employed per household.[2]

That said, servant-keeping in London households was general practice. Additionally vast numbers of servants were required for all the inns with which London and Westminster abounded. The great London houses of the leading nobility, certainly in the sixteenth century, contained large assemblies of household staff; the Earl of Leicester, for example, in the 1580s boasted between 100 and 150 servants on his payroll. (An extended epitaph on the subsequent decline of such large establishments and the old-style culture of service they represented was provided in *A Health to the Gentlemanly Profession of Servingmen*, 1598.) Servants could be seen everywhere on the streets of the capital. Jonas Hanway estimated in 1767 that one in thirteen of London's population was employed as a servant. Henry Thrale, the wealthiest brewer in London in the last quarter of the eighteenth century, kept eighteen to twenty household servants at his house in Streatham. John Baker, successful London lawyer of the same period, employed a staff of eleven. Horace Walpole's household at Strawberry Hill in 1781 was run by ten servants. Smaller households, however, abounded. At the very end of the seventeenth century 57 per cent of London homes kept only one servant and a further 21 per cent had two. But the cumulative implications were staggering. A writer in the *London Chronicle* in 1762 went so far as to claim that the capital 'would soon become depopulated if it was not for the waggon loads of poor servants coming every day from all parts of this kingdom'.[3]

Estimates for provincial towns and cities in the seventeenth century show similar high proportions of servants in the urban populations. Bristol and Stafford had 13 per cent, York 10 per cent, Leicester and Lichfield 8 per cent. Bath and other fashionable spas and watering places by the eighteenth century relied on large contingents of servants – both those accompanying their employers and those waiting to receive them – to make them function in the ways expected. Country houses of the aristocracy and gentry required large complements of domestic staff. In the sixteenth century feudal households still supported large numbers of retainers; a peer like the Earl of Northumberland had no fewer than 166 servants in 1521. The Bishop of Ely had 100 in 1533. At Stowe, country house of the Temple family, thirty-one servants were employed c. 1635. At the end of the 1650s Sir Ralph Verney, back at Claydon House, Buckinghamshire, after his unhappy Interregnum exile, maintained a household staff of eleven, together with two jobbing gardeners and an upholsterer. More impressively Sir Richard Newdigate of Chilton Coton, Warwickshire, had twenty-eight servants in his employ in 1684. In the late seventeenth century the Russells kept a staff at Woburn, Bedfordshire, which included a receiver-general, auditor, steward, housekeeper and eleven or twelve footmen. By 1771 the Russells' payroll for their servants comprised forty-two names with new kinds of employee listed – confectioner, butler, under-butler, hairdresser – advertising the age of opulence and comfort in which such aristocratic families now lived. The Duke of Norfolk brought thirty servants with him to Arundel in 1775. Lord Hardwicke employed the same number in 1778. Lower down the social scale, country gentry like Henry Purefoy in the period 1735–53 made do with seven. William Heathcote (a successful East India merchant who converted some of his commercial wealth into a landed estate at Hursley, Hampshire) kept an indoor staff of twelve in the last decades of the eighteenth century. Clergy like the Rev. James Woodforde in Norfolk in the same period, on an annual income of about £300, was able to maintain five servants. Large numbers of clergymen, however, had to function and keep up appearances with a much smaller staff. The Rev. William Holland in Stowey, Somerset, dispensed with one of his maidservants in 1804, consoling himself with the thought that 'by experience we find that one servant will do as much as two'. The advice to gentry and professional men, in any case, was that they should not be overburdened with servants. 'Keep no more cats than will kill mice,' was the pithy recommendation of Josiah

Dare in 1710. Though the servant-keeping habit spread in the late seventeenth and early eighteenth centuries, most servants in the provinces, as in London, were employed in small households containing one or two hard-pressed household staff. The 'maid of all work' was a ubiquitous figure.[4]

The general presence of such servants by the early eighteenth century was an accurate reflection of two general trends: the extension of the servant-keeping habit in society and the feminisation of service. Taxation of male servants later in the same century accentuated the trend still further. At Knole, Kent, in the 1620s the Countess of Dorset kept a household that was over 80 per cent male in its composition. By the end of the eighteenth century menservants, far from being commonplace, had become a defining index of high rank and luxury. The gender balance of the household staff of the Russell household changed noticeably in the course of the eighteenth century; under-staff in the kitchen, for example, came to be predominantly female. The servant tax returns for the 1780s – useful at least to historians as some guide to the overall gender balance if not to actual numbers – show menservants in a small minority; even in London, according to the tax returns at least, only thirty-two households kept more than five menservants. Even at the beginning of the century, it has been estimated, 81 per cent of the capital's household servants were women, representing 40 per cent of the female population of the city. In Edinburgh at the same point in time women accounted for 75 per cent of household servants. Southampton's total in the same period was 55 per cent.[5]

The presence of increasing numbers of foreign-born servants was being repeatedly remarked on in the course of the eighteenth century. Richard Steele in his play *The Tender Husband* (1705) has one of his characters say, 'the English are so saucy with their liberty – I'll have all my lower servants French. There cannot be a good footman born outside an absolute monarchy.' Such approbation, even expressed in satire, was uncommon. Sir John Fielding warned in 1762 that the mingling of foreign with English servants was almost always disruptive in its effects, since 'the former are too often beheld by the master or mistress with a partial eye'.[6] French servants were generally denounced – especially when England was at war with their country – since their 'religious and political principles have an apt and natural tendency to the subversion of our religion, laws, government and obedience'. A letter to the *London Chronicle* in October 1757 denounced them as 'spies to France'. Fashions for French cooks with their newfangled dishes were undermining the tried and trusted standards of wholesome English cuisine. (English hostility to the French was frequently remarked on. D'Archenholz, a foreign visitor at the end of the eighteenth century, believed that 'The English populace call every foreigner a Frenchman, whether Swiss, German, or Italian'.) The parallel influx of German servants – in the Hanoverian wake – was also resented, since in the view of one commentator at least (in 1744) they were merely 'drones . . . who had promoted themselves from lice and laziness into laced liveries and profitable places'. A xenophobic £5 tax on all foreign servants was proposed in 1750 by a spokesman for their opponents long before servant taxes had been first canvassed and introduced.[7]

Immigrant servants from other parts of Europe clearly abounded in eighteenth-century England, and by that period, as a consequence of imperial expansion and the growth of the slave trade, black servants were becoming more common. There are isolated references to negro servants in England from the mid-sixteenth century; I. Habib's *Black Lives in the English Archives, 1500–1677. Imprints of the Invisible* (London, 2008) has painstakingly brought them together. They include Henry Blackemer, servant to Mr Lording of All Hallows, Bread Street, London, in 1548 and other blacks who figured in the households of Spanish and Portuguese traders and diplomats. Nicholas Wichelhalse of Barnstaple in his will of 1570 passed on a black slave as a bequest. The burial records of the Baptist-inclined Church of Christ in Broadmead in 1640 contain a blackamoor maid called Frances, 'a poor Ethiopian'; Samuel Pepys employed a black cook-maid in 1659. Seventeen black servants were listed in the 1695 census of the central London parishes. Negro slave pageboys, with pet names, featured increasingly in the London and country houses of the aristocracy and were valued, until they lost their youth and charm, by mistresses as ornaments or toys. At Knole in Kent from the sixteenth century a succession of such boys adorned the house, each of them given the same name (John Morocco). Country gentleman John Verney in Buckinghamshire had a black pageboy, Peregrine Tyam, baptised when he came to England in 1689 aged about six. He was buried in September 1707. The presence of Henry Friday, a black boy, is recorded at Wentworth Woodhouse, Yorkshire, in 1770. There were evidently enough black slaves in employment for Matthew Dyer, maker of 'silver padlocks for blacks or dogs' to offer his wares in the *London Advertiser* in 1756. Court cases involving black servants crop up periodically. A runaway 'black-amoor' servant was returned to her master in Weymouth, Dorset, in the early seventeenth century. The Bishop of Exeter's black maid, Margaret

Paul, was prosecuted for fornication with another servant in January 1641. In London in 1692 Edward Frances, 'a blackmore servant', was charged with attempting to poison his master in order to gain his liberty. In Egham, Surrey, in June 1770 Caesar, negro servant to Philip Dacre, of Thorpe, was accused of attempted rape.[8]

An article in the *Gentleman's Magazine* in 1764 spread alarm by claiming that there were probably 20,000 black servants in London – an impossibly high estimate – and that since they were generally 'sullen, spiteful, treacherous and revengeful' the capital was resting on a powder keg. Four years later John Fielding warned of the dangers of importing black slaves from the West Indies plantations into English households. Almost inevitably, he said, the blacks 'put themselves on a footing with other servants, become intoxicated with liberty, grow refractory, and either by persuasion of others, or from their own inclinations, begin to expect wages according to their own opinion of their merits'. Rumours circulated among the black fraternity that baptism or marriage in England would automatically confer freedom. And when such people returned to the West Indies, Fielding said, they invariably caused trouble by spreading knowledge of the liberties which English servants enjoyed.[9]

Black servants figured in art from the seventeenth century onwards, as David Dabydeen has shown. They made appearances in literature. The first dialogue in Vol. II of Defoe's popular and much reprinted *The Family Instructor* included Toby, a negro servant boy brought in from Barbados and kept in ignorance of religion by an indifferent white master. Samuel Richardson's *Pamela* (1740) has a reference to a black servant boy of about ten years of age sent as a gift but who fell victim to smallpox and died. James Townley's popular but divisive farce *High Life below Stairs* (1759) includes black servant characters among the reprobate crew depicted.[10]

A few black servants, it is clear, found favour with their employers and were cherished. The tombstone of Charles Pompey, Lady Thomas's negro servant, who died aged about twenty-four in 1719, praised a young man who had been brought up by his mistress in the Christian faith and who became a paragon of honesty, loyalty and diligence, much loved and respected by others in the same household. Francis Barber, born in Jamaica and brought to England in 1752, became Dr Johnson's trusted and devoted servant for thirty-four years and – as a further manifestation of this employer's affection for this man and his general hostility to slavery – a major beneficiary under the terms of his will. At Erdigg, near Wrexham, two negro coachboys were memorialised in verse and art; if only they had encountered 'Massa Wilberforce', the doggerel poem declared, what good things might have happened! High Court Judge Lord Mansfield took into his household as a companion/servant the half-caste illegitimate daughter, Dido, of his nephew, Sir John Lindsay. Julius Soubise, brought from the West Indies as a child, became the favourite servant and then protégé of Catherine Hyde, Duchess of Queensberry, who had him painted by Gainsborough. It all went to his head, unfortunately. Fame was too much for him and he sank into the debauched, miserable life of a spendthrift fop. Gainsborough also, in 1768, painted a well known portrait of Ignatius Sancho, a black servant who later prospered as a London grocer and cut a figure in London society.[11]

Black servants arrived in England directly or indirectly as a result of the slave trade. European servants either came of their own volition in search of a job or because of unsettled conditions at home, or were picked up by English employers on the Grand Tour. How the rest of household servants in England were recruited and from how far afield they were drawn are closely related questions. In the provinces they tended to come chiefly from the local area – if the family had more than one country seat that, of course, enlarged the choice – and were taken on as a result of direct recruitment or as a result of recommendations from friends or neighbours. Some employers found jobs as servants for poor relations. A Retford maltster in 1632 employed Elizabeth Smith, 'my late wife's kinswoman and now my servant', and left her a modest bequest in his will. Rising civil servant Samuel Pepys reluctantly employed his sister in a maidservant capacity and left her in no doubt of her subordinate position in his household; she was consistently excluded from the inner circle of the family. Most of the seventeenth-century servants employed in the small town of Retford in Nottinghamshire had come from within a five-mile radius. 'Rawness' in a servant was often seen as an advantage, since such a recruit was unlikely to be already corrupted and was considered to be more amenable to rigorous training. The Barringtons in Essex in October 1631 took on a maidservant from Hertfordshire, evidently well recommended, and paid a carter 6s 9d to fetch her. But she quickly proved a disappointment and was dismissed by the end of the following month with such wages as had accumulated during her brief stay. The carter received a further payment to return her from whence she came.[12] William Harte wrote in December the same year to Hester, Lady Temple to thank her for taking his daughter into her service. In February 1650 Lady Temple was also contacted by John Swaine seeking employment for a kinswoman and asking her if she would recommend his nominee to 'any lady or gentlewoman of quality who wants a servant'.[13] In the following century Lord Fitzwilliam wrote from London in May 1700 to his steward at Milton, Northamptonshire, requesting him before his next visit to recruit new household staff for the country house, including 'two working maids, one for the kitchen and the other for the house ... [London maids being] too fine fingered for country business'. Cookmaids were also needed, he signalled in September 1702, for the Northamptonshire house 'because they are all here such sluts or whores or thieves or drunken beasts that we dare hardly bring any of them down', Daniel Eaton (1698–1742), steward to the third Earl of Cardigan, wrote in May 1725 recommending his younger sister, Theophilia, as a lady's maid, confident that 'with two or three months instructions she would be perfect in it as some that have been at it several years'. Nicholas Blundell in Lancashire recorded in his journal in September 1724 records two potential maidservants coming to his home seeking employment. At the end of the following year he mentioned that 'Joseph Rigby brought Barnaby Hargrave to be my butler but he is too little'.[14]

Many letters survive in the Purefoy archive relating to servant recruitment for the family home at Shalstone, Buckinghamshire. Elizabeth Purefoy wrote, for instance, in February 1743 to the mother of a prospective maidservant requesting a testimonial, saying that travelling expenses would be paid, and reminding her that the girl's brother – perhaps the source of a recommendation? – was already employed by them. Another letter of around the same date, sent directly to a would-be cookmaid, queried the accuracy of the dates given in her past employment record. In February 1750 the same mistress was asking a correspondent to recommend a maid. 'She must sew plain work, wash fine linen and iron and to help to send in dinner in extraordinary days. I should like her never the worse if she was forty years old.' This employer, like others, had had enough of younger maidservants getting pregnant. Someone who was older might reasonably be expected to have fewer 'followers' and be less likely to get into trouble.[15]

At Dunham Massey in Cheshire in the late eighteenth and early nineteenth centuries some servants were drawn in from the family's other estate at Enville, Staffordshire. Generally speaking, recruitment of new servants to this household was through personal contacts, word of mouth and direct approaches by would-be servants to the land agent. Only specialist staff were recruited by more extensive searches.[16] The Rev. James Woodforde, newly establishing himself in Norfolk in the 1770s, generally relied on recommendations for maidservants from the wife of a local clergyman and drew his servants from the local area; in fact only one manservant (William Coleman, who hailed from Somerset) seems to have been drawn from outside the region. Mrs Thrale in Streatham asked a correspondent to find her a new housekeeper, one 'such as you *know* will suit us; a good country housewife who can salt bacon, cure hams, see also to the baking etc. and be an active manager of and for a dozen troublesome servants'. Amanda Vickery has made a careful study of servant recruitment patterns in a group of late eighteenth-century northern households. Elizabeth Shackleton at Alkincoats, near Colne, Lancashire, sent or received a total of thirty-six letters on this subject between 1770 and 1781, her correspondents consisting chiefly of other gentlewoman, shopkeepers and a doctor's wife. Three incoming letters were from servants themselves or from their parents. Most of the servants this demanding mistress recruited came from within a sixteen-mile radius. Religious tests tended to be applied; Roman Catholics and Methodists were generally bypassed, due either to her own prejudice or to the belief that the specific demands of their worship would make too many inroads into their work routines. Household servants for Charlecote, Warwickshire, in the late eighteenth and early nineteenth centuries were chiefly recruited locally either through informal contacts or, sometimes, at hiring fairs.[17]

Hiring fairs – chiefly used in connection with servants in husbandry rather than household servants – still figured, of course, in Thomas Hardy's Wessex and, vestigially, into the twentieth century. (An American visitor in the 1880s seeing such a fair on his travels described it as 'a labour exchange open for a day'.) But by the end of the eighteenth century would-be servant maids from respectable families were being advised against attending them. 'What crowds of drunken men are there who will hardly suffer a modest girl to pass along unmolested . . . A discreet girl would hardly wish to be seen in those which are in or near London.'[18]

Like hiring fairs, though for different reasons, register offices (i.e. labour exchanges), much used in London from the second half of the eighteenth century, also acquired a very chequered reputation. Hard-to-please spinster employer Gertrude Savile, who had first looked to such places as a way of addressing her constant 'servant problem', soon grew to despise them. A short-lived maidservant, recruited in this way, was dismissed after only five months in 1755 with scorn poured out on 'Fielding's vile office . . . I will never more have anything to do with those offices . . . How much mischief they do.' (On Savile see pp. 74, 159, 177–9.) Joseph Reed's ribald farce of 1761, *The Register Office*, satirised such an institution, directed in this instance by the appropriately named Mr Gulwell. Peopled with deluded females in search of imaginary positions, duped employers, bawds and lusting mistresses like Lady Wrinkle in search of a 'handsome, well-bred young fellow [preferably tall, since] nothing adds more to the dignity of an equipage than the size and stateliness of one's domestics', the play paints a bleak and sordid picture. John Trusler in 1786 had come to believe that 'it is the refuse of servants in general that apply to these offices. You must not take the recommendation of the office keeper, who is paid also by the servant for procuring the place.' Samuel and Sarah Adams, with a long record of household service going back to the same period, were of the same opinion. 'Very good employers and very good servants seldom need apply to common register offices.' An early nineteenth-century North American commentator dismissed register offices as 'necessary but vicious instruments'.[19]

It had once been very different; high hopes had been entertained of register offices when they were first launched. Prototypes were tried out in fifteenth- and sixteenth-century Nuremburg and Strasbourg and there were various seventeenth-century experiments with agencies of this kind in London and Edinburgh. Inns on the main thoroughfares leading into the capital, because of their strategic location, sometimes became unofficial labour exchanges.[20] Henry Fielding, however, is credited with the first organised professional register office, launched in London in February 1750. A wide range of business was transacted and competitors soon came on to the scene but it was the hiring of servants which was its principal specialism. Operated 'for the common good', as its publicity material took pains to emphasise, by public-spirited gentlemen, Fielding's register office prided itself on acquiring full and reliable information about actual and would-be servants – age, experience, present post and employer, marital status, health record and available references – and having information on file about unsatisfactory servants who could thus be prevented from securing further employment. The plan had much in common, therefore, with Christopher Tancred's proposals to Parliament earlier in the eighteenth century. (See pp. 201–2.) Unlike Tancred's scheme Fielding's actually got off the ground but it was difficult, if not impossible, to vouch for the accuracy of all the information stored. Fielding's personal connection with the office was short-lived, and less scrupulous competitors fairly speedily brought the whole experiment into considerable disrepute.[21]

Servants' testimonials were always one of the issues in the credibility of register offices and indeed with the employment of servants in general. As early as 1559 a reform programme had proposed an obligatory system of authenticated testimonials for servants, with stiff penalties for infringement. Quarter sessions records show JPs up and down the country wrestling with the problem thereafter. Tancred in 1724 optimistically proposed the setting up of an all-inclusive central registry for copies of all servants' testimonials where they could be properly stored and systematically checked.[22] Some employers at least, it is clear, took the giving of character references for servants very seriously. Roman Catholic Lancashire squire Nicholas Blundell, for example, wrote in December 1704 to a Cheshire gentleman on behalf of his wife's chambermaid to assist her in getting a new position. 'She is a Catholic and a brisk mettled workwoman, gets up linen both fine and coarse very well, rubs well, and is a neat cleanly lass.' Towards the middle of the eighteenth century newly gentrified Yorkshireman William Gossip (1705–72) made no bones about the crucial value of honest testimonials for servants. Such documents, he insisted, are 'a debt from one gentleman to another and if they would be more exact in discharging it faithfully it might be one means of putting a stop to the misconduct of servants so much complained of'. Equally, a good reference, honestly earned and supplied, was a servant's prized possession, a valuable passport to future employment. 'A servant's good name is his life,' declared the writer of *The Footman's Looking Glass* in 1747. 'It is all he has to live upon. His character is his property, to which he has as good a right as to his wages.'[23]

Other employers were more lax and glossed over the failings of servants either just to be rid of them or to prevent slanderous revenge being taken by disgruntled former employees. 'We recommend sluts and thieves and drones and saucy insolent fellows and wenches . . . to one another,' wailed the inveterate campaigner Daniel Defoe in 1722, 'without any concern for our neighbours' safety or peace.' William Windham II of Felbrigg, Norfolk, in 1752 dismissed one of his London footmen for drunken, violent behaviour against some of his own servant maids. Despite this, however, Windham still saw fit to recommend him a few months later, after some agonising, to another employer in his home county. John Gabriel Stedman in late eighteenth-century Devon is another case in point. He wrote very disparagingly in January 1786 of his servant John, who 'drinks, whores, lies and skulks. I scold him in a damnable manner.' Only two months later, however, Stedman parted with him, 'giving him an excellent character'. The problem with testimonials continued into the nineteenth century and beyond. Mrs Beeton joined the chorus of denunciation of such bad practices. Without reliable testimonials, complained a writer to the *Covent Garden Journal*, the whole system of employing servants broke down.[24] The problem was compounded by servants themselves, especially in London, counterfeiting much better character references than the ones they had been given by past and present employers. 'Such things in London are procured from friends and often forged,' sighed John Trusler in 1786. John Huntingford complained of the same entrenched malpractice four years later.[25]

Unreliable testimonials, since they debased the currency of such documents, undoubtedly contributed to the perennial 'servant problem'. Long-suffering spinster employer Gertrude Savile was resigned to the fact that character references were often not worth the paper on which they were written. John Barlow was taken on as a servant in July 1755 'without a character; the best, I find, signifies nothing', but was discharged within a year, 'one of the worst fellows I have ever had . . . a scandalous whoremonger', Sarah Howard, a housemaid, arrived in the Savile household in March 1756 but, again, lasted less than a year. 'Had her character from a boarding school . . . but characters signify nothing at all.' Savile and other employers bemoaned the giving of bland, routine, superficial, generalised character references to servants. The lack of available training, except in charity schools, for young girls destined for service was also an issue of some importance. It was a deficiency which continued into the next century and beyond. In 1862 eagle-eyed social commentator Harriet Martineau concluded of household service that 'there is no other department of industry in which skill is expected without anything being done to create it'.[26]

Gertrude Savile's diary makes constant reference to the comings and goings of an endless stream of menservants and maids, some of them in post for less than a month. She had no fewer than five different footmen in the course of 1727. There were six changes to her household staff in July 1755 alone. The equally fastidious employer Elizabeth Shackleton of Alkincoats, Lancashire, witnessed twenty-nine women servants pass through her household in 1772, ten of them staying for less than thirty days. William Gossip in York was alarmed to see a total of fourteen temporary cooks arrive and depart between 1732 and 1740; of his household staff only his valet stayed for very much longer. During her residence in London in 1715 Scottish gentlewoman Lady Grisell Baillie saw eight cooks come and go. At the London Foundling Hospital the median period of service for female domestics between 1759 and 1772 was twenty weeks, and only ten weeks for scullery maids. Many young female servants, said a mid-eighteenth-century wit, 'are as restless as a

new equipage running from place to place . . . If their mistress but gives
them a wry word . . . they are as ready to be gone as a relieved guard
or a discharged jury.' The womanising footman John MacDonald later
in the century had twenty-eight masters in the space of thirty years. A
high turnover of household servants, of course, was nothing new in the
eighteenth century. Servant mobility (especially of female servants with
fewer prospects) was commonplace and was encouraged by the practice
of annual contracts. Reasons for accelerated mobility were as varied as
the servants themselves. Inter-servant rivalries and hostilities in larger
households could play a part. Resentment of severe regimes imposed
by employers was certainly another cause. Desire for betterment, especially in the bustling market place of London, played its part. The family
circumstances of young servants might change and call them back to the
parental home. Pregnancies and marriage took even more female servants out of their employment. How typical was the fairly small London
household of Samuel Pepys which had thirty-eight servants between 1660
and 1669, thirteen of them staying for less than six months? We do not
know.[27]

Not all employers and writers of household manuals, it has to be
said, were opposed to servant mobility. *The Ladies Cabinet Enlarged and
Opened* (4th edn. 1654) was one publication which recognised advantages
in having frequent renewals, since long-serving staff might grow slack
and feel that they were entitled to indulgence. At the end of the following century, reflecting on the abrupt departure of a serving man who
had been with him for nine years, the Rev. James Woodforde mused that
that extended period of service was 'much too long for any Norfolk
servant for they will get pert, saucy and do as they please'.[28]

Generally speaking, however, long service was valued and seen as bringing the benefits of stability and loyalty to a household. 'The master that
often changeth his servants receiveth great dishonour thereby,' declared
a commentator in 1607, 'and withall sheweth himself an impatient man
and hard to please.' Long service went on being advocated throughout
the eighteenth century, and at different times schemes were devised for
rewarding it. 'Stay long in your place,' was the pious advice given in *The
Servants' Friend* in 1780, 'for long service shows worth, as quitting a good
place through passion is folly . . . The servant that often changes his place
works only to be poor.' Charles Jones, footman, in his autobiography
(1797) advised others that 'the more years you continue in one service
the more you are respected by your master and the world. A good family
considers an old servant as one of themselves . . .' Very much later, in

the 1930s, *The Times* started publishing brief obituaries of long-serving household staff to give them some public recognition and hold up their example to inspire others.[29]

What was preached was also practised. In the 1630s Sir Richard Grosvenor in Cheshire recommended three long-standing servants to his son 'to be cherished and better provided for'. Francis North recalled how his grandfather greatly valued 'a venerable old steward . . . faithful and diligent for love rather than for self interest . . . one of a race of humankind heretofore frequent but now utterly extinct'. An epitaph in Tilsworth, Bedfordshire, memorialised John Quinny, who died in August 1669 aged seventy-two, having been servant to Sir Henry Chester for fifty-six years. Mary Lemon, who died in 1742, had been employed in service in Southampton for fifty years. The Leghs of Lyme in Cheshire employed the same male cook from 1693 to 1757. The Jackson family of Wesenham Hall, Norfolk, in 1756 had a housekeeper who had been in service for fifty-one years, a butler for at least thirty-two and a lady's maid for twenty-four. At Dunham Massey, Cheshire, wage increments rewarded long-serving staff, while some of them also received preferential long leases on estate property. The Yorke family at Erdigg, near Wrexham, immortalised their long-serving household and estate staff in verse and in portraits. Jane Ebrell, who arrived as a housemaid there in the 1720s, broke all records in this family by still being there in service seventy years later.[30]

But long service among servants, especially maidservants, was not the norm. Servant marriage was a thorny issue with many employers and commonly marked the point at which a female servant left employment. ('You were a nobody,' observed one early twentieth-century maidservant at a time when the issue remained largely the same as in earlier centuries. 'Marriage was the way out of it.')[31] Sir William Wentworth in 1604 was not in favour of servants marrying. 'Not good,' he declared tersely, 'to keep those that will marry long for they will be confederate.' In 1673 Hannah Woolley, drawing on her own service experience, firmly advised against hasty marriage among servants. 'By inconsiderately marrying you may have one joyful meeting and ever after a sorrowful living and have time to repent of your rash matching.' In the following century Thomas Gossip in Yorkshire expressed severe displeasure with his 'undutiful and ungrateful' maidservant Mary, who 'very foolishly threw herself away into the hands of a soldier [of all people] without giving me the least notice.' Marriage to a chambermaid was never advisable, so jested a tract of 1783:

They bring nothing with them but a few old clothes of their mistress's, and for housekeeping few of them know anything of it; for they can hardly make a pudding or a pie, neither can they spin or knit, nor wash, except it be a few laces to make themselves fine withall.[32]

Servant marriage was still being frowned upon in the late nineteenth century. To many employers a married butler was anathema. Family responsibilities, it was thought, would make too many inroads into time which should rightfully be at the disposal of employers, and might encourage pilfering of food and other household goods for the benefit of his own family.[33]

Some servants judged the best policy was to keep their marriage hidden from view. In late seventeenth-century Edinburgh some married menservants lived out of their employers' households, an early example of the separation of workplace and home. Much later, in the 1830s, man-servant William Tayler, whose rare and revealing diary survives, kept his marital status secret from his employers. So did Hannah Cullwick, Munby's maid-of-all-work spouse.[34]

Other employers, however, had a more benevolent attitude to servant marriage, and in some cases actually helped to facilitate it in the face of opposition. A master from Brimpton, Somerset, in the early seventeenth century, fearful that he might lose his lovelorn servant Robert Avoke, who was planning to elope with his sweetheart in the face of her step-father's immovable opposition to a match between them, engineered their formal betrothal. Another employer, this time in London in 1635, pro-tected the best interests of his wife's maidservant by pushing her dila-tory suitor into a promise of marriage in the presence of a clergyman. Thomas Mort of Dam House in Lancashire gave his maidservant Genet Bowker the equivalent of a quarter's wages when she married in the early eighteenth century. After some soul-searching the Rev. George Woodward in East Hendred, Berkshire, allowed his long-standing ser-vants Joe and Sarah to stay on in April 1760 after they announced their intended marriage, 'for I verily believe there cannot be two people of more upright principles in all respects'. He was confident that Sarah's age guaranteed that no offspring would result, but to his evident dismay a child was born in December the following year. Even with this new, unlooked-for addition to the household, however, all turned out well. 'We have not found that inconvenience which might have been expected ... [The baby] is the quietest thing that ever was for it is very seldom we hear it cry.' The Rev. William Cole in Buckinghamshire observed contentedly in August 1766, 'I married my old servant Will Travel to

Elizabeth Hickes, Thomas Billington's niece – a match that has been in hand fourteen years to my knowledge.' He had had a long time to accustom himself to the impending nuptials. John Gabriel Stedman in Devon noted in his journal on 16 December 1791, 'My servant Betty Norman goes away to her husband to whom I wish every good and give the whole family a dinner.' Sarah, the much loved maidservant of Anne Hughes, whose intriguing *Diary of a Farmer's Wife, 1796–1797* was first published in 1937, married the newly arrived, raw young parson with her employer's consent. Her mistress grieved for the loss of such an ideal young woman even though she and her husband and mother-in-law showered her with wedding gifts.[35] Though servant marriage was still generally disapproved of in the late nineteenth century, some employers, at least, took the view that a married butler was likely to be 'steady'.[36]

In a society in which there was no clearly defined end point for working life old age, and the issues which came with it, like servant marriage, elicited mixed responses from employers. Shakespeare's 'Old Adam' in *As you like it* (1603) neatly illustrates the point. All too often, as a ballad observed in the 1630s, there was a stark contrast between the serving man in his youth and in old age. 'In prime of years he'll roar and swagger/ And being grown old grows a beggar.' And so it continued. Prince Albert in 1849 pointed out that 66–70 per cent of the adult inmates of the St Marylebone workhouse were ex-servants. Moralising handbooks exhorted masters to care for faithful servants in old age. William Hinde in his life of John Bruen, published in 1641, dwelt on the special, caring relationship which developed between this godly master and an old family retainer, nearing eighty years old and no longer capable of sustained hard work, and held it up as a model to be followed by others. All too often, he declared,

> merciless and prophane masters . . . deal no better with . . . their impotent and old servants than they do with their old dogs. First they grow weary of them and then they turn them off their land without any means or maintenance to live on a commons or die in a ditch.

Long service was recommended to servants as a passport to a secure old age. A late eighteenth-century set of instructions to servants declared roundly that 'an old tried servant is looked upon as a relation, is treated with little less respect, and perhaps a more hearty welcome; and, further, will never want friends'. Charles Jones, footman, said much the same in 1797. Bridget Holmes, still working at the age of ninety-six in the royal household and immortalised in John Riley's late seventeenth-century portrait, must surely win the prize for longevity in service. Jane Ebrell, still employed at Erdigg in her eighties at the end of the eighteenth century, is another good example. Long-serving household staff were remembered in employers' wills with bequests of money, the setting up of annuities and the provision of pensions and housing. Roughly 16 per cent of London testators in the late seventeenth and early eighteenth centuries made bequests to servants, especially those of long standing.[37]

John Quinny, who died in 1669 and had been servant for fifty-six years to Sir Henry Chester, received an annuity of £8 a year under the terms of his master's will. Sarah, Duchess of Marlborough (d. 1744) bequeathed three annuities of £200 apiece to three long-serving staff. When John Baker gave up his house in Horsham, Sussex, in 1777 he settled a pension of £21 a year on his well respected housekeeper. Lydia Miller, who was in service with two branches of the same family for upwards of forty years, was rewarded in old age with an almshouse, and died in August 1814. The Rev. Peter Beauvoir of Downham Hall in 1821 left a bequest of almost £300 to his housemaid of forty years' standing. But even fairly newly arrived servants, if they had made their mark and aroused gratitude and affection, could benefit handsomely from employers in their wills or even in their lifetimes. In 1671 Lady Powys was obviously shocked that her sister had given '£500 to a waiting woman that served her but two years'. But this was a mere trifle compared with the Earl of Devon's later bequest in 1835 of his Charenton estate and a house in Paris to his coachman/butler.[38]

Though appeals were constantly made to the better nature of employers to remember rather than discard faithful old servants, the principle of self-help was also underlined as well; thrift was held up not simply as a virtue in servants but as a necessity. Richard Lucas in *The Duty of Servants* (London, 1685) roundly declared, 'I think it is the extremity of folly in a servant to expect . . . to eat the bread of his old age at the courtesy of others when, if he pleases, he may eat his own. This cannot but prove a very strong inducement to thrift.' Oliver Grey in 1760 put the same point even more strongly. 'If [the servant] has saved nothing to support himself he must crawl to the workhouse.' David Barclay in 1800 in yet more advice to servants urged them to 'save your money for that will be a friend to you in old age. Be not expensive in dress nor marry hastily.' Short-term thrift was encouraged by the standard practice of quarterly or even annual payment of wages, but over longer periods masters often acted as bankers for their servants, thus encouraging the habit of saving. Joyce Jefferies in Herefordshire in the 1640s paid quarterly or half yearly 'use' or interest to some of her servant maids both on accumulating wage funds or on other investments they had lodged with her. Mrs Monk's maids at Chawton, Hampshire, availed themselves of their mistress in this way in the eighteenth century, drawing most of their accumulated earnings only when they left her employ; one maid stayed, and saved up, for ten years. The introduction of penny savings banks in the nineteenth century was aimed at workers of all kinds, servants included.[39]

Servants' wages varied considerably over time, from place to place, and depended on their occupational function, and on household size. Generalisations are difficult to make, and historians who have written on the subject previously have been wisely cautious. Hecht's classic book provides eight pages of examples of wages, drawn chiefly from London, but even these reveal considerable variations and oscillations. Two different valets in 1770–71 had starkly contrasting wages of £15 and £30. In the same year one butler had £10 while another had thirty guineas. Wages to cooks in 1760–61 varied from £6 to £20. The subject of wages was not central to Bridget Hill's later investigation, which moved chiefly in other, non-quantitative, directions. Jane Holmes's valuable regional study of servants and servant-keeping in Yorkshire found fewer differences between servants' wage rates in Yorkshire and London than might have been expected, though no doubt this is partly explained by the fact that she was looking mainly at elite households in the northern county. Some servants – young boys in larger households and poor relations taken on as servants to give them a roof over their heads – were largely unpaid. Women – housekeepers and sometimes cooks excepted – were invariably paid much less than men, often half as much. Wage rates, however, were market-oriented and responded in the sixteenth and early seventeenth centuries to the driving force of inflation. George Booth in Cheshire complained in January 1609 about 'the excessive wages of servants' while in 1642 Henry Best in Yorkshire bemoaned the fact that whereas in recent memory a maid could be contracted for 18s a year 'now of late we cannot hire a good lusty servant-maid under 24s and sometimes 28s', Employers in the North Riding of Yorkshire also were evidently having to pay more for their servants in the early years of the seventeenth century. Wages for the household staff of the Stapley family, of Hickstead Place, Twineham, Sussex, in 1647 ranged from £5 to £1 per year. The Barringtons in Essex in 1665 were paying £10 a year to their housekeeper, £4 a year to a maid, £3 to a cook-maid, and £2 10s to under-maids. When in the eighteenth century inflation greatly subsided, wage rates in the provinces – even in counties close to the capital – changed far more slowly than they did in London itself. In Lancashire, far away from the London orbit, Nicholas Blundell in 1709 was paying his steward a mere £6 a year, £3 15s a year to a man who doubled as gardener and butler, £3 a year to his wife's maid, £2 a year to a chambermaid and the same amount to the cook. Sergeant Kite in Farquar's play *The Recruiting Officer* (1706), set in Shropshire, targeted among others 'servants with too little wages' (Act I, scene 1). William Heathcote, at Hursley Park, near Winchester, was slow to increase the wages his servants received: his butler had exactly the same annual salary (£14) in 1745 as he had been given in 1727. Another Hampshire employer, Robert Kingsmill, hired a servant in 1778 at an agreed wage of £5 5s a year. He quit and was taken back in October the following year for only 75 per cent of this rate. 'He tried to get a better place,' Kingsmill recorded in his account book, 'but he could not, therefore on his promising to behave well in every respect I took him again at the above wages of 4 guineas.' Mrs Shackleton at Alkincoats, Lancashire, between 1762 and the 1770s was paying annual wages of £5 to cook/housekeepers and not very much less (£4 4s) to maidservants, perhaps to encourage them to stay. At Downham Hall in Essex servants' wages remained largely unchanged over a forty-year period. The same housemaid who had been taken on for £8 per year in 1782 was receiving precisely the same amount in 1821. John Baker in Sussex in the 1770s was paying annual wages of £8 8s to a housemaid, £12 12s to his cook, £15 to £18 to a valet, and twenty guineas to his devoted housekeeper. The Rev. James Woodforde in more remote Norfolk, surrounded by different market conditions, in 1798 was paying his footman £8 a year, his cook/dairymaid £5 5s and the same to his housemaid.[40]

As the nation's epicentre of wealth and polite society it was natural that London should contain by far the largest concentration of household servants. Demand for servants outstripped the supply. Turnover of household staff was high as both menservants and maidservants exploited a labour market that, by the late seventeenth century at least, operated in their favour. Wages were forced up stimulating loud complaints about the distorting economic effects of the trend and the poor quality of many of those being so grossly overpaid. Daniel Defoe (1660–1731), normally an advocate of higher wages and their economic benefits, led the chorus of complaint in the early eighteenth century about a wage trend which in this case appeared to be spiralling out of control. Servants, bad ones at that, insisted Defoe – ever the alarmist – were holding the capital's unfortunate employers to ransom. Within living memory servants' wages in London, he insisted, had doubled or even trebled. Servants' unruliness and insubordination increased in proportion to their wages; democracy of the ugliest and most rampant kind was raising its head in the capital. The more cynical Bernard Mandeville was content to see higher, but all-inclusive, wages for servants but insisted that, as a corollary, perks of all kinds should be abolished.[41]

Alarm at London's servant problem and escalating wage rates was expressed repeatedly in the course of the eighteenth century. Only a few dissenting voices dared to suggest that the anxieties and complaints might be exaggerated. Elizabeth Carter, the late eighteenth-century bluestocking, was one of them. Radical William Godwin went further in attacking those who hypocritically complained about London servants and their wages. 'The wealth of servants,' he declared, 'amounts perhaps to ten or fifteen pounds a year and it is not infrequent to hear persons of ten to fifteen thousand a year exclaim upon the enormousness of wages'. Servants' so-called 'high wages' were entirely relative. These workhorses – who 'had nothing to do but obey' – were still to be pitied. Anthony Heasel rallied to their defence in another, much more practical, way in 1773 with his *Servants' Book of Knowledge*. This rehearsed in familiar fashion the roles and responsibilities of different officers in medium to large households and the text contains some conventional moral platitudes. But mostly this short book, only eighty-seven pages long, written (according to the preface) by a 'menial servant' himself, is consistently practical and down-to-earth; the clearest indicator of this is that, unusually, he devotes more pages to the varied work routines and daily challenges of chambermaids than to any other kind of household servant. Uniquely, however, in a publication aimed directly at servants themselves (and specifically those in London) and not their masters, Heasel included page after page of wage tables, patiently instructing imperfectly educated readers how they could calculate exactly, down to the last farthing, the wages due to them when they left their employer. Servants must surely have found Heasel's little book eminently useful and empowering and have constantly thumbed through its pages. *The Servants' Book of Knowledge* was a democratic tool for hard-working and not-to-be-cheated servants – the very title announced this – and it probably enjoyed a large initial print run. But there appear to have been no reprints and, ironically, a publication which was once probably in wide circulation among servants themselves has now become a rarity. Only one known surviving copy, in fact – in Yale University Library – has been traced.[42]

London employers of servants like Samuel Pepys in the 1660s and Gertrude Savile from the 1720s to 1740s said much about their servants; their diaries, especially Savile's, are running commentaries on household problems and servant life. But they said little or nothing about wages. That information, presumably, was contained in account books which no longer survive. Abundant records of this kind, however, are to be found in the papers of James Brydges, first Duke of Chandos (1673–1744), and they make rewarding reading. Brydges, like others of his rank, kept a London home as well as a country seat (Canons, at Edgware, Middlesex) with a substantial roll-call of staff. In 1725, one of the years for which a full listing survives, he paid his house steward £48 a year. The porter's boy, at the opposite end of the scale, had £2 in wages. The housekeeper and 'His Grace's gentleman', the groom of the chamber and the duchess's principal lady's maid were all on a par at £20 a year. The butler received £17, somewhat less than the cook, who had the rather odd salary of £18 4s 7d. The gentleman usher had £15 a year and the Duke's valet £12. Footmen had annual wages of £7. The head laundry maid got £6 a year for her pains; kitchen maids and housemaids received £5. That this was an establishment where fine fare was highly valued is demonstrated by the fact that the duke's confectioner enjoyed a high salary of £26 per annum. Music, however, it should be noted, had an even higher value attached to it in the Chandos household. The composer John Christopher Pepusch (1667–1752) enjoyed the princely annual retainer of £100 for a number of years after 1712, giving place eventually in 1718 to the much more illustrious George Frederick Handel (1685–1759), who gratefully dedicated his Chandos anthems to his wealthy patron.[43]

Comparisons can be drawn between the London wage rates the Duke of Chandos was paying his household servants in the 1720s with those provided by Thomas Coke, Earl of Leicester in the same period. Coke's house steward on £30 a year was paid considerably less than Brydges' but he had an assistant on £20 a year to share the work load. The earl's favoured valet had a salary of £20 (£8 more than in the other aristocratic household). His housekeeper's £20 a year was exactly the same as in the Brydges' residence. The butler here received £12, £5 less than in the previous set of figures. The earl's cook, however, luxuriated in an annual salary of £40, which shot up to sixty guineas in 1725 when a fashionable Frenchman was appointed to take gourmet fare to new heights. The porter, ultimately responsible for controlling access to the earl, had very respectable wages of £10 a year. Footmen in this household received either £8 or £7 according to rank. Cook-maid and upper laundry maid received £6, exactly on a par with those in the Brydges' establishment. Housemaids were also on an equal footing at £5. In this household as in the other casual supplementary staff were also periodically employed on daily rates.[44]

In the third quarter of the eighteenth century the records of the Russells, Earls of Bedford, covering their London establishment in Bloomsbury showed a stark upward trend in servants' wages. In 1753 for a household staff of forty at Bedford House the annual wage bill was £637 8s. By 1771, with forty-two now on the London payroll, the annual running costs had soared to £859 16s. The house steward's salary in the eighteen-year interval had gone up to £100 from £80. The clerk of the kitchen was now, strangely, placed on a par with the steward, with the same salary, whereas previously he had been allowed £60. The butler's salary, even more oddly, remained fixed at its earlier level. The wages of footmen – evidently in increasingly short supply – had doubled or, in some cases, almost trebled. In 1786 John Trusler in his *London Adviser and Friend* suggested that valets and butlers might get £30 a year wages, footmen £14, ladies' maids £12–£20, cooks £12 – Trusler evidently did not have French cuisine in mind – and housemaids £7 to £9.[45]

Money wages, of course, did not represent a household's servant's total pay, and for lesser servants they might indeed amount to less than the amount derived from other, supplementary, sources. Live-in servants necessarily were supplied with accommodation and food. (See below, pp. 97–104.) Prosperous employers operating both a London and country household paid board wages – to allow staff to buy food with which they were not being supplied in the employer's absence – to the skeleton staff of servants who were left behind. Thomas Coke, Earl of Leicester, when he was absent from his London home for nineteen weeks in 1719, paid board wages of 10s per week to his cook and butler, 7s per week to a porter and footman, 6s per week to laundry maids, housemaid, cook-maid and housekeeper's maid and 3s a week to 'Old John' Grayer, an odd-jobbing helper. James Brydges, Duke of Chandos, also paid board wages, but the accounting system employed in this household – lump-sum payments often paid retrospectively for unspecified time periods to senior staff for distribution to lesser servants – generally prevents a clear sense of weekly rates from emerging. Hecht's figures on board wages show valets getting between 10s 6d and 12s a week in the 1770s, footmen 10s 6d, housemaids and laundry maids 6s. Count Friedrich von Kielmansegge, visiting London in the early 1760s, observed that board wages for household servants had gone up in recent years from 7s to 10s 6d per week.

In 1786 Trusler thought that 10s 6d per week for upper servants and 7s per week for lower servants represented the norm.[46]

Abuse of the practice of board wages, as of much else relating to household servants, was many times complained of. *The Spectator* in 1711 denounced board wages as the road to ruin; the practice placed too much ready money in servants' pockets and encouraged idleness and drunkenness. 'This one instance of false economy is sufficient to debauch the whole nation of servants.' The periodical *The World* in 1756 was in full agreement and spoke of the curse of giving board wages to improvident footmen. The Rev. William Cole complained bitterly in January 1766 of servants taking advantage of his absence from home:

> I found out today that my maid to whom I allowed handsome board wages in my absence, the use of a cow, beer, ale, coals and candles and other things with half a crown per week, had not left me one onion or potato though there [were] three bushels of the last and one of the former when the gardener brought them into the house for the winter's use.

Further investigation brought to light information about those who had been helping themselves.[47] James Townley's farce *High Life below Stairs* (1759) depicted servants on board wages in their master's absence luxuriating in a frenzy of freedom, partying and helping themselves greedily to his stocks of fine food and wine. At the end of the nineteenth century a much-used publication rehearsing *The Duties of Servants* (1894) advised against the practice of board wages as anything other than an occasional expediency. 'It renders servants in a way independent of their masters and mistresses; they lose the feeling of being members of one household and dependent upon the kindness and consideration of its master and mistress.'[48]

Although it is not well documented, some household servants, we know, somehow carved out enough time to practise by-employments which brought in extra income over and above the wages they received from their employers, generally with their full knowledge and approval. The early sixteenth-century chronicler John Hooker painted a vivid picture of servant involvement in the local textile industry in Devon. 'Wheresoever any man doth travel,' he wrote, 'you shall find at the foredoor of the house the wife, their children *and their servants* at the turn spinning or at their cards carding and by which commodity the common people do live.' Research by Elizabeth Ewan on sixteenth-century Scottish towns has represented maidservants' by-employments as one significant expression of their striving for a degree of independence; free choice of marriage partners and collective self-defence when pressured or challenged were others. Part-time laundry work was one option, often combining extra items given to them for washing with the household load they were doing anyway for their mistress. Occasional brewing was another resort where the use of their employers' equipment was recompensed with a share of the brew. Ewan also found a number of cases of maidservants engaged in petty moneylending, sometimes one of the most risky forms of penny capitalism which might result in their having to go to law to reclaim unpaid debts. Servants' miniature local networks and routine multi-tasking, built up in and through their regular employment, clearly could be spasmodically utilised for other purposes. In the 1640s a former maidservant of Joyce Jefferies in Herefordshire took up part-time dres-making as well as assisting her husband in his shop.[49] Very much later in the West Riding of Yorkshire Phoebe Beatson, maidservant to the Rev. John Murgatroyd, whose poignant life story has been explored by Carolyn Steedman, somehow combined her many tasks as a maid-of-all-work with tending a garden and with employment as a worsted out-worker for a local clothier, spinning consignments of wool which she received from him at regular intervals.[50]

Servants' by-employments were often hidden from view and tended to become visible, certainly in the case of petty moneylending, only if financial and/or legal problems arose. Servants, however, enjoyed other sources of supplementary income, other bonuses. A benevolent employer like the unmarried seventeenth-century Herefordshire gentlewoman Joyce Jefferies seems to have treated her maidservants as surrogate daughters, rewarding them with occasional treats, and special gifts when they married. The good relations often continued even when such servants had left her employ; it appears that Jefferies became godmother to some of their offspring and provided further presents. The link with one such maidservant, Anne Davies, was particularly close. She was given a fine silk wedding gown in June 1641 when she married. Jefferies paid for the midwife's and nurse's charges when Davies gave birth to a daughter the following year and picked up the bill for the cakes and wine served at the time of her churching. Beatrice, Davies's daughter, became a firm favourite of the maid's former employer, who had coats and dresses made for her and had her stay with her at her home. (Jefferies seems to have been especially warmhearted and generous. She gave money to a Hereford baker whose house burned down in a fire and even rewarded a young boy who pleased her by singing like a blackbird.) Some employers, like Sir John Vanbrugh, rewarded good service with extra payments –

'godspennies' on top of the agreed annual wages. But such payments, it was felt, had to be seen as the occasional freewill 'extras' that they were, and not as some kind of regular entitlement. It was a fault in servants, Richard Vaughan, had said at the beginning of the seventeenth century, to try to wheedle such 'booty' from their employers.[51] Servants from larger households, sent to buy household supplies, often received 'poundage' – a percentage of the bill – from shopkeepers, which was then charged as a concealed mark-up to their employers. Other shopkeepers sometimes rewarded with liquor servants who brought them their master's trade, the concealed cost of which was also included in the master's account. Middlesex JPs received complaints about the practice in 1725. At the end of the nineteenth century poundage as a perk to cooks was being actively resisted. *The Duties of Servants* (1894) recommended that discovery of the practice should be taken as sufficient grounds for dismissal.[52]

Within the household there were other regular perks to be had. Some employers allocated servants an agreed ration of tea and sugar, and encountered bitter resentment if they did not follow the practice, which by the late eighteenth century was coming to be viewed as a right. Stedman's diary for 24 October 1785, for instance, angrily records the case of two washerwomen who 'ran off in a most impertinent manner because they could have no sugar to their tea'.[53] Butlers and cooks felt entitled to any leftover wine, cooking fat, meat scraps, bread and candle ends; it was still common practice at the end of the nineteenth century to allow cooks in larger households to claim the dripping from roast joints of meat as their standard perk.[54]

Mistresses' cast-off clothes came to be viewed as the rightful perk of ladies' maids if not servant maids, though in time the practice came to be disapproved of, since it blurred social distinctions.[55] 'Christmas boxes', in the form either of outright seasonal gifts from employers to servants or of licence to solicit token gifts from family members, guests and neighbours were another established practice. Walpole's porter, it was said, raised as much as £80 in this way. Isabella, maid-of-all-work to an insolvent East End of London debtor, in 1746 bargained with lodgers and neighbours over her Christmas box 'entitlement' and shamed one man into increasing his contribution from half a crown to 3s.[56] A running grievance in the eighteenth century among employers in larger households was the time-honoured practice among footmen of collecting 'card money' for new packs of cards distributed at domestic gambling parties.[57]

But all this was nothing as compared with the way in which the entrenched practice of vails became a *cause célèbre* in the course of the eighteenth century. Vails were tips intimidatingly extracted from departing guests in larger households and, like gratuities to waiters and waitresses in today's restaurants, were the direct consequence of low wages. Sir Joshua Reynolds once engaged a servant for £5 a year but informed him that 'the door', that is, vails, would be worth £100. Attention has been drawn to other similar examples. Sir Edward Gascoigne, visiting Nunnington Hall, Yorkshire, in July 1729 doled out £3 16s 6d in total to housekeeper, butler, cooks, footmen, coachman and groom, chambermaid and postillion.[58]

Foreign visitors to England, unused to vails in their own countries, complained vociferously about the practice, which they first mistakenly thought was a xenophobic infliction only upon them and not imposed in blanket fashion upon all guests, regardless of nationality, in elite households. César de Saussure, for example, in the second half of the 1720s, was one of them:

> If you wish to pay your respects to a nobleman and to visit him you must give his porter money from time to time or else his master will never be at home for you. If you take a meal with a person of rank, you must give every one of the five or six footmen a coin when leaving. They will be ranged in file in the hall, and the least you can give them is one shilling each. Should you fail to do this you will be treated insolently the next time. My Lord Southwell stopped me one day in the park and reproached me most amicably with my having let some time pass before going to his house to take soup with him. 'In truth, my Lord,' I answered, 'I am not rich enough to take soup with you often.' His Lordship understood my meaning.[59]

A very similar complaint from another foreign visitor appeared in *The Gentleman's Magazine* in 1748. An increasing number of Englishmen concurred with this hostile view. John Shebbeare (1709–88), writing under pseudonym B. Angeloni in 1755, saw vails directly undermining servants' deference to their masters. If a major part of their income no longer came from their wages but was picked up from visitors, how could it be otherwise? The author of a 1754 tract lamented that although the case against them was self-evident vails might have become too deeply entrenched to be capable of abolition.[60]

Jonas Hanway (1712–86), however, was one who refused to accept that vails were a permanent fixture and he campaigned vigorously to bring them to an end. 'This hydra,' he declared, 'is not invincible.' The practice, in his view, represented a foolish abdication of authority on the part of masters, allowing servants, as a result, to use vails as part of their power base. These tips were, he said, in a striking phrase, 'a republican tyranny', He found it inexplicable that many masters appeared to turn a blind eye to the disgraceful practice, which was nothing less than a maliciously levied private tax on friendship and hospitality. It was positively shameful, in his view,

> to observe the master of the house with all the adroitness he can exert shun the sight of his guests when they leave his doors that he may not be a spectator of a practice at which he is equally ashamed and scandalised notwithstanding the universality of it.

Vails were self-evidently a 'national folly' and England was 'too wise a nation to prefer slavery to freedom though we frequently play the fool for a time'. Common sense was bound to prevail sooner rather than later, and higher wages would produce the inevitable and eagerly anticipated extinction of vails. Due to concerted action by employers Scotland was already pointing the way which England might follow.[61] D'Archenholz, another foreign commentator, believed that at the time he was writing (1791) the 'scandalous practice of giving vails so much in vogue twenty years ago is now almost entirely banished'.[62]

This was far too optimistic. Vails, though by now much less widespread, in fact continued into the twentieth century. Ernest King, valet to the de Winchfields in the 1920s, could accumulate £16 in a single week from this source when there was a houseful of guests, considerably more than his entire annual salary in his previous employment. *Gosford Park*, the 2001 film about country house living in the inter-war period, accurately depicted vail-giving as one of many old-style practices that were still alive and well, much to the annoyance of the financially hard pressed Lady Constance, who found the stubbornly immortal practice to be one of the greatest challenges of country house visiting.[63]

NOTES

1 Majorie K. McIntosh, *Working Women in English Society, 1300–1620* (Cambridge, 2005), p. 46; D. Baker (ed.), *The Inhabitants of Cardington in 1782*, Bedfordshire Historical Record Society, 52 (1973), p. 44. The characteristic age structure of household servants was a European, not just English, phenomenon. Even in the early twentieth century in Czechoslovakia only 2.3 per cent of servants were over sixty. (Ludmila Fialova, 'Domestic staff in the Czech Lands at the turn of the nineteenth and twentieth centuries', in Fauve-Chamoux, *Domestic Service*, p. 158.)

2 D. V. Glass (ed.), *London Inhabitants within the Walls, 1695*, London Record Soc., II (1966), p. xxvi.

3 P. Earle, *The Making of the English Middle Class. Business, Society and Family Life in London, 1660–1730* (London, 1989), p. 219; J. F. Merritt, *The Social World of Early Modern Westminster. Abbey, Court and Community, 1525–1640* (Manchester, 2005), pp. 174–5; L. Schwarz, 'English servants and their employers during the eighteenth and nineteenth centuries', *Economic History Review*, 52 (1999), 236–56, 237; Hecht, *Domestic Servant Class*, p. 6; Glass, *London Inhabitants*, p. xxvi; quoted in Hecht, *Domestic Servant Class*, pp. 8, 12.

4 D. Souden, 'Migrants and the population structure of later seventeenth-century English provincial cities and market towns', in P. Clark (ed.), *The Transformation of English Provincial Towns* (London, 1984), p. 150; Hecht, *Domestic Servant Class*, p. 4; Huntington Library, San Marino, CA, Temple STT Personal Box 99 (16); Frances P. Verney (ed.), *Memoirs of the Verney Family during the Civil War* (4 vols., London, 1892), III, p. 449; S. Hindle, 'Sir Richard Newdigate and the "Great Survey" of Chilvers Cotton', in C. Dyer and Catherine Richardson (eds.), *William Dugdale, Historian, 1605–1686* (Woodbridge, 2009), p. 165; Gladys Scott Thomson, *Life in a Noble Household, 1641–1700* (London, 1937), pp. 113–24; Thomson, *The Russells in Bloomsbury, 1669–1771* (London, 1940), pp. 239, 226, 227; Hecht, *Domestic Servant Class*, pp. 5, 7; Pamela Horn, *Flunkies and Scullions. Life below Stairs in Georgian England* (Stroud, 2004), pp. 7, 12; Josiah Dare, *Counsellor Manners his last Legacy to his Son* (London, 1710), p. 67.

5 Pamela Horn, *The Rise and Fall of the Victorian Servant* (London, 1975), p. 5; Thomson, *The Russells in Bloomsbury*, pp. 226–7; Schwarz, 'English servants and their employers', 241; Elizabeth Ewan, 'Mistresses of themselves? Female domestic servants and by-employments in sixteenth-century Scottish towns,' in Fauve-Chamoux, *Domestic Service*, p. 413; Froide, *Never Married. Single Women in Early Modern England*, p. 89.

6 Quoted in L. Stone, *The Road to Divorce. England, 1530–1987* (Oxford, 1990), p. 218; quoted in Horn, *Flunkies and Scullions*, p. 79.

7 J. E. Tierney (ed.), *The Correspondence of Robert Dodsley, 1733–1764* (Cambridge, 1988), p. 80; quoted in Horn, *Flunkies and Scullions*, p. 79; *Hell upon Earth, or, The Town in an Uproar* (London, 1729), p. 32; D'Archenholz, *A Picture of England* (Dublin, 1791), p. 230; Horn, *Flunkies and Scullions*, p. 80; *The State and Case of the Native Servants [of Ireland]* (Dublin, 1750), p. 1.

8 Habib, *Black Lives*, pp. 48, 86, 204, 213; Waterfield, *Below Stairs*, p. 140; Glass, *London Inhabitants*, p. 332; Vita Sackville-West, *Knole and the Sackvilles* (London, 1931), p. 191; *Memoirs of the Verney Family during the Civil War*, IV, pp. 469–70; Holmes, 'Domestic Service in Yorkshire', p. 51; D. Underdown, *Fire from Heaven. Life in an English Town in the Seventeenth Century* (London, 1992), p. 101; D. Dabydeen, *Hogarth's Blacks. Images of Blacks in Eighteenth-Century English Art* (Manchester, 1987), p. 21; D. Cressy, *England on Edge. Crisis and Revolution, 1640–1642* (Oxford, 2006), p. 54; Amanda Flather,

Gender and Space in Early Modern England (Woodbridge, 2007), p. 65; Elizabeth Silverthorne (ed.), *Deposition Book of Richard Wyatt, JP, 1767–1776*, Surrey Record Soc. 30 (1978), p. 90.

9 Quoted in Gretchen Gerzina, *Black England. Life before Emancipation* (London, 1995), p. 41; Fielding, *Extracts from such of the Penal Laws as particularly relate to the Peace and Good Order of this Metropolis* (new edn, London, 1768), pp. 143–4.

10 D. Defoe, *The Family Instructor* (15th edn., 1761), II, pp. 290–7; Richardson, *Pamela*, p. 504.

11 J. W. Streeten, *Epitaphia, or, A Collection of Memorials inscribed to the Memory of Good and Faithful Servants* (London, 1826), p. 7; Gerzina, *Black England*, pp. 43–52; P. Yorke, *Crude Ditties* (Wrexham, 1802), pp. 30–1; Carolyn Steedman, 'Lord Mansfield's women', *Past & Present*, 176 (2002), 137; Gerzina, *Black England*, pp. 54–67; Waterfield, *Below Stairs*, p. 135.

12 D. Marcombe, *English Small Town Life. Retford, 1520–1642* (Nottingham, 1993), p. 98; *Court of Good Counsell* (London, 1607), unpaginated, chapter 27; W. Addison, *Essex Heyday* (London, 1949), p. 93.

13 Huntington Library, Temple Additional Mss. HM 46489. Box 1; *ibid.*, Box 2.

14 Quoted in Sambrook, *Keeping their Place*, p. 4; Joan Wake and Deborah C. Webster (eds.), *The Letters of Daniel Eaton to the third Earl of Cardigan, 1725–1732*, Northants Record Soc., 24 (1971), p. 18; *Blundell Diaries*, III, pp. 140–1, 200.

15 L. G. Mitchell (ed.), *The Purefoy Letters, 1735–1753* (London, 1973), pp. 146, 149, 150.

16 Sambrook, *Country House at Work*, pp. 66, 68.

17 Ann Haly (ed.), *The Complete Servant, by Samuel and Sarah Adams*, with an introduction by Pamela Horn (Lewes, 1989), p. 8; Vickery, *The Gentleman's Daughter. Women's Lives in Georgian England* (New Haven, CT, and London, 1998), appendix 5, pp. 135–6, 141; Alice Fairfax-Lucy, *Charlecote and the Lucys* (Oxford, 1958), *passim*.

18 Stratford on Avon, Warwickshire, still had a 'runaway mop' fair – the relic of a hiring fair – in the 1970s. (C. B. Patten), *England as seen by an American Banker* (Boston, MA, 1885), pp. 119–21; Ann Taylor, *The Present of a Mistress to a Young Servant* (10th edn., London, 1832), pp. 61, 63.

19 Saville, *Secret Comment*, p. 308; Reed, *Register Office*, p. 20; Trusler, *The London Adviser and Guide* (London, 1786), p. 266; Adams, *Complete Servant*, p. 32; Clarissa Packard, *Recollections of a Housekeeper* (New York, 1834), p. 22.

20 Merry E. Wiesner, *Working Women in Renaissance Germany* (New Brunswick, NJ, 1986), pp. 83–4; Merritt, *Early Modern Westminster*, p. 174, F. A. Norman and L. G. Lee, 'A further note on labour exchanges in the seventeenth century', *Economic History Supplement to Economic Journal*, I (1928), 399–402, M. Dorothy George, 'The early history of registry offices,' *Economic History*

Supplement to Economic Journal, I (1929), 570–90; Helen Dingwall, *Late Seventeenth-Century Edinburgh. A Demographic Study* (Aldershot, 1994), p. 48, R. A. Houston, *Social Change in the Age of the Enlightenment. Edinburgh, 1660–1760* (Oxford, 1994), p. 90; Fauve-Chamoux, *Domestic Service*, p. 290.

21 Fielding, *A Plan of the Universal Register Office, 1751* (repr. Middletown, CT, 1988), pp. 6, 8, 9. On Tancred see pp. 201–2.

22 R. H. Tawney and Eileen Power (eds.), *Tudor Economic Documents* (London, 1924), I, p. 325; J. C. Atkinson (ed.), *Quarter Sessions Records*, North Riding Record Soc., I (1884), pp. 61, 69; Tancred, *A Scheme for an Act of Parliament for the better Regulating of Servants* (London, 1724), pp. 15, 19.

23 *Blundell Diaries*, I, p. 69; B. Harrison, 'The servants of William Gossip', *Georgian Group Journal*, 6 (1996), 138; *Footman's Looking Glass*, p. 26.

24 Defoe, *Religious Courtship* (London, 1722, 10th edn, 1796), p. v; R.W. Ketton-Cremer, *Felbrigg. The Story of a House* (London, 1986), pp. 139–41; S. Thompson (ed.), *The Journal of John Gabriel Stedman* (London, 1962), pp. 271, 275; Isabella Beeton, *The Book of Household Management* (London, 1861, rpr. 1986), p. 7; Hecht, *Domestic Servant Class*, p. 83.

25 Trusler, *The London Adviser and Guide*, p. 47; Huntingford, *The Laws of Masters and Servants Considered* (London, 1790), p. 98.

26 Saville, *Secret Comment*, pp. 308, 315, 313, 328; Martineau, 'Modern domestic service,' *Edinburgh Review*, 115 (1862), 434.

27 Saville, *Secret Comment*, pp. 88, 252, 255, 293–4, 308; Vickery, *Gentleman's Daughter*, p. 137; Harrison, 'Servants of William Gossip', 135; R. Scott-Moncrieff (ed.), *The Household Book of Lady Grisell Baillie, 1692–1733*, Scottish History Soc., new ser. I (1911), p. li; Horn, *Flunkies and Scullions*, p. 14; *Satan's Harvest Home* (1749), p. 4, quoted in P. Seleski, 'Women, work and cultural change in eighteenth and early nineteenth-century London', in T. Harris (ed.), *Popular Culture in England, c. 1500–1850* (Basingstoke, 1995), p. 150; Earle, *English Middle Class*, pp. 177, 221.

28 *Ladies' Cabinet*, pp. 51–2; J. Beresford (ed.), *James Woodforde. Diary of a Country Parson* (5 vols., London, 1931, rpr. 1981), IV, p. 124.

29 *Court of Good Counsell*, unpaginated, chapter 23; *The Servants' Friend*, pp. 2, 21; *History of Charles Jones*, p. 14; Horn, *Life below Stairs in the Twentieth Century*, p. 43. Because of its elite readership *The Times* developed a particular association with servant-keeping. A free advertisement service offered to servants seeking a placement began in 1913. (*Ibid.*, p. 161.)

30 R. Cust (ed.), *The Papers of Sir Richard Grosvenor, first Baronet, 1585–1645*, Record Society of Lancashire and Cheshire, 134 (1996), p. 33; A. Jessopp (ed.), *The Lives of the Norths* (3 vols., London, 1890) I, p. 30; Munby, *Faithful Servants*, p. 2; Lynn Botelho and Pat Thane (eds.), *Women and Ageing in British Society since 1500* (Harlow, 2001), p. 100; Hecht, *Domestic Servant Class*, p. 82; Sambrook, *Country House at Work*, p. 61; Waterson, *Servants' Hall*, p. 25. Much later Annie Jones, who died in the 1950s, had been in service with the

Cook family of Bristol for eighty years since she started out with them as an orphan skivvy. (Horn, *Rise and Fall of the Victorian Servant*, p. 138.)

31 Quoted in Sambrook, *Keeping their Place*, p. 166.

32 J. P. Cooper (ed.), *Wentworth Papers, 1597–1628*, Camden Soc., 4th ser., 12 (1973), p. 15, Woolley, *The Gentlewoman's Companion*, p. 208; quoted in Holmes, 'Domestic Service in Yorkshire', p. 131; *A York Dialogue between Ned and Harry* (1783), pp. 15–16, quoted in Hill, *Servants*, p. 110.

33 *The Duties of Servants. A Practical Guide to the Routine of Domestic Service* (1894, repr. East Grinstead, 1993), pp. 51–2.

34 Dingwall, *Late Seventeenth-Century Edinburgh*, p. 48; Wise, *Diary of William Taylor*, *passim*; Hudson, *Munby*, *passim*; Stanley, *Diaries of Hannah Cullwick*, *passim*.

35 *Wanton Wenches*, pp. 45–6; Gowing, *Domestic Dangers*, pp. 150–1; Dorothy Bowen, 'Thomas Mort of Dam House', *Huntington Library Quarterly*, 8 (1944–45), 330; D. Gibson (ed.), *A Parson in the Vale of White Horse. George Woodward's Letters from East Hendred, 1753–1761* (Stroud, 1982), pp. 128, 150; F. G. Stokes (ed.), *The Blechley Diary of the Rev William Cole, 1765–1767* (London, 1931), p. 78; Thompson, *Journal of John Gabriel Stedman*, p. 364; *The Diary of a Farmer's Wife, 1796–1797* (Harmondsworth, 1982).

36 *Duties of Servants*, p. 53.

37 Richard Clemsell, *A Pleasant New Dialogue, or, The Discourse between the Servingman and the Husbandman* (London, c. 1635); Harriet Martineau, 'Modern domestic service', *Edinburgh Review*, 15 (1862), 425; Hinde, *A Faithfull Remonstrance of the Holy Life and Happy Death of John Bruen of Bruen Stapleford in the County of Chester, Esq.* (London, 1641), p. 61; *Advice to Servants* (Bath, n.d.), single A3 sheet; *History of Charles Jones*, p. 14; Waterfield, *Below Stairs*, p. 56; Waterson, *Servants' Hall*, p. 25; Earle, *English Middle Class*, p. 321.

38 Munby, *Faithful Servants*, p. 2; Hecht, *Domestic Servant Class*, p. 175; P. C. Yorke (ed.), *The Diary of John Baker* (London, 1931), p. 56; Taylor, *The Present of a Mistress to a Young Servant*, pp. 6–23; Horn, *Flunkies and Scullions*, p. 213; W. J. Smith (ed.), *Herbert Correspondence . . .* , Board of Celtic Studies, University of Wales History and Law series, 21 (1968, 1998), p. 31; Horn, *Flunkies and Scullions*, p. 213.

39 Lucas, *Duty of Servants*, p. 193; Grey, *An Apology for the Servants* (London, 1760), p. 19; Barclay, *Advice to Servants* (c. 1800), p. 7; British Library, Egerton Mss 3054, Joyce Jefferies Account Book, *passim*; Horn, *Flunkies and Scullions*, pp. 192–3.

40 Hecht, *Domestic Servant Class*, pp. 142–9; Hill, *Servants*, has a chapter on 'The moral economy of servants' but does not dwell for any length of time on wages as such; Holmes, 'Domestic Service in Yorkshire', pp. 87–8; J. H. E. Bennett and J. C. Dewhurst (eds.), *Quarter Sessions Records. County Palatine of Chester, 1559–1760*, Record Soc. of Lancashire and Cheshire, 94

(1940), p. 68, D. Woodward (ed.), *The Farming and Memorandum Books of Henry Best of Elmswell*, British Academy Records of Social and Economic History, new ser. 8 (1984), p. 138; Atkinson, *Quarter Sessions Records* (North Riding of Yorkshire), pp. 122, 209; E. Turner, 'On the domestic habits and mode of life of a Sussex gentleman', *Sussex Archaeological Collections*, 23 (1871) p. 48; Addison, *Essex Heyday*, p. 94; *Blundell Diaries*, I, p. 203; Horn, *Flunkies and Scullions*, p. 195; Hampshire Record Office 19/M61/1441; Vickery, *Gentleman's Daughter*, p. 137; Horn, *Flunkies and Scullions*, p. 197; *Diary of John Baker*, p. 53; *Diary of a Country Parson*, V, p. 94.

41 Defoe's views on the servant problem, especially in the metropolis, were expressed in a stream of overheated publications. See pp. 46–7, 180–4, below. Mandeville, *Fable of the Bees* (London, 1729, repr., 1981), II, p. 56.

42 Hecht, *Domestic Servant Class*, p. 11; P. Clemit (ed.), *Political and Philosophical Writings of William Godwin*, V, *Educational and Literary Writings* (London, 1993). 'The Enquirer' Part 2, Essay IV, 'Of servants', pp. 169, 171. I am exceedingly grateful to Yale University Library for providing me with a photocopy of Heasel's scarce publication.

43 Huntington Library, San Marino, CA, ST 82 James Brydges, first Duke of Chandos, Payments to tradesmen and servants, 1722–32; ST 87 Wages notebook, 1718–20; Oxford *DNB*, Pepusch and Handel.

44 Mortlock, *Aristocratic Splendour*, pp. 195, 196, 198, 200, 201.

45 Thomson, *Russells in Bloomsbury*, p. 239; Trusler, *London Adviser*, p. 48. Housemaids in remote Anglesey could be had for £13 a year as late as the 1920s. (Horn, *Life below Stairs in the Twentieth Century*, p. 182.)

46 Mortlock, *Aristocratic Splendour*, p. 208; Hecht, *Domestic Servant Class*, p. 154; *Diary of a Journey to England in the Years 1761–1762 by Count Kielmansegge* (London, 1902), pp. 19–20; Trusler, *London Adviser*, p. 48.

47 G. G. Smith (ed.), *The Spectator* (4 vols., London, 1907), I, p. 273; *The World*, quoted in Marshall, 'Domestic servants of the eighteenth century', 19; *Blechley Diary of the Rev. William Cole*, p. 11.

48 *Duties of Servants*, pp. 26–7.

49 W. J. Blake (ed.), 'Hooker's *Synopsis Chorographical of Devonshire*' in *Reports and Transactions of the Devonshire Association*, 47 (1915), p. 346, quoted in E. Duffy, *The Voices of Morebath. Reformation and Rebellion in an English Village* (New Haven, CT, and London, 2001, 2003), p. 9; Elizabeth Ewan, 'Mistresses of themselves? Female domestic servants and by-employments in sixteenth-century Scottish towns', in Fauve-Chamoux, *Domestic Service*, pp. 412–13, 430, 428; British Library, Egerton Mss 3054, Joyce Jefferies Account Book, f. 61.

50 Steedman, *Master and Servant*, chapter 2, *passim*.

51 British Library, Egerton Mss 3054, Account Book of Joyce Jefferies, ff. 44, 49, 50, 65, 44, 41; Holmes, 'Domestic Service in Yorkshire', p. 71; R. Vaughan, *The Golden Grove* (London, 1608), unpaginated, chapter 17.

52 J. P. Malcolm, *Anecdotes of the Manners and Customs of London during the Eighteenth Century* (2nd edn., 2 vols., London, 1810), I, p. 139; *Duties of Servants*, p. 9.
53 *Stedman's Journal*, p. 267.
54 *Duties of Servants*, p. 83.
55 *Ibid.*, p. 106.
56 *A Foreign View of England in 1725–1729. Letters of César de Saussure* (London, 1992, 1995), p. 121; T. Hitchcock, *Down and Out in Eighteenth-Century London* (London, 2004), p. 183.
57 Hecht, *Domestic Servant Class*, pp. 169–70.
58 M. Dorothy George, 'The early history of registry offices', *Economic History Supplement to Economic Journal* (1929), 584; Turner, *What the Butler Saw*, p. 53; Holmes, 'Domestic Service in Yorkshire', p. 93.
59 Saussure, *Foreign View*, pp. 120–1.
60 Angeloni, quoted in Marshall, 'Domestic servants', 24; Horn, *Flunkies and Scullions*, p. 207; *Public Nuisance Considered*, p. 45.
61 Hanway, *Eight Letters to his Grace the Duke of – on the Custom of Vails giving in England* (London, 1760), pp. 61, 49, 12; Hanway, *The Sentiments and Advice of Thomas Trueman, a Virtuous and Understanding Footman* (London, 1760), pp. 44, 55.
62 D'Archenholz, *A Picture of England* (Dublin, 1791), p. 207.
63 Horn, *Life below Stairs in the Twentieth Century*, pp. 37, 61–2.

5

HOUSING, DIET, DRESS, WELFARE, RECREATION AND EDUCATION

I am not against using the forecourt for common passage of servants but on one side only and not in the principal walk.
(Roger North, 'On planning a country house', in H. Colvin and J. Newman, eds., *Of Building. Roger North's Writings on Architecture*, Oxford, 1981, p. 129)

Decency and neatness are sufficient ornaments for servants . . .
(Nicholas Zinzano, *The Servants Calling*, London, 1725, pp. 21–2)

Servants require more than masters and mistresses can afford and what madness is it to encourage them in this by industriously increasing at our cost that knowledge which they will be sure to make us pay for again.
(Bernard Mandeville, *The Fable of the Bees*, ed. P. Harth, Harmondsworth, 1970, p. 307)

Live-in servants, of course, were housed and fed – that was one of the major attractions of this field of employment, especially for teenagers newly departed from their own homes. The younger they were the smaller their money wages would be. For the youngest, like John Baker's poor relation maidservant mentioned in the previous chapter, there might be no wages at all. In such cases having a roof over their heads, somewhere to sleep, regular diet, and often clothing provided, was literally all-important. But for the majority of servants, with the notable exception of those high-ranking employees in large households, it was the wages, not the room and board, which constituted the 'extras'. That fact was emphasised by the infrequency with which wages were actually paid; quarterly or half-yearly intervals were common. With their daily needs provided, servants were judged by many commentators and employers to be safely cushioned against any prevailing harsh external economic realities. What did higher prices of provisions and household necessities mean to people who did not have to pay for them? Tax-paying employers, sometimes hard pressed themselves, were shouldering all the financial burdens, so it was piously claimed, and providing their servants with a carefree, protected, insulated miniature world in which they lived and worked at no cost to themselves. It was rank ingratitude, so employers, churchmen and other commentators had it, if servants did not recognise their enviable lot in life. 'Let none repine at being servants who through Grace have such a liberty and freedom as this,' declared Richard Mayo in 1693. The same refrain echoed through the following decades. Servants, insisted one commentator in 1754,

> have no care, they have the necessaries of life provided for them and a yearly sum for their encouragement to lay by for their better support at a proper time. [They] have really nothing but a very easy duty to perform, and all that is required of them beyond that is but to behave with humility and obedience to their superiors as becomes their station.[1]

Separate, dedicated accommodation for servants was almost unknown, even in greater households, before the second half of the seventeenth century, as Amanda Flather and others have shown. No separate bedrooms, even dormitory-style, were provided for them. They slept where they could on folding truckle beds (which could be removed when not in use) in halls, kitchens, passageways, closets, cellars, barns, or in or near their employers' bedrooms, where they could be at their beck and call. Couch or settee bedsteads stood in passageways at Erdigg in the 1720s so that servants could sleep close to where they would be needed. Sometimes young maidservants as well as nurses shared a bed with the employer's own children, occasionally with tragic consequences. Isaac Archer, noting the sad death in infancy of his own daughter in 1682, observed the child had 'a tender hearted nurse but we fear 'twas overlaid as many that saw it did positively say, there being four in the bed'. Sometimes maidservants slept at the foot of their master and mistress's bed. It was not uncommon for vulnerable, anxious mistresses who had experienced physical abuse from their husband to have a maid sleep with them in the same bed for extra security and to try to keep their spouse at bay. Servants were expected to stay up until their master and mistress were abed, to air their beds and carry candles before them as they turned in for the night. In some larger households young menservants were commonly expected to sleep, like human watchdogs, across the inside of doorways. Only in the course of the seventeenth century do references to separately designated, usually gendered, sleeping accommodation (maids' chambers and men's chambers) begin to appear in household inventories and other records. Since the rooms were characteristically shared, it was exceedingly rare for servants to possess keys of their own to control access to the place where they slept; in the course of her research on this topic Flather found only one example of a maidservant having a key to her own room. Employers, therefore, had easy access to where servants slept, a fact which encouraged prying, domination and, at times, sexual exploitation. In a 1621 Essex court case it emerged that a mistress, Isobel Collin, 'suspecting [her servant] Margaret to be lousy did one day go into her chamber and searching her bed did find the same full of lice'. At an Old Bailey court case in 1750 it emerged that a young maidservant, Mary Thursel, had been raped by her employer, whose bedroom she had been obliged to share, and who had then given her money to keep quiet about the incident. The most personally controlled 'space' the majority of sixteenth and early seventeenth-century servants could aspire to was their own lockable box containing their personal possessions. Other valuables were constantly carried about in pockets and pouches.[2] The ultimate degradation for inmates of the Wimbledon workhouse in the late eighteenth century was to be deprived of the key even to their own chest or box. The final scene of Hogarth's 'Harlot's progress' (1732) depicts the unfortunate woman's box being rifled as she lies dying.[3]

Servants' quarters in larger houses, first in the countryside and then in London, became more common in the course of the seventeenth century as architectural changes accommodated the growing desire among the employing classes for more privacy. The rebuilding of Woburn after 1626 on the Russells' Bedfordshire estate to Inigo Jones's designs incorporated not only extensive new kitchen quarters, but living accommodation for servants and a servants' hall. Subsequent adaptations of their Bloomsbury mansion even provided upper servants with small suites of rooms. The house steward and housekeeper each had three rooms they could call their own. The butler had two. Lesser servants invariably had to share rooms, kitchen maids on the ground floor close to their workplace, housemaids in the attic, and footmen in lofts above the stables. Roger North refashioned his old house in Norfolk, since he could not afford to build a completely new one, providing designated servants' quarters for the first time. As an architect for others and a writer on house design North always advocated the provision of separate living accommodation for servants; it was more economical in the long run and kept them out of sight.

> As for servants I know it is usual to clutter them all into a kitchen, partly to save fire, and partly for want of room. But that is not consistent with good economy, because not only the waste of meat and drink from the petulance of idle fellows who will be sponging but it also hinders the passage and management of the servants assigned to the kitchen employments.

North argued, however, that the servants' hall should be kept away from the main rooms of the house, 'for the noises will be insupportable', and there was much to be said in his view for keeping servants' living quarters below ground rather than in attics, 'for all offensive things fall rather than rise'. Isaac Ware, another leading architectural pundit of the time, agreed and recommended that such basement rooms should at least have floorboards, for the 'necessary care of these people's health'.[4]

Other architects of the period, Sir John Vanbrugh and Sir Roger Pratt among them, proceeded in a likeminded way, creating not only servants' quarters in their new commissions, but corridors, extra doors (sometimes skilfully concealed) and back or side staircases to keep servants invisible and to provide more privacy for their employers. But even with the new improvements servants still heard and saw too much for comfort of what went on around them in the household context and for this reason were commonly called upon to give evidence in matrimonial dispute cases. (See p. 198.) By the early eighteenth century bell systems further emphasised social and spatial separation between employers and employed and removed the need for noisy summonses. Horseheath, near Cambridge, Kingston Lacy in Dorset and Coleshill in Berkshire, some of Pratt's best known creations, followed this pattern of territorial separation of master and servant. The benefits were obvious. Separate living accommodation and internal routes for domestic staff guaranteed that 'no dirty servants may be seen passing to and fro by those who are above, no noises heard, nor ill scents smelt'. Even valets, lodged in small rooms near their masters, were obliged to use the back stairs so that they 'need not foul the great ones and whatsoever is of use may be brought up or carried down the back way'.[5]

At Dunham Massey, Cheshire, a new servants' court, with a servants' hall, was added to the house around 1720. Here, as elsewhere, the degree of comfort in servants' bedrooms varied according to their status in the household hierarchy. Later in the century the new house built at Seaham, County Durham, by the Milbankes in 1791 included ample quarters for servants – a servants' hall, housekeeper's room, kitchens, larders, and with bedrooms above these for servants. Shared sleeping accommodation in such households for lesser servants was the norm until well into the nineteenth century. An advertisement in a London newspaper in 1781 for rented accommodation stipulated that there must be a room for a lady's maid and 'a garret for common servants'. At Charlecote, Warwickshire, menservants and maidservants had dormitory-style bedrooms in separate attics which were locked at night by the housekeeper, a custom still in force at the end of the Victorian period. Housemaids at Newby Hall, Yorkshire, in the early eighteenth century shared bedrooms and sometimes beds. At Everingham Hall in the same county even the housekeeper shared her bedroom with two maidservants and occasionally also with her lover as an additional, unofficial, occupant.[6]

Newly built houses in London by 1700 had basements containing kitchens and servants' rooms and they were provided with servants' staircases. Such houses, however, as Tim Meldrum has reminded us, were by no means always in single occupancy, a fact which undoubtedly complicates our understanding of the impact of changing architectural design and room use. D'Archenholz when travelling in England around 1780 assumed too readily that new properties in the fashionable West End contained only one household, observing that they 'have each of them two storeys underground to which light is communicated by means of a forecourt. The servants are lodged, and the kitchen, storerooms etc. are placed there, so the rest of the house is entirely at the disposal of the master.' John Evelyn's late seventeenth-century design for a scholars' retreat for the Royal Society was entirely in line with current architectural thinking by planning for service quarters and living accommodation for servants which, stowed away in basement and attic, meant that menials were entirely hidden from view. Increasingly by the first decades of the eighteenth century in provincial towns and cities and even in rural farmhouses servants were being segregated from the master's immediate family.[7]

Spatial segregation of masters and servants, the new ideal of the late seventeenth and eighteenth centuries, was no less boldly expressed in the public setting. Bath, with its huge seasonal influx of employers and their staff, not to mention the large number of those regularly engaged in service capacities in the pump room, baths, assembly rooms and other fashionable meeting places and lodging houses, and as sedan chair men, struggled to achieve some measure of social zoning. So in the first half of the eighteenth century did the proprietors of the new York Assembly Rooms, the original design of which included an entirely separate vault for footmen and other attendants. That made it understandably more difficult for their masters to summon them, so a ground-floor passageway was added to the main part of the building. That, unfortunately, worked all too well and facilitated a flood of unseemly and noisy servant traffic into the Assembly Rooms themselves, which greatly annoyed the fashionable company. The steward and his assistants were called upon in 1750 to flush out the servant influx and to restore decorum.[8]

Within elite houses servant comforts varied according to the size and wealth of the establishment. Footmen and housemaids at Canons, Middlesex, home of the Duke of Chandos, enjoyed feather beds, and in some rooms chests of drawers, chairs and inlaid tables. The Russells provided their London staff with something similar or even better; fine but old furniture and furnishings which had previously seen use in the main part of the house ended up, recycled, in the servants' quarters. The housekeeper's breakfast room, for instance, contained a mahogany table and mirror, a Persian rug and a good clock. John Evelyn noted that in the post-Restoration households of Lord Arlington and the Countess of Sutherland 'servants never lived with more ease and convenience' and that 'the meanest servant is lodged so neat and cleanly'. But elsewhere menial servants' living accommodation might be spartan in the extreme – straw pallets to lie on, for example, and benches rather than chairs on which to perch at mealtimes. In the Elizabethan period William Harrison's classic account of social conditions had it that common servants could expect little or nothing in the way of comfort. 'If they had any sheet above them it was well, for seldom had they any under their bodies to keep them from the pricking of the straw that ran oft through the canvas of the pallet and rased their hardened hides'. Such conditions, however, could be judged by servants themselves only in comparison with what they had been previously been accustomed to. Loud complaints about living conditions came only later and even then usually through the mouths of social critics rather than from servants themselves. William Godwin, for instance, writing at the very end of the eighteenth century, berated employers for providing faithful servants with living quarters that were often damp, evil-smelling, cramped, meanly furnished and uncomfortable. With servants themselves, however, regular, plentiful meals usually appeared to have weighed more in their expectations than feather beds.[9]

Servants were workhorses, so it was counterproductive as well as unjust for employers to supply them with too little to eat. 'Feed your household servants with honest common fare without delicacies,' was the advice given in one of the earliest household manuals in 1531. To give them too much was equally reprehensible. 'For the servant that is made a glutton shall never after mend his manners.' The servant's right to a sufficiency of plain, wholesome food became a recurring refrain in household manuals thereafter. It was included, for example, in the English translation of della Casa's *The Arts of Grandeur and Submission* (London, 1665). 'I have always thought it a most uncomfortable thing to keep house in so sparing a manner as to pinch the belly of servants,' declared another writer in 1669. 'Hospitality hath ever been a great honour to this nation.' Servants should not be singled out for exclusion from its benefits. Hannah Woolley, writing a few years later, was in full agreement. 'Let there be a competent allowance for the servants that they have no just cause to complain nor so much superfluity as that they may entertain a sort of loose gossip in corners, the very bane and spoil of servants.' Mean-spirited employers who starved their servants attracted comment from others of their class and, unsurprisingly, loud complaint from the victims. That such cases appear to have been relatively rare, if the surviving record is a reliable indicator, suggests that the majority of servants were not short-changed. Even in middling households, it may be safely assumed, many servants enjoyed a better diet than they would have been used to in the parental home. In elite households this would have been invariably the case.[10]

Exceptions there were, however, though, it seems, relatively few in number. In a late seventeenth-century court case in which a London merchant, William Coles, and his wife figured, servants appeared to have good cause for complaint about their meagre rations. The master and mistress and immediate family, it was said by an observer well placed to judge,

> did usually feed very high of the best sorts of food but as to servants he kept an extraordinary bad house, for the servants did very rarely eat of any of the meat . . . but what was left at [the employer's] table above stairs was generally locked up and very seldom (only some few scraps) brought down to the servants. And the food wherewith the servants were generally fed was very coarse, stale, mouldy bread and rank salt butter with some pottage made of the meat that the [merchant] and his wife ate above stairs and scraps of fish and sometimes dumplings very dry and with very little suet or other ingredients in them. And if it chanced that the servants had any of the meat it was often stale and corrupt and so stinking that they could scarcely eat it but yet were forced to eat it for mere necessity . . . And the bread and butter and also if there were at any time any cheese (which was very seldom and but ordinary) it was immediately so soon as they had dined constantly locked up so that the servants could not come at it. The said servants very seldom had any breakfasts or suppers allowed them and, if they had, it was of such ill food as they were not able to eat to any content . . . All the victuals were constantly locked up and the beer kept above stairs.

It was a complaint which revealed much about servants' expectations. Not to have plentiful meat regularly and not to have ready access to cheese and beer infringed the entitlement they felt was theirs. A late eighteenth-century clergyman's wife, it was observed by a parson from a neighbouring parish, 'used to weigh the victuals [behind] locked doors lest their servants should think they begrudged them victuals'. Parson Woodforde recorded in his diary on 8 December 1801 that servants at nearby Weston House had launched a complaint to their master against the housekeeper who was keeping them on short rations.[11]

Servants' diet varied enormously from one household to another and ultimately depended on the generosity of the employer as well as on the size of the establishment. Even in the smallest of households practice was far from uniform. In some, servants ate with the employer's own family and enjoyed the same menu; this was Thomas Turner's practice in Sussex. In others servants had to make do with left-overs or with cheaper alternative meals. We know too little about servants' actual experience in this respect as in many others. Account books for the largest elite households survive – those for Holkham, for example – but usually only list total quantities of household provisions consumed, thus preventing the social historian from knowing with certainty what servants themselves had set before them. Upper servants in any case could reasonably have expected more luxury than the minions and they took their meals, or part of their meals at least, in the steward's or housekeeper's room. Meat figured conspicuously in the servant diet of elite households especially. Precise accounting at Canons in the eighteenth century makes it clear that each servant had no less than 21 oz of beef for dinner on Tuesdays, Thursdays and Sundays and the same quantity of mutton on Wednesdays and Saturdays. Fourteen ounces of pork apiece sufficed for the other two days of the week. Pastries, jellies and fresh fruit also abounded. In the face of such gastronomic profusion Eliza Haywood's *A Present for a Servant-Maid* was one of a number of manuals which saw the need to caution servants about the sin of gluttony. Ale flowed freely to quench servants' thirst; six gallons a day was supplied to the servants' hall at Canons. In the same household cider was sometimes provided as an alternative, and upper servants could certainly expect wine. Experiencing such a diet at first hand, with the innovations introduced by French chefs and others, undoubtedly contributed to the social diffusion of the changing fads and fashions in food consumption which Joan Thirsk has explored in her study of the subject. In this respect as in others servants functioned as cultural amphibians; they took with them, either to imitate or adapt, as they moved on from their place of employment either to another household or eventually to set up home on their own account the novelties they had first encountered in service. Nothing like this rich diet, of course, could be expected in households below the top rank. In the early eighteenth-century Scottish household of Lady Grisell Baillie, for example, servants' breakfast consisted of a daily ration of oat or rye bread swilled down with beer or milk. For the main meal of the day servants here were given boiled beef and broth three times a week, broth and herring twice a week, broth and two eggs on Wednesdays, and on Saturdays broth with cheese or haggis or pudding. Tea and buttered toast was the standard breakfast for servants, as it often was for their masters, in smart London town houses by the later decades of the eighteenth century.[12]

For the most part, servants' diet was not a contentious issue. It was quite otherwise with servant dress, especially that of maids, as a succession of tract and treatise writers as well as employers vainly tried to counter the mounting tide of fashion. Arthur Dent in *The Plain Man's Pathway to Heaven* (London, 1612) railed against all vanities of dress and against mistresses who spent half the day preening themselves before venturing forth 'with their pedlar's shop upon their back . . . They do so exceedingly swell with pride that it is to be feared they will burst with it as they walk in the street' flaunting their painted faces, dyed hair and naked breasts. (Women's clothes, it is worth underlining here, were their own property, not their husband's, and for that reason had a special value attached to them.) Small wonder, he moaned, that maidservants too, flouting all sumptuary laws and aping their mistresses, were starting to over-dress and forget their humble station in life. (Dent would have been left speechless, presumably, if he had encountered the extraordinary case of Thomas Hall, a cross-dressing bisexual servant in Virginia in 1629 who changed his gender identity and clothing to suit different needs and opportunities. After a court appearance and physical examination of Hall the perplexed authorities reluctantly agreed to allow him to wear both a man's breeches and a woman's apron! And Dent, presumably, would have been in full agreement with the penance imposed on another cross-dressing manservant, Thomas Salmon, of Great Tew, who in 1633 was accused and convicted of donning women's clothes and breaking all gender taboos by attending a childbirth.) But the general trend which Dent had denounced proved unstoppable. Socially conservative Adam Martindale was horrified by the growing democratisation of fashion that was taking place around him somewhat later in the seventeenth century and contrasted it with what he remembered had been the earlier norm.

'Now every beggar's brat,' he lamented, was rushing to wear a smart gown, hood or scarf, attire which in his youth would have been considered unthinkable for those of their rank. In the second decade of the following century Defoe favoured the enforced wearing of liveries by maidservants to proclaim their dependent position and to stop such 'pert sluts' in their tracks. Such an imposition, however, was impossible to achieve. De Saussure on his travels in the same decade observed that he saw few women dressed in woollen gowns. 'Even servant maids wear silks on Sundays and holidays, when they are almost as well dressed as their mistresses.' Erasmus Jones, writing in 1737, concurred. 'Servant wenches turn up their noses at yard wide stuffs and substantial camblets; every trollop of five pounds a year appears in her silk nightgown'. Samuel Richardson, later author of *Pamela*, in his very first publication, *The Apprentice's Vade Mecum* (London, 1734) had lamented that 'pride in dress is one of the epidemic evils of the present age, immersed from the highest to the lowest in luxury and sensuality . . . The vice has inverted all order and destroyed distinction.'[13]

All that Eliza Haywood could do in the following decade was to appeal to maidservants' better nature and to try to cajole them into believing that 'nothing looks so handsome in a servant as a decent plainness':

Enquire of your mothers and grandmothers [she went on] how the servants of their times were dressed, and you will be told that it was not by laying out their wages in these fopperies they got good husbands but by the reputation of their honesty, industry and frugality in saving what they got in service.

Donning lewd fashions, Thomas Broughton continued in the same vein, invariably had the effect of making maidservants look like common harlots. But he and others like him could have saved their breath. London maidservants, said Grosley in 1772, were often so smartly dressed that 'if the mistress be not known it is no easy matter to distinguish her from her maid'. Henry Fielding's farce *The Intriguing Chambermaid* (1750) declared that the same was true of menservants and their masters; swaggering in their fashionable clothes and wigs, swearing, gambling and drinking, they competed with each other to draw attention to themselves. Soame Jenyns in 1790 was in full agreement. 'The *valet de chambre* cannot be distinguished from the master but by being better dressed.' Similar disapproving comments continued to be made throughout the nineteenth century. 'A dressy servant is a disgrace to a house,' insisted Ann Taylor, 'and renders her employers ridiculous as well as herself.' The lost battle over servant dress was still being fought in rearguard actions in the twentieth century.[14]

As with the social diffusion of changing diet, so also servants, especially in London and in major provincial towns and cities, made a major contribution to the spread of new fashions in dress in the seventeenth and eighteenth centuries. Social commentators bemoaned the fact and some employers became increasingly nervous about it. It has to be said, however, that they themselves often directly assisted the trend. In fashionable households well dressed servants were seen as an asset to the master's reputation. 'We are obliged to take the lowest of the people,' said the perceptive Soame Jenyns in 1790, 'and convert them by our own ingenuity into the genteel personages we think proper should attend us.' In better-off establishments giving cast-off clothes to servants was established practice and was regarded by domestics as a legitimate, regular perk of their employment. Even in farmers' households, Henry Best noted in 1642, 'some servants will (at their hiring) condition to have an old suit, a pair of breeches, an old hat, or a pair of shoes; and maidservants to have an apron, smock, or both . . .'. Joyce Jefferies in Herefordshire provided her maidservants with new clothes and kept their shoes in good repair. Her coachman's livery was periodically replaced and when he retired she gave him £4 to buy himself a new outfit. Lady Grisell Baillie in 1693 provided servants with coats, hats, shirts, waistcoats, cravats, aprons, bonnets and underclothes. Favoured servants, like Sarah, the much loved late eighteenth-century maidservant in Anne Hughes's *Diary of a Farmer's Wife*, fared even better, receiving choice items of clothing for special outings and again when she married. Parson Woodforde presented new pea-green gowns to his two maidservants in 1783. In 1789 each maid received a cotton gown, bought in London for £1 8s and his manservant, Ben, a waistcoat worth 6s. Further purchases of waistcoats for servants were made in 1801 and pink and white cotton gowns for his maidservants. One eighteenth-century Yorkshire serving man had 5s added to his wages 'because he wore his own breeches sometimes'. William Clift's sister, however, reported to her brother in 1795 that one of her fellow maidservants in the household where she worked was chastised and dismissed when discovered wearing her mistress's fine clothes. Young pauper servants taking up their first place were frequently provided with decent clothes by parish overseers in cases where the cost involved was deemed to be beyond the reach of their own families.[15]

Occasionally the records afford tantalising glimpses of maidservants purchasing items of dress on their account rather than relying on hand-outs from their mistresses. The account books of Hampshire drapers Mary Medhurst and Thomas North show the bills run up by a number of maidservants in the period 1764 to 1770 for purchasing various items of clothing and trimming – satin hats, stockings, mitts, handkerchiefs, lace, silk ribbons and linen. Another set of such instances derives from the household accounts of Robert Heaton (1726–94), a Yorkshire worsted manufacturer. Heaton as a rule employed two or three live-in female servants, most of whom stayed with him for less than three years and received wages on a scale which extended from 52s in the 1760s to 91s in the early 1790s. On top of this, of course, they were housed and fed, and enjoyed heating, light and soap at no cost to themselves. Heaton, clearly 'a most indulgent master' – in the words of John Styles, his historian – advanced credit to his servants to allow them to buy items of clothing which had caught their eye. Most of these servants whose purchasing habits are revealed in the master's account books spent annually as much, if not more, than they earned in the year. Alice Hutchinson, for example, hired in 1781 at an annual wage of 78s, ended the year in debt, since she spent 92s on items of clothing in the first twelve-month period of her employment. Very noticeably few of these servant purchases were second-hand: the maids could presumably expect to get such things free of charge as the perks of their job. They had clearly set their sights on new goods and new fashions. They spent more on gowns than on any other item of dress. Some bought relatively expensive whalebone stays; others made do with the cheaper leather variety. Neckcloths and handkerchiefs were other common purchases.[16]

In elite households, the most visible of menservants – footmen, pages, grooms, coachmen, porters and the like – were constrained to continue in an attenuated fashion the medieval practice of wearing liveries, an ostentatious flourish which chiefly advertised the importance of their employer. In the largest of households such servants were present chiefly for display and provided one indicator of how the employer's worth might be judged by society.

> It is not only the decency and aptitude of the clothes which gives the character of a person [declared Erasmus Jones in 1737] but his servants, his equipage, his horse, his furniture and his table; all these ought to be modelled and proportioned to his quality.

The Russells lavished a huge sum – £245 – on new liveries for their servants in 1660 at the Restoration. This was obviously a special effort, since even in the middle of the next century new liveries in this household were being bought for £100 less than this. Sir Richard Temple's household accounts for December 1680 record expenditure of £2 5s on three coats for footmen and a further 18s 'for the coachman's campaign coat, being better than the rest'. In the same year a Scottish gentleman, Sir John Foulis, of Ravelston, laid out £1 16s for a pair of evidently rather expensive stockings for Malcolm, his footman. The Coke household in Norfolk placed regular annual orders for blue and red broadcloth for suitings and facings for its servants' livery. Lace and other decorations added substantially to the total bill, which in 1725, for materials alone, came to almost £90. At Dunham Massey, Cheshire, the bill for liveries in June 1821 was a staggering £365.[17]

That wearing livery in a real sense often brought fine clothes which those wearing them would have found impossible to purchase on their own account is beyond question. Nonetheless the archaic practice of liveries increasingly aroused resentment in the later eighteenth century and, at times, downright hostility in the nineteenth. Robert Dodsley, ex-servant himself, who rose to be a newspaper proprietor and publisher, found himself in dialogue with a correspondent to the *London Chronicle* in December 1757 who had insisted that 'an Englishman in livery is a kind of monster . . . He is a person born free with the obvious badge of servility . . . He who wears another's habit, though for pay, forfeits his freedom.' Dodsley agreed with the 'badge of servility' label but not with the rest of the sentiments expressed in the letter to the newspaper. The liveried servant, he declared, was no slave. Wearing the uniform did not involve the immediate loss of individual freedom. But livery remained a sensitive issue. In Kent in the late eighteenth century the Rev. Joseph Price was advised, 'let your man wear no livery, only fustian'. At Dunham Massey early nineteenth-century servants obliged to wear livery clearly felt the stigma attached to that form of dress and those who received promotion in the household hierarchy were unquestionably relieved to be emancipated from the requirement. Mourning dress (a temporary livery), however, was commonly bought for servants to wear in elite households on the death of their master. In making such provision the Verney and Russell households were simply conforming to established practice. It was expected that in death as in life an elite master should be surrounded by a noticeable display of deference and dependence.[18]

There were some variations, as we have seen above, in the provision of accommodation, diet and dress which servants experienced. The same was probably even more true in respect of welfare and health care. Writers of household manuals from the sixteenth century onwards consistently exhorted employers to care for their servants in sickness as in health. Those who declined to do so, said one of them, were 'cursed and hard-hearted persons; and pity it is that ever good servants should step over their thresholds'. Some servants, indeed, found themselves on the receiving end of unwanted medical attention at the hands of masters and their friends. Oxford scientists Christopher Wren and Timothy Clarke, in pursuit of their anatomical experiments apparently attempted in 1657 at the London residence of the French ambassador to inject an infusion of a toxic emetic (antimony sulphate) into 'an inferior domestic that deserv'd to have been hanged' to test how quickly the poison would take effect. Fortunately for the poor servant the 'hazardous experiment' was given up in the face of his resistance and fainting; the scientists had to make do with similar experiments on dogs. Such startling deviations were presumably highly exceptional. Good practice in medical care by masters for their servants frequently coincided with the injunctions of the domestic manuals. Model master John Bruen in late sixteenth-century Cheshire showed exemplary concern for sick and aged servants in his household. In the late 1630s and 1640s Joyce Jefferies, an unmarried Herefordshire gentlewoman, had a benevolent concern for her servants which extended to paying for sometimes expensive medical treatment for them when they were sick; the bill for one such consultation in March 1639 came to 40s. When Adam Martindale's daughter Elizabeth, away from the family home in Lancashire in service near Lichfield, fell seriously ill after taking cold in 1672, 'her master and mistress took great care of her, as if she had not been a servant but a child, making use of a doctor in Lichfield betimes'. Servants in the Russell household seem also to have been well cared for. A 1675 listing in the account books sets out the various cordials, antiscorbutic juices, purging oils, St John's Wort oil, gargles and ointments obtained on servants' behalf and treatments prescribed for bites, sprains, toothache and broken limbs. The Verneys, too, in the same period showed great consideration to their servants when they were ill.

> I sent him out of the house in a chair (and that a sedan) [wrote Lady Verney of one of them], to a good nurse keeper who tended my Lady Gardiner's children; my uncle Dr Denton has been with him and is his physician. If he were my own I could do no more for him, he shall want for nothing.

In the following century William Mawhood, London woollen draper, allowed his maidservant Sarah her full wages during a period of sickness and used his patronage to have her treated as an out-patient at a

London hospital in the early 1770s. In health care as in other matters Parson Woodforde in Norfolk showed genuine concern for his servants, providing them, in 1783 for instance, with medication and paying for doctors' visits. Molly, a maidservant who fell sick the following year, was sent away with her expenses paid to convalesce at home. 'Poor Molly,' Woodforde wrote, 'is as good a girl as ever came into a house. I never had a servant that I liked better . . .' Servants in the Dunham Massey household readily received medical treatment on request. Edinburgh servants around 1700, however, mindful of the value of self-help, advanced a collective scheme for insurance against sickness and unemployment.[19]

Smallpox, perhaps more than anything else, highlighted the contrast between considerate and uncaring employers. The Russells were among those displaying good practice. Isolation of the patient to prevent the spread of infection and the provision of proper medical care and attention were all in evidence at Woburn and Bloomsbury. In 1662, for example, long before inoculation came into use, account books show that £2 7s was laid out for apothecary's bills for Richard Petty, a smallpox-suffering servant in the Russell household. A chamber was rented for him for his one-month convalescence at a cost of £1 8s and nursing expenses were paid amounting to £5 3s. In 1687 Thomas Peake, one of the grooms, was similarly cared and paid for when he contracted smallpox. Again a nurse was found and paid for – often such nurses were wives of estate workers – and Peake himself was put on board wages. A later Duke of Bedford in the mid-eighteenth century insisted on all his servants being inoculated against smallpox; he was also one of the benefactors who set up the first smallpox hospital in the capital. Parson Woodforde in Norfolk took pains to have his servants inoculated. Pock-marked servants – except those in very visible household positions – may actually have been more employable, since the facial marks were their badge of future immunity. But some, undoubtedly, were less fortunate. Earl Fitzwilliam in the first part of the eighteenth century enquired about one of his Northamptonshire footmen who was recovering from smallpox. His concern was not about the man's health but was entirely based on a refusal to have anyone with facial disfigurement occupying a front-line position in his house. 'I would not have unsightly servants.' A footman/groom taken on at the Heathcote household in Hursley, Hampshire, in the early 1720s was made to understand that 'if he should have the smallpox he was to go away and be at his own charges'. In the Purefoy household in Buckinghamshire in the years between 1735 and 1753 newly employed servants were made to sign an undertaking to quit their service there if they contracted smallpox. The managers of the Edinburgh Royal Infirmary loudly complained in 1759 about the cruelty of some masters who (almost literally) dumped on the streets servants infected with smallpox or fever.[20]

With the exception, perhaps, of footmen in large elite households whose function was principally ornamental, servants had long, often never precisely defined, hours of employment. Holidays were few. Servants' time, as they were often pointedly reminded, was not their own but their master's; 'maid of all work' was an unhappily accurate description of many of their number and the apparently unremitting work routines which enslaved them. House-cleaning, certainly as the eighteenth century approached, was often a fetish among mistresses of households, obsessed with outward display. Richard Baxter in 1662 thought that, already, the trend had gone too far; vanity had taken over from necessity. 'So much washing of stairs and rooms, to keep them as clean as their trenchers and dishes and so much ado about cleanliness and trifles was a sinful curiosity and expense of servants' time.' But the trend became even more emphatic as Wesley and others in the following century proclaimed a correlation between cleanliness and godliness. A French visitor to London in the 1720s was frankly bemused by what he saw:

> Not a week passes but well kept houses are washed twice in the seven days and that from top to bottom; and even every morning most kitchens, staircases and entrances are scrubbed. All furniture and especially all kitchen utensils are kept with the greatest cleanliness. Even the large hammers and the locks on the door are rubbed and shine brightly.[21]

The English, he thought, were almost as notorious as the Dutch in this respect. Scotland, however, renowned for its filth and stench, stood aloof from the new niceties.

Allowing servants too much time for sleep, even the fair-minded William Gouge insisted in the 1620s, was unnecessary and unwise. Later in the same century Caleb Trenchfield observed that 'it is hard not to declaim against the intemperate use of sleep, it being indeed . . . the abatement of our life'. Time was a precious, finite, commodity and should not be squandered. 'Be not fond of increasing your acquaintance,' was one piece of related advice offered to servants around 1800, 'for visiting leads you out of your business, robs your master of your time, and often puts you to an expense you cannot afford.' Nonetheless, servants – some of them, at any rate – contrived to create intervals or spaces in the daily rhythm of their working lives. That some servants ingeniously added their own income-generating by-employments to their regular household routines has been already noted. (See pp. 85–6.) Multi-tasking in many households in any case could bring welcome relief from relentless, repetitive drudgery and often brought points of contact for servants outside the home. Fetching water, delivering messages and going to market all directly contributed to the increasing sociability of servants and to the creation and consolidation of mini social networks. Furthermore, especially in smaller establishments, versatility was needed and servants were often called upon to act in different capacities. A nineteenth-century Sussex antiquary documenting the life of the Stapley family of Hickstead Place, Twineham, in that county in the Stuart period was struck that the menservants of that age were quite unlike 'the pampered menials of the present day'. In the seventeenth century the household staff as well as serving meals 'could also, when not so employed, turn their hands to anything that might be required of them, either indoors or out'. A new coachman appointed by Sir Ralph Verney in France during his mid-seventeenth-century exile was required 'to do anything that I appoint him'. Sir Walter Calverley in Yorkshire in 1704 sought a manservant who could combine an extraordinarily wide range of duties – stabling, gardening, cleaning, brewing, driving a carriage and waiting at table! When William Gossip, of York, recruited a gardener in 1750 it was made clear that he would be expected to take on other tasks as needed, including waiting at table on Sundays. Another gardener had to double up as a valet when his services were required. A visitor to the Holkham household in 1792 observed 'a fine group on the lawn of valets, footmen, grooms, cooks, women and labourers to the amount of sixty persons, all busy getting hay up into cocks'.[22]

Church attendance by servants commonly occupied an ambiguous position in their lives. Some devout servants, it is clear, were held up as godly paragons; John Bruen's faithful old retainer (see pp. 135–7) is a case in point. Very much later the tower of Soberton church in Hampshire was reputedly funded by donations from servants in the surrounding area. David Taylor, footman to Selina, Countess of Huntingdon, was sponsored by his mistress as an evangelist and rehearsed his missionary skills in her servants' hall. For other servants, however, obliged to accompany their employers to Sunday services – a practice masters were always exhorted to follow by writers of household manuals – church attendance must sometimes have been seen as yet a further imposition of control over their lives. The resentment must have been fuelled by the fact in many churches they were required either to stand at the sides or at the back or crowd together in galleries, since the main (rented or owned) pews were reserved for their social superiors. Small wonder that some servants misbehaved even though their employers were responsible for their good conduct in church. A Stratford upon Avon man charged in 1622 with creating a disturbance in the parish church admitted that 'he did swing the [servant] boy by the ear because the said boy did fight and jostle with another boy and did disturb the congregation'. And if servants strayed into church seating that was not theirs, loud complaints were bound to result. A church court case of 1701 originating in Thame, Oxfordshire, dealt with 'several servants and other young persons who are not house-keepers [who] do intrude and thrust themselves into several seats within the parish church aforesaid and do thereby exclude several parishioners that pay the rates and other duties to the church and to the poor'. Pew arrangements in churches reinforced the social order, in which servants were at the margins. Their masters, too, as Amanda Flather has shown, could sometimes become locked in parochial disputes over church seating and their place in local hierarchies. A violent dispute, for example, broke out at Hatfield Peverel church, Essex, in 1573 between contenders (backed up by their servants) for the same pew. Similar contentions over church seating in Essex parishes arose at Upminster in 1600 (resulting in the excommunication of the offenders) and at Hornchurch in 1616. The local politics of pews was something that mattered in this period, and servants, both directly on their own account and as reinforcements, were drawn into disputes.[23]

For some servants, church attendance was simply an unwanted obligation imposed from above. 'Common ignorant people and servants', for example, in Aberdeen in 1604 were required to attend a Sunday school to be instructed in the basics of the reformed faith. Nor did servants who went to church necessarily participate fully in all parts of the service. Taking communion, it seems, for them may not have been usual practice, as the researches of Michael Snape and Carolyn Steedman have revealed. Non-attendance of servants at divine worship in fact seems to have been common, though for this employers were often to blame. Charged at Stratford upon Avon in August 1622 with failing to come to be catechised, a servant explained, 'he would have come but his master, William Richardson, would not suffer him, but did send him about his business two Sundays together'. Recurring instances of the same phenomenon came frequently before the ecclesiastical courts. Household manual writers were well aware that it was a major obstacle which lay in the path of creating godly households and a godly commonwealth. Complications of other kinds arose in the matter of servant attendance at church as religious fracturing occurred during the Civil Wars and as Nonconformity and Dissent spread from the later seventeenth century. Anglican employers and chapelgoing servants sometimes made a very uncomfortable mix, and some masters and mistresses even in the second half of the nineteenth century discountenanced religious individualism among their household staff and struggled to maintain religious uniformity. Roman Catholic masters like Nicholas Blundell in Lancashire tried to recruit co-religionists to be his servants. Quaker servants found it an advantage to have Quaker employers.[24]

Ambiguities in its significance apart, church attendance unquestionably took servants for a short time away from their place of employment and provided a break from the regular routines of work. Servants needed some time for recreation, advised Thomas Hilder in 1653, and worked all the better for it. Knitting and sewing among maidservants in any spare time they might have was common but could well be quasi-work-related. Church ales and maypole dancing provided occasional light relief. In the eighteenth century tea drinking promoted socialising among servants. Parson Woodforde records an instance in June 1783 when maidservants from a neighbouring house came to join his own to drink the increasingly esteemed beverage. Nine years later an entry in his diary records that:

> there was a frolic given to the servants etc. at Weston house this afternoon, tea and supper etc. Our servants were invited. Betty and Breton went about five in the afternoon and stayed until eleven at night. Our people said they were never at a better frolic.

Some London servants frequented the outdoor theatres of Shakespeare's time; there is even evidence of servants and apprentices forming rival gangs at playhouses. London footmen in the eighteenth century enjoyed free gallery seating until their rowdiness provoked a backlash. Even provincial servants, however, enjoyed theatre visits as a special treat; Nicholas Blundell's house staff, for example, attended plays with their master and his immediate family in 1708 and 1712. A threepenny hop near Piccadilly – 'a notable nursery for the gallows', according to a hostile commentator – attracted footmen, servant maids, apprentices and others. Card playing and gambling among servants, especially in London and in fashionable provincial centres like Bath, was no doubt frequent, though frowned upon by employers and social critics. Servants' right to recreation was still being contested in the nineteenth century. What was there to fear, asked one sympathetic commentator in 1874? 'A box of crayons on the kitchen table in the evening would not spoil the pastry in the morning and a piano below stairs would sound no more inharmoniously than a piano above stairs . . .'. The emancipating effects for servants of cheap bicycles and the cinema still lay far ahead.[25]

For a very long time any promotion from above of education for servants was linked with catechising and to the Bible and religious tracts. Such was the regime undoubtedly practised in godly households like those of John Bruen and Lady Anne Clifford. (See pp. 135–7.) Lady Anne, in fact, bought multiple copies of favourite religious texts to distribute to her servants as gifts or loans. Some of these tracts presented themselves as being 'very fit for all children and servants . . .' But as servant literacy spread – though this was subject to gender variations – the range of their reading matter widened. (More than 75 per cent of servants in the Russell's London household in 1753 were literate.) Chapbooks and romances and later novels – Richardson's *Pamela*, for example – became standard fare and the shared experience of reading aloud assisted those with lesser capacities. Servants, indeed, sometimes figured as heroes and heroines of such popular literature. Cotton Mather deplored the low standards of servants' reading habits.

These romances usually beget in the unwary readers of them very false notions of love, honour and virtue, and the images of servants occurring in them are usually full of wickedness. Besides the most of these romances are such foolish tales that the readers instead of being the wiser or the better for them have their minds very sensibly thereby tainted with a frothy vanity.[26]

Mary Frend, one of many servant maids to the hard-to-please spinster employer Gertrude Savile, was described by her mistress in 1750 as being 'very proud of her capacity and learning (which was indeed more than common for one of her station, having read a great deal) which occasioned her being very touchy and scornful'. The good-natured and benevolent Parson Woodforde, however, was paying 4s 6d per quarter in 1776 for two of his young male servants to be taught to read and write. In the same decade the Rev. Joseph Price, vicar of Brabourne, Kent, was informed that Wiltshire clergymen when taking on a new manservant often asked applicants if they could write with a good hand, so that they could copy out their masters' sermons while they went hunting. A household manual of 1800 on maidservants was in no doubt that 'writing added to reading renders a servant valuable to the family'. 'Hire no servant that cannot read and keep a common account,' advised *The Housekeeper's Oracle* in 1829. In April 1802 Mrs Boon explained to a prospective employer of her former footman that the reason she parted with him was that 'he could neither read nor write which is particularly inconvenient to her'.[27]

Unanimity was lacking, however, among employers and social commentators about the wisdom of educating servants. Mandeville was against what he considered to be an unnecessary and harmful practice; charity schools, in his view, constituted a major cause of the 'servant problem' with which his society was wrestling. (See pp. 184–5.) Sarah Trimmer in 1792 thought that a safe compromise would be to reserve charity school education for those children who would progress to employment as servants in respectable households. On the other hand those children destined to become 'common servants' and work in the 'other inferior offices of life' such as factories needed practical training only and not irrelevant book learning. Even in the early twentieth century some employers resisted the idea of educating servants beyond the bare minimum. 'I have invariably found that the more education the worse the servant,' said one mistress in her reply to a questionnaire on domestic service conducted in 1916.[28]

Religion and education, as Mandeville and some others feared, were indeed potentially empowering to servants, and those who eventually got into print spoke for the rest. (See chapter 3 *passim*.) Few servants attracted much attention, and even fewer rose in society; Stephen Duck and Robert Dodsley in their different ways were both highly exceptional. (See pp. 49–50, 45–7,) For most servants religion and education were chiefly valuable in providing refuge, diversion and solace. Mary Collier, the Hampshire maidservant, told in her fragments of autobiography how she came to be an avid reader. Through her own writings she achieved only a temporary claim to attention in the immediate locality in which she lived. She remained locked into the precarious economic circumstances of those in her position and she died in poverty. (See pp. 47–50.) Life in service had attractions and advantages, as we have seen. Servants had relative security, they were much in demand, especially in London, mobility of employment was theirs for the taking, and their money wages were usually accompanied by free lodging and food. Other perks were theirs as well. Experience varied from household to household, of course, and there were gender differences. Some servants – especially those in livery in large households – had an easier life than others, and undoubtedly there were individual servant–employer collisions and casualties. But there are few signs in this period, as there undoubtedly are later, in the nineteenth and twentieth centuries – when alternative forms of employment opened up and class consciousness heightened – that servants felt any stigma attached to their *occupation* as such. Barker, a higher servant in the household of Samuel Pepys (like Munby's Hannah two centuries later), completely mystified her master by expressing a preference for hard manual labour. 'She did always declare that she would rather be put to drudgery and wash the house than to live as she did like a gentlewoman.' The sheer lack of ambition astonished her employer, a man on the make. William Basse bemoaned the unenviable lot of the servant in his *Sword and Buckler, or, The Servingman's Lament* (London, 1602):

> But see how hateful is but lately grown
> This fateful title of a serving man
> That every dunghill clown and every drone
> Nor wise in nature nor condition
> Spares not to vilify our name and place
> In dunsical reproach or blockish phrase . . .
> I have but two sons, but if I had ten
> The worst of them should be no serving man.

How representative a spokesman he was is unclear. More than a century later Defoe's Moll Flanders, who as a child had had 'a thorough aversion to . . . that terrible bugbear of going into service' was, apparently, at that time out of the ordinary. Not so the demoralised Charles Bennett in 1863. 'How [can] any human being habitually wear a face of impossible vacuity, to assume an air of formal subserviency . . . to bear the gawdy badge of servitude without taking secret revenge upon society which dooms him to such a fate?' Many of the respondents to a national survey of servants and servant-keeping undertaken in 1916 were similarly depressed with their condition. One maidservant on that occasion spoke for many when she declared that 'a servant has no social status whatever. She is always spoken of slightingly and with contempt. She is absolutely nothing and nobody.' Another, quite senior and relatively well paid, went further and described household service despairingly as 'prison without committing crime'.[29]

In the early modern period, by contrast, close bonds between employers and live-in servants were frequently noted and celebrated, though for workers employed on a casual, daily basis it was a different story. The number of such daily paid workers probably increased in this period. They certainly featured in the late seventeenth and early eighteenth-century Brydges household as supernumeraries. The fact that the word 'charwoman' was coined at this time presumably suggests that a new term was needed to describe one sector of a growing phenomenon. The employer of one such female servant in York, giving evidence in a court case of 1576, explained that the casual worker in question was 'but my servant for a while and I cannot tell when she will go away, for she will be here tonight and away tomorrow'.[30] Such freelancing was never well received by those in authority, obsessed with the potential dangers of masterless men (and women).

Regularly employed, long-serving servants, by contrast, could be treasured. The poet Robert Herrick held his cook, Prudence Baldwin, in high esteem, and hoped that after her death violets would bloom on her grave. Samuel Pepys developed a close, trusting relationship with his long-serving manservant William Hewer. Much later, Yorkshire master Richard Wedell increased the pay of his manservant, George Cooke, in 1761 'in consideration of the small advantage he had from him last year at Newby and the greater trouble he now has in attending me as I grow old and more helpless'. But gratitude and generosity could flow the other way as well. Ann Arnold, 'faithful servant to Mr Charles Brereton', who died in 1760 in Gloucestershire, 'ordered by her will that the little fruits of her labour should at length return to the family in which she had earned them . . .'.[31]

Epitaphs proclaimed the strong bonds between faithful servants and their employers, though often in these cases a general didactic purpose combined with specific memorialisation. Elizabeth Nickhols, over seventy years of age when she died in 1703, was celebrated in a memorial tablet placed in All Saints Church, Hertford, which pointedly praised her as 'laborious and faithful in all service, a pattern for all servants to follow'. James Bentley, aged sixty-five at his death in 1716 at Buckland, near Farringdon, Berkshire, was similarly held up as 'sober, faithful and diligent in his station leaving behind him a good example to all future servants'. A long-serving Shropshire mercer's maidservant was also immortalised on the same grounds and with the same aims in 1742:

> Ye servants all who look upon this grave,
> Follow the good example which she gave.
> Serve God your maker, in him put your trust
> and be, as she was, to your master just.

A memorial tablet in Romsey Abbey, Hampshire, commemorates the aptly named Honest Gaspar, who died in May 1785 aged seventy-two, sixty years a servant in the household of his master and a model to 'the rising generation in his line of life'. Fulsome praise, if in doggerel verse, was also given by the Rev. William Price of Epsom, Surrey, to his 'friend and servant' Samuel Cane in November 1782:

> Here lies a pattern for the human race,
> A man who did his work and knew his place;
> A trusty servant, to his master dear,
> A good companion and a friend sincere.
> In spite of bribes and threats, severely just,
> He sought no pension and he broke no trust.
> Truth warmed his breast, he lived without disguise,
> his heart was grateful and his actions wise.
> In him through life all social virtues shone.
> O, blush, ye great, by CANE to be outdone.[32]

Verses like this make it clear that specific commemoration of an individual servant and his close bond with his master easily merged with more general purposes; the depiction of an ideal instance of servanthood in such cases was designed to have a wider application. Some employers, indeed, when erecting gravestones for former employees, betrayed the real subtext by carefully wording inscriptions which primarily drew attention to themselves and their well managed households. The servant was mentioned not chiefly as an individual but as part of the surrounding domestic context and as an example to others.

NOTES

1 Mayo, *A Present for Servants* (London, 1693), pp. 63, 68; *Public Nusance Considered* (London, 1754), p. 39.

2 Flather, *Gender and Space in Early Modern England*, pp. 68–73; Waterson, *Servants' Hall*, p. 98; M. Storey (ed.), *Two East Anglian Diaries, 1641–1729. Isaac Archer and William Coe*, Suffolk Record Soc., 36 (1994), p. 166; Horn, *Flunkies and Scullions*, p. 40; Amanda Vickery, 'An Englishman's home is his castle? Thresholds, boundaries and privacies in the eighteenth-century London house', *Past & Present*, 199 (2008), 150; Flather, *Gender and Space*, pp. 48, 47.

3 Vickery, 'An Englishman's home', p. 173, 164.

4 Thomson, *Life in a Noble Household*, p. 24; Thomson, *Russells in Bloomsbury*, pp. 230–32; Stone, *Open Elite*, p. 307; H. Colvin and J. Newman (eds.), *Of Building. Roger North's Writings on Architecture* (Oxford, 1981), pp. 138, 89–90; I. Ware, *Complete Body of Architecture* (London, 1768), p. 347, quoted in Emily Cockayne, *Hubbub. Filth, Noise and Stench in England, 1600–1770* (New Haven, CT, and London, 2007), p. 151.

5 Patricia Meyer Spacks, *Privacy. Concealing the Eighteenth-Century Self* (Chicago, 2003), pp. 197–8, 201; R. T. Gunther (ed.), *The Architecture of Sir*

Roger Pratt (Oxford, 1928), pp. 125, 93; C. Platt, *The Great Rebuilding of Tudor and Stuart England* (London, 1994), pp. 39, 41, 42.

6 Sambrook, *A Country House at Work*, pp. 24, 35, 70; M. Elwin, *The Noels and the Milbankes. Letters for Twenty-five Years, 1767–1792* (London, 1967), p. 387; Hecht, *Domestic Servant Class*, p. 103; Alice Fairfax-Lucy, *Charlecote and the Lucys*, p. 92; Holmes, 'Domestic Service in Yorkshire', p. 96.

7 Saussure, *Foreign View of England*, p. 43; Meldrum, *Domestic Service and Gender*, pp. 82–3; D'Archenholz, *Picture of England*, p. 81; Platt, *Great Rebuilding*, pp. 135, 99, 158; U. Priestley and Penelope Corfield, 'Rooms and room use in Norwich housing, 1580–1730,' *Post-medieval Archaeology*, 16 (1982).

8 P. Borsay, *The English Urban Renaissance. Culture and Society in the Provincial Town, 1660–1770* (Oxford, 1989), pp. 294, 293. For a fuller account of the development of Bath and its social scene see R. S. Neale, *Bath. A Social History, 1680–1850* (London, 1981).

9 Hecht, *Domestic Servant Class*, p. 107; quoted in Marshall, *The English Domestic Servant in History*, p. 14; G. Edelen (ed.), *The Description of England by William Harrison* (Washington, DC, and New York, 1994), p. 201; P. Clemit (ed.), *Political and Philosophical Writings of William Godwin* (London, 1993), V, *Educational and Literary Writings. The Enquirer*, Part 2, essay 4, 'Of servants', p. 170.

10 R. Whitford, *A Work for Householders* (London, 1531), unpaginated; della Casa trans. H. Stubbe, *Arts of Grandeur and Submission*, p. 60; *Observations and Advices Oeconomical* (London, 1669), p. 76; Woolley, *The Gentlewoman's Companion, or, A Guide to the Female Sex* (London, 1673), p. 110.

11 The Coles case is cited in P. Earle, *The Making of the English Middle Class. Business, Society and Family Life in London, 1660–1730* (London, 1989), pp. 279–80; G. M. Ditchfield and B. Keith-Lucas (eds.), *A Kentish Parson. Selections from the Private Papers of the Rev. Joseph Price, Vicar of Brabourne, 1767–1786* (Stroud, 1991), p. 151; Woodforde, *Diary of a Country Parson*, V, p. 355.

12 Hecht, *Domestic Servant Class*, pp. 112–13; Vaisey (ed.), *The Diary of Thomas Turner 1754–1765, passim;* Mortlock, *Aristocratic Splendour*, chapter 10; Joan Thirsk, *Food in Early Modern England. Phases, Fads and Fashions, 1500–1760* (London, 2007), *passim;* R. Scott-Moncrieff (ed.), *The Household Book of Lady Grisell Baillie, 1692–1733*, Scottish History Soc., new ser. 1 (1911), pp. 277–8; J. Lucas (ed.), *Kalm's Account of his Visit to England on his Way to America* (London, 1892), p. 14.

13 Dent, *Plain Mans Pathway*, p. 19; Kathleen M. Brown, *Good Wives, Nasty Wenches, and Anxious Patriarchs. Gender, Race, and Power in Colonial Virginia* (Chapel Hill, NC, 1996), pp. 75–8; D. Cressy, *Travesties and Transgressions in Tudor and Stuart England* (Oxford, 2000), pp. 92–6; R. Parkinson (ed.), *The Life of Adam Martindale*, Chetham Society, 4 (1845), p. 7; Defoe, *Everybody's Business is Nobody's Business* (4th edn., London, 1725), pp. 16–17,

7; Saussure, *Foreign View of England*, p. 127; Richardson, *The Apprentice's Vade Mecum* (London, 1734), Augustan Society reprint 169/70 (London, 1975).

14 Haywood, *Present for a Serving Maid*, pp. 24–5; Broughton, *A Serious Advice and Warning to Servants* (London, 1763), p. 22; M. Groseley, *A Tour to London* (3 vols., London, 1772), I, p. 81; Fielding, quoted in Dorothy Marshall, 'The domestic servants of the eighteenth century', *Economica*, 9 (1929), 21; Jenyns, quoted in Hecht, *Domestic Servant Class*, p. 122. Anne Taylor, *The Present of a Mistress to a Young Servant* (10th edn., London, 1832), p. 130; Mrs C. S. Peel, *Waiting at Table. A Practical Guide* (London, 1929), pp. 4–5.

15 Jenyns, quoted in Hill, *Servants*, p. 217; Woodward, *The Farming and Memorandum Books of Henry Best of Elmswell*, p. 134; British Library, Egerton Mss 3054, Joyce Jefferies Account Book, ff. 26, 28, 46, 59v; *Household Book of Lady Grisell Baillie*, p. 117; *Diary of a Farmer's Wife, passim;* Horn, *Flunkies and Scullions*, pp. 198–9; Holmes, 'Domestic Service in Yorkshire', p. 90; F. Austin (ed.), *The Clift Family Correspondence, 1792–1846* (Sheffield, 1991), p. 110; F. Sokoll (ed.), *Essex Pauper Letters, 1731–1837*, Records of Social and Economic History, new ser. 20 (Cambridge, 2001), *passim*; K. D. Snell, *Parish and Belonging. Community, Identity and Welfare in England and Wales, 1700–1950* (Cambridge, 2006), p. 248.

16 Horn, *Flunkies and Scullions*, p. 199; J. Styles, 'Involuntary consumers? Servants and their clothes in eighteenth-century England', *Textile History*, 33 (2002), 11, 12, 16, 13, 14, 15.

17 Jones, *The Man of Manners, or, The Plebeian Polished* (London, 1737), p. 13; Thomson, *Life in a Noble Household*, p. 84; Thomson, *Russells in Bloomsbury*, p. 237; Huntington Library, San Marino, CA, ST 175, Sir Richard Temple, third baronet, Day Book; A. W. C. Hallen (ed.), *The Account Book of Sir John Foulis of Ravelston, 1671–1707*, Scottish Historical Soc., 16 (Edinburgh, 1894), p. 44.

18 Mortlock, *Aristocratic Splendour*, pp. 197–8; Sambrook, *Country House at Work*, p. 64; J. E. Tierney (ed.), *The Correspondence of Robert Dodsley, 1733–1764* (Cambridge, 1988), p. 498; Ditchfield and Keith-Lucas (eds.), *Kentish Parson*, p. 164; Sambrook, *Country House at Work*, p. 65; *Memoirs of the Verney Family*, IV, pp. 436–7; Thomson, *Life in a Noble Household*, p. 42.

19 T. Hilder, *Conjugall Counsell* (London, 1653), p. 159; Lisa Jardine, *On a Grander Scale. The Outstanding Career of Sir Christopher Wren* (London, 2002), pp. 124–5. I am indebted to Dr A. J. Partridge for this reference. On Bruen and his celebration by biographer William Hinde, see pp. 135–7. British Library, Egerton Mss 3054, Joyce Jefferies Account Book, ff. 31, 44, 64; *Life of Adam Martindale*, p. 208; Thomson, *Life in a Noble Household*, pp. 313–15; quoted in Marshall, *English Domestic Servant*, p. 24; E. E. Reynolds (ed.), *The Mawhood Diary. Selections from the Diary Notebooks of William Mawhood, Woollen Draper, of London, 1764–1790*, Catholic Record Soc., 50 (1956), p. 31; *Diary of a Country Parson*, II, pp. 86–7, 158; Sambrook, *Country House at Work*,

p. 93; R. A. Houston, *Social Change in the Age of Enlightenment. Edinburgh, 1660–1760* (Oxford, 1964), p. 89.

20 Thomson, *Life in a Noble Household*, pp. 320–1; Turner, *What the Butler Saw*, p. 72; Cockayne, *Hubbub*, p. 23; Horn, *Flunkies and Scullions*, pp. 52, 195; L. G. Mitchell (ed.), *The Purefoy Letters, 1735–1753* (London, 1973), p. 135; Houston, *Social Change*, pp. 88–9.

21 Quoted in K. Thomas, 'Cleanliness and godliness in early modern England', in A. Fletcher and P. Roberts (eds.), *Religion, Culture and Society in Early Modern Britain* (Cambridge, 1994), p. 67; Saussure, *Foreign View of England*, p. 98.

22 Gouge, *Of Domesticall Duties*, p. 674; Trenchfield, *A Cap of Gray Hairs* (London, 1671), p. 17; *Advice to Servants*, para. XXI; Sheila McIsaac Cooper, 'From family member to employee: aspects of continuity and discontinuity in English domestic service, 1600–2000', in Fauve-Chamoux, *Domestic Service*, p. 282; E. Turner, 'On the domestic habits and mode of life of a Sussex gentleman', *Sussex Archaeological Collections*, 23 (1871), p. 41; quoted in Slater, *Family Life in the Seventeenth Century*, p. 113; Horn, *Flunkies and Scullions*, p. 134; Harrison, 'The servants of William Gossip', 137, 138; Hecht, *Domestic Servant Class*, p. 9.

23 R. Dutton, *Hampshire* (London, 1970), p. 153; Turner, *What the Butler Saw*, p. 39; E. R. C. Brinkworth (ed.), *Shakespeare and the Bawdy Court of Stratford* (Chichester, 1972), p. 150; P. Hair (ed.), *Before the Bawdy Court* (London, 1972), p. 62; Flather, *The Politics of Place. A Study of Church Seating in Essex, c. 1580–1640*, Friends of the Department of English Local History, 3 (1999), pp. 45, 51, 48.

24 E. Patricia Dennison *et al.* (eds.), *Aberdeen before 1800. A New History* (East Linton, 2002), p. 299; Snape, *The Church in an Industrial Society. The Lancashire Parish of Whalley in the Eighteenth Century* (Woodbridge, 2003), pp. 16–19; Steedman, *Master and Servant*, p. 96; Brinkworth, *Shakespeare and the Bawdy Court of Stratford*, p. 156; Anon., 'On the side of the maids', *Cornhill Magazine*, 171 (1874), 302; *Blundell Diaries, passim*; P. S. Belasco, 'Note on the Labour Exchange idea in the seventeenth century', *Economic History Supplement to the Economic Journal*, 1 (1926–29), 277, 279.

25 T. Hilder, *Conjugall Counsell* (London, 1653), p. 157; *Diary of a Country Parson*, II, p. 76; quoted in Marshall, *English Domestic Servant*, p. 25; A. Gurr, *Playgoing in Shakespeare's London* (3rd edn, Cambridge, 2004), pp. 63, 77, 149, 225 *et seq.*; *Blundell Diaries*, I, p. 167, II, p. 23; J. P. Malcolm, *Anecdotes of the Manners and Customs of London during the Eighteenth Century* (2nd edn, 2 vols., London, 1810), I, p. 291; 'On the side of the maids', *Cornhill Magazine*, 171 (1874), 302.

26 Heidi Brayman Hackel, *Reading Material in Early Modern England. Print, Gender and Literacy* (Cambridge, 2005), p. 230; Margaret Spufford, *Small Books and Pleasant Histories* (London, 1981), p. 212; Thomson, *The Russells in Bloomsbury*,

p. 238; *ibid.*, p. 153, T. Harris, *Popular Culture in England, c. 1500–1800* (London, 1995), p. 82; on *Pamela* see pp. 39, 68, 115, 159. B. Reay (ed.), *Popular Culture in Seventeenth-Century England* (London, 1985), p. 201. Bridget Hill includes a chapter on 'Literate and literary servants in eighteenth-century fact and fiction' in her book on *Servants* (Oxford, 1996), pp. 225–50; Mather, *A Good Master Well Served* (London, 1696), p. 49.

27 Saville, *Secret Comment*, p. 294; *Diary of a Country Parson*, I, p. 194; Ditchfield and Keith-Lucas, *A Kentish Parson*, p. 153; *Hints to Masters and Mistresses respecting Female Servants* (London, 1800), p. 12; W. Kitchiner, *The Housekeeper's Oracle* (London, 1829), p. 126; Sambrook, *Keeping their Place*, p. 23.

28 Trimmer, *Reflections upon the Education of Children in Charity Schools* (London, 1792), pp. 7, 11, 20–2; C. V. Butler, *Domestic Service. An Enquiry by the Women's Industrial Council* (London, 1916), p. 26.

29 Quoted in Earle, *The Making of the English Middle Class*, p. 227; William Basse, *Sword and Buckler, or, The Servingman's Defence* (London, 1602), stanzas 18 and 21; *Moll Flanders*, quoted in Hill, *Servants*, p. 114; Butler, *Domestic Service*, pp. 39, 29.

30 Quoted in D. M. Palliser, *Tudor York* (Oxford, 1979), p. 132; Marjorie K. McIntosh, *Working Women in English Society, 1300–1620* (Cambridge, 2005), p. 75.

31 Thirsk, *Food in Early Modern England*, p. 91; Holmes, 'Domestic Service in Yorkshire', p. 125; J. W. Streeten (ed.), *Epitaphia, or, A Collection of Memorials inscribed to the Memory of Good and Faithful Servants* (London, 1826), p. 20.

32 Streeten, *Epitaphia*, pp. 4, 6, 15, 45.

6

℧

SERVANTS, GODLY HOUSEHOLDS
AND SOCIAL ENGINEERING

Let not the Christian servant murmur nor grudge at suffering if it be laid
upon him.
(Thomas Fosset, *The Servants Dutie, or, The Calling and Condition of Servants*,
London, 1613, p. 21)

Good servitudes are those colleges of sobriety that check in the giddy
and wild-headed youth from his uneven course of life by a limited
constrainment.
(George Alsop, *A Character of the Province of Maryland*, London, 1666,
p. 28)

How grievous a sin the disobedience of servants is. 'Tis a downright
contempt of God's revealed word . . . a violation of the law of nature.
(Richard Lucas, *The Duty of Servants*, London, 1685, p. 88)

In England from the 1590s – a troubled, disjointed decade in which inflation, harvest failures, enclosure riots and the destabilising effects of war
all featured – and for over 100 years thereafter, an uninterrupted succession of manuals for the improvement of relations between masters
and servants and the well ordering of households appeared in print.[1]
Invariably written by clergymen, many of them London-based, these books
blended doctrine with the fruits of first-hand experience gained in
particular ministries. The pre-Civil War decades produced the largest
single crop of such publications. A significant sub-group appeared in the
1650s under the Republic. A larger number followed in the later decades
of the seventeenth century to confront the looser morals of the new post-
Restoration age. The genre was still flourishing in the early eighteenth
century and, indeed, Edmund Gibson's *Family Devotion* (1726), one of
the most successful of all these manuals, was still being reprinted in the
middle of the nineteenth century. Puritans were in the vanguard of the
authors of such texts and, unquestionably, William Perkins's *Christian*

Oeconomie (1590) and Robert Cleaver's *Godly Forme of Household Government* (1598) did much to define the characteristics of this kind of writing in the first place. William Gouge's *Of Domesticall Duties* (1622), Thomas Carter's *Christian Commonwealth* (1627), Philip Goodwin's *Family Religion Revived* (1655) and Richard Baxter's *The Poor Man's Family Book* (1675) were later landmarks in the tradition. Though puritan writers predominated and set the pace, however, they did not monopolise such publications. *Bethel, or, A Forme for Families* was written by Matthew Griffith (1599?–1665), a Royalist who was sequestered of his London living in 1642 and later involved in the stubborn and protracted defence of the besieged Basing House in Hampshire (home of the Marquess of Winchester) in 1645.[2] Much later, Edmund Gibson author of *Family Devotion* was successively Bishop of Lincoln and Bishop of London.[3]

The post-Reformation spiritualisation of the household, to which Louis B. Wright, Christopher Hill and other historians have drawn attention, was indeed one of the hallmarks of early modern England.[4] At its most basic level puritan organisation rested on a molecular network of family cells (of which servants were part) which also provided the setting for the exercise of the puritans' godly discipline. Therefore the family, declared John Downame in *A Guide to Godlynesse* (1629), is like 'a particular church . . . and the master of the family representeth the minister and the rest of the house the people in the congregation'.[5] In the larger picture godly families underpinned both church and state. If only the godly discipline were practised in all households, Lewis Bayly insisted in 1613, churches would be filled to capacity, the number of lawsuits would plummet, prisons would be empty and the streets would be cleared of drunkards, swearers, whoremongers and other undesirables.[6] 'A household is, as it were, a little commonwealth,' declared Robert Cleaver in his influential treatise mentioned above, 'by the good government whereof God's glory may be advanced.'[7] But godly rule in the state could not be expected without the prior establishment of godly households. 'An error in the foundation,' declared William Perkins in 1590, 'puts the body and parts of the whole building in apparent hazard.'[8] Writing more than sixty years later, Thomas Hilder in his *Conjugall Counsell* (1653) was in complete agreement. 'Every family,' he confidently echoed, 'is a little nursery to the great orchards of church and commonwealth.'[9] Thus the family was seen as a training ground, the most natural and regular setting in which sound religion and principles of good conduct could be instilled. The larger units of church and state reaped the benefits of family instruction. The household, declared William Perkins, is:

the seminary of all other societies. It followeth that the holy and righteous government thereof is a direct means for the good ordering of church and commonwealth . . . For this first society is, at it were, the school wherein are taught and learned the principles of authority and subjection.

John Downame's *A Guide to Godlinesse* (1629) offered the same message about the fundamental religious and socio-political importance of families. As 'the seminary of the church and commonwealth' they functioned as a kind of 'private school wherein children and servants are fitted for the public assemblies, as it were the universities, to perform when they meet together'. George Swinnock's *The Christian Man's Calling* (London, 1668) was no less insistent. 'The way to make godly parishes and godly countries [that is, counties] and godly kingdoms is to make godly families.'[10]

These household manuals or conduct books were clearly written to inspire. 'Good and holy books,' said Robert Cleaver, 'are as ladders to climb up to heaven.' In one after another the duties of husbands and wives and parents and children were set forth. Indeed, in some of these publications this represented almost the full extent of their coverage; Thomas Gataker's *Marriage Duties* (1620) is the prime example. But households in this period, as historians have long recognised, did not consist only of blood relations. Servants and apprentices were considered integral members of families and the concept of the godly household embraced them no less than the master and his immediate circle.[11] Master–servant relations occupied a secure place in the great majority of these publications. Indeed, some of them – Thomas Fosset's *The Servants Dutie* (1613), Abraham Jackson's *The Pious Prentice* (1640), Richard Lucas's *The Duty of Servants* (1685), Richard Mayo's *A Present for Servants* (1693) and Cotton Mather's *A Good Master Well Served* (1696) – focused exclusively on the role and duties of servants and on the religious imperatives which ought to inspire and frame their labour.[12]

Godfearing servants and masters were constantly advised to seek out each other. 'Thus godly servants will go through difficulties to get into such families where religion is,' declared Philip Goodman in 1655, 'putting themselves into such houses where they may honour God and have helps for heaven.'[13] Richard Lucas advised servants in search of a place that they would find 'that family the best for you which is in itself the most religious, the best for your temporal and the best for your eternal interest'.[14] The initiative in employing servants, however, most commonly lay with masters and it was their responsibility to ensure that they recruited the most suitable staff. Robert Cleaver in 1598 advised 'religious and godly masters [to] be very wary and circumspect when they hire and entertain any servants into their service that they be such as are godly, honest and religious'. William Gouge in his influential treatise *Of Domesticall Duties* (1622) heartily agreed and underlined the practical advantages. 'When good servants are chosen there is hope of receiving the more good from them and doing more good unto them. They will be pliable to all good admonition, docible by all good instruction, serviceable in all things they take in hand.'[15] Gouge recognised, however, that godly servants, if they could not be found, could certainly be *trained*. 'Take such,' he advised, 'as are of mean and poor estate and know not how to maintain themselves but by service. Thus will a double work of charity be done therein, and thus mayest thou look for better service, for commonly such are most industrious and most obedient to their masters.' Robert Cleaver, cited earlier, had said as much. Though godly masters ought always to be on the lookout for godly servants; if they were simply unavailable masters would have to make do with 'such at least [as] will be tractable and obedient to such good order and godly government'. Servants known to be unrepentantly committed to sinful ways were best avoided. 'It were better to be without servants [an unthinkable prospect in that service-dependent age] than to have such as hate goodness.'[16]

That so many manuals on household government were published in this period is indicative of the importance attached to the subject by clergymen authors and to the ready market for such publications. (Soon after his marriage Nehemiah Wallington, the puritan London wood turner, bought a copy of Gouge's *Of Domesticall Duties* (1622) and distilled from it a list of thirty-one articles 'for my family and for the reforming of our lives'. All adult members – servants included – set their hands to it in agreement.[17]) Most obviously, however, the attention given to master–servant relations bears witness also to the ubiquity of servants and the practice of servant-keeping in society in this period. It was also a recognition of the indisputable fact that household servants underpinned the labour-intensive, hierarchical society of early modern England and were vital to its functioning and well-being.

'Tis by [servants] the order and beauty of the world in a great measure subsists [declared Richard Lucas in 1685] for where there are no servants there could be no masters. 'Tis by [their] travail that not only the necessities of mankind in general are supplied but also the pleasure and grandeur of states supported. 'Tis by [servants] we enjoy the studies of the learned and the prudence of the statesman.[18]

Lucas's frank admission of the dependence of masters on their servants, though perfectly accurate, did not follow through the implications of his own logic to recognise the potential vulnerability of the propertied classes, but the statement may have disconcerted some of his readers unused to the recital of such painful truths. Nor was he alone in making such statements. Service, insisted William Fleetwood in a treatise published in 1705, was 'absolutely necessary ... The world could not be governed and maintained without it and it is fallen to the [servants] to be instrumental to the public good in that station.'[19]

Given the seminal importance attached to households and household religion, writers of manuals, unsurprisingly, waxed eloquent about the proper conduct, routines and management of families. Frequently they took their cue from key verses in St Paul's letters to the Ephesians, Colossians, and Timothy and Titus, which set out unambiguously what was expected of both servants and masters. The God-given authority of masters and the natural hierarchies of husbands and wives, parents and children, masters and servants were taken for granted in all these publications.

> God in general ordaineth degrees of superiority and inferiority [declared William Gouge in 1622], of authority and subjection, and in particular he gave to masters the authority which they have and put servants in that subjection where they are ... Masters by virtue of their office and place bear Christ's image and stand in his stead by communication of Christ's authority to them.[20]

Decades later James Janeway in his *Duties of Masters and Servants* (1676, 2nd edn. 1726), taking Ephesians 6:5–9 as his text, was still fervently repeating the same theme:

> God advanceth one above another and yet with no injustice or wrong to any but for the mutual help one of another ... What a chaos and heap of confusion would the world be without government? And how can government be without superiority and inferiority?
>
> How unreasonable and blasphemous [he went on] are the repinings of some that are ready to quarrel with their maker and to impeach Him as guilty of partiality, cruelty and injustice that hath not advanced them to a higher, richer and more honourable condition than they are in. Shall the thing formed say unto Him that formed it, why hast thou made me thus? What diabolical pride and arrogance is this for the creature to accuse and condemn his creator? ... He that breaks his rank to get a higher and safe place may be likelier to meet with destruction than promotion.[21]

Within the patriarchal household the duties of servants to their masters were carefully and pointedly rehearsed in an unbroken series of injunctions from the late sixteenth century onwards.[22] Almost invariably the early publications – Cleaver, Perkins, Gouge *et al.* – addressed the subject impersonally. Thomas Carter's *Christian Commonwealth* (1627) and William Whately's *Prototypes* (1640), however, began the new trend of addressing servants directly. By the early eighteenth century this was standard practice and recognised the usable reality of rising literacy rates. Eliza Haywood's *A Present for a Serving Maid* (1744), many times reprinted, is a prime example. Thomas Broughton's *Serious Advice and Warning to Servants*, which reached its fifth edition in 1787, was clearly marketed with an eye on its being distributed among servants by masters, clergymen and moral improvement societies: a hundred copies of the tract could be bought for only £1. Thomas Fosset, author of one of the early manuals, had complained in 1613 that, all too often, servants appeared not to know their duties.[23] Unremittingly bombarded on the subject on all fronts in the decades which followed, later generations of servants would find it increasingly difficult to plead ignorance.

Robert Cleaver in 1598 provided a convenient summary of household servants' duties to their masters:

> To love them and to be affectioned towards them as a dutiful child is to his father; to be reverent and lowly to them in all their words and gestures, to suffer and forbear them, to obey with ready and willing minds all their lawful and reasonable commandments, to fear them and to be loath to displease them, to be faithful and trusty to them and theirs in deeds and promises, to be diligent and serviceable, to speak cheerfully, to answer discreetly . . .

No later writer on the subject deviated in the least from these high principles but re-emphasised them at every opportunity. The same catalogue of necessary virtues and duties in household servants was still being rehearsed in the mid-nineteenth century.[24] The need for servants to show humility, obedience, diligence, honesty, loyalty, discretion and piety, and to shun self-will, sin, arrogance, deviousness and vice, was constantly underlined. Cleanliness and decency of dress were necessary accompaniments of service which ought to be taken for granted; moral cleanliness, however, took pride of place before personal cleanliness, understandably perhaps in the sixteenth and seventeenth centuries before the coming of cheap soap. Commitment to their masters' service, proclaimed William Gouge in 1622, ought always to be absolute. 'While the time of their service lasteth [servants] are not their own, neither ought the things which they do to be for themselves. Both their persons and their actions are all their master's, and the will of their master must be their rule and guide.' Since 'the master is God's vice-regent in his family', declared Thomas Carter five years later, a servant's disobedience ranked, in effect, as rebellion against God.[25]

St Paul in Ephesians 6:6 denounced servants who went in for mere 'eye service' – working hard only when watched by their master – as 'men pleasers'. It was a theme taken up repeatedly by the clergymen authors of household manuals when they wrote about servants' duties. 'Eye servants,' bemoaned William Whately in 1640, 'that cared no further to do [their] duty than [they] conceived [their] masters should know of [their] carriage otherwise not caring how [they] loitered out the time' were an undesirable encumbrance to any household.[26] Cotton Mather in his *A Good Master Well Served* (1696), written with the New England experience of labour scarcity in mind, was firmly convinced of the fact and sternly pointed his accusing finger at those miserable specimens of humanity,

> those eye servants who will obey your master no longer than the eye is upon you. Know it that the eye of the all-seeing and almighty God is upon you to condemn you for this disobedience . . . There is nothing more offensive than a servant that stays loitering upon his errands. Let servants go and come nimbly and be upon the wing in the errands of their masters.[27]

In fledgling colonies where all were expected to pull their weight working hours were far too precious a commodity to be squandered. It had been a matter of pride in the model godly household of John Bruen in early seventeenth-century Cheshire that 'amongst [his servants] there was not one idle and unprofitable person'. Every cog in the machinery of this well ordered household was in good working order.[28]

Idleness was deemed a cardinal sin in servants. 'Nothing more infecteth the mind of man,' thundered Walter Darell in 1578, 'than the horrible monster idleness.'[29] Thomas Floyd in *The Picture of a Perfit Commonwealth* (1600) was even more emphatic:

> Idleness [he insisted] is a fear of labour desisting from necessary actions both of body and mind. It is the only nurse and nourisher of sensual appetite and the sink which entertaineth all the filthy channels of vices and infecteth the mind with many mischiefs and the sole maintainer of youthly affections.[30]

Arthur Dent's *The Plain Mans Pathway to Heaven* (1612) left his readers in no doubt that idleness had no place in the spiritual itinerary he was advocating. How could it? 'Fie of this idle life. Many profane serving men do falsely suppose that they were born only to game, riot, swear, whore, ruffle it, roist it out, and spend their time in mere idleness.'[31] 'An idle household,' declared Matthew Griffith in 1633, was 'a shop for the Devil to work in.'[32] 'Idle and untrusty servants,' concluded William Whately in 1640, 'quickly bring [a house] to naught.'[33] Reflecting on his fate, one of two servants about to be executed in Boston, Massachusetts, on 18 March 1674 for the murder of their master, declared that he had 'lived an idle, slothful, vagrant life . . . His idleness had ruined him.'[34] Another writer at the end of the century roundly condemned the prevalence among servants of 'unnecessary sleeping, curious gazing, idle talking'.[35]

'A good servant,' declared Philip Goodwin in 1655, 'must not only be as a working ox but as a flying eagle with wings of heavenly thought about earthly works' – surely not the easiest combination of attributes to cultivate.[36] Like all other kinds of employment household service was automatically dignified by the godly into a 'calling' if it was first dedicated to God. George Herbert's famous poem 'The elixir' (1633) summed it up:

> A servant with this clause
> Makes drudgery divine:
> Who sweeps a room, as for thy laws,
> Makes that and th' action fine.
>
> This is the famous stone
> That turneth all to gold:
> For that which God doth touch and own
> Cannot for less be told.[37]

To have no legitimate calling was to have no properly anchored place in the commonwealth. 'There be far too many which follow no honest calling,' Arthur Dent had moaned in 1612, 'live to no use; nobody is the better for them. They do no good either to the church or commonwealth. They are like drone bees; they are unprofitable burdens of the earth.'[38]

The fixed concept of the servant's calling reverberated down the century. 'The servant must persuade himself that he obeys God in obeying his master,' declared Richard Lucas in 1685. 'He must look upon himself as placed in his station by God . . .'[39] Cotton Mather (1663–1728), a leading voice among the late seventeenth-century New England puritan clergy, told servants roundly:

> You may sanctify all your servile employments by doing them under this consideration, the Lord Jesus Christ hath commanded me to obey my master and my mistress . . . Truly the meanest work you have to do in your

service, though it be in the stable or the kitchen, you may thus render very glorious.[40]

John Bunyan in his *Christian Behaviour* (1663) had accepted no less absolutely the axiom that the servant's calling was 'God's ordinance' and 'as acceptable to Him in its kind as is preaching'.[41] Lofty words indeed, prayerfully echoed by many others:

> O Lord God Almighty, it is the wise appointment of Thy providence [so ran a prayer for servants issued in the early eighteenth century] that there should be various orders and degrees of men and that I should be disposed of in the station where I now am . . . [I] desire with content and thankfulness to accept of my portion how low and mean soever in the world . . . If I faithfully discharge the duties of my place I know I shall be acceptable to my God as any that enjoy the highest station. If I be found in the way of righteousness I shall be exalted in due time, however abated for the present . . . O let it not be so much my care to get higher in the world as to get more in Thy favour, wherein is life . . . Make me true and faithful, careful and diligent, humble and obedient, doing the business of my place.[42]

Godly servants, the household manuals stressed, had duties towards each other. Richard Baxter in *The Poor Man's Family Book* (2nd edn. 1675) urged servants to provoke one another to remember and practise their responsibilities, to grow together in knowledge, to guard each other from sin and temptation, to be loving and supportive to each other, to receive little injuries from fellow servants uncomplainingly and to correct each other in a loving, mutually supportive manner, enlisting the master's intervention only as a last resort.[43] Twenty years on, Richard Mayo reminded household servants of the good they could do each other. 'How easily may two or three well disposed servants carry away [from church] a whole sermon in their memories when they shall repeat over the heads to each other as they go along or when they come home.' Literate servants could teach others less fortunate than themselves to read the Bible. 'And how sweet it is for servants to get into a corner and pray together. What a blessing they will be to one another and to the family and neighbourhood where they live!'[44] God's wrath and vengeance, another preacher insisted, would inexorably fall on those servants who betrayed their calling and led others astray.[45]

The ideal of the godly household set forth in these domestic manuals presupposed that masters and mistresses would take the lead and set an example. Servants, the majority of whom were young anyway, were to be treated in the same way as children.[46] 'Remember,' declared Thomas Carter in 1627, 'that the charge of the servants which are committed unto you is not small but that a great account you must give unto God how you have governed those souls committed unto you.'[47] Much was expected of the godly master; inadequacies were pilloried. 'He that cannot rule his own family,' Thomas Hobbes (inveterate opponent of anarchy) insisted, 'is much more incapable to direct a multitude.'[48] Perkins provided the blueprint. A good master, he preached, should rule over his household in justice and require from his servants labour 'proportionable to their strength and yield them sometimes intermission and rest'. William Gouge concurred. Appropriate wages should be paid to servants promptly at the agreed times and in full, and accommodation, food and other benefits should be provided as a matter of course. Servants should be properly cared for in sickness and old age. 'It is but just and equal,' Matthew Griffith opined in 1633, 'that if they labour for you in their health you should labour for them in their sickness.'[49] A good master should govern wisely and humanely and administer an appropriate level of correction in the right spirit. 'You must not give correction to manifest your authority or to be revenged on them for crossing you,' Thomas Hilder continued in 1653, 'but sincerely to kill sin in them, to subdue their exorbitant lust, to make them more fit to glorify God and to perform service unto men.'[50] No servants should be commanded to do anything that was ungodly. The master, no less than the servant, had a calling. Baxter and others elaborated its particulars.[51] Thomas Hobbes, approaching the subject from a very different starting point, had much wise advice to offer on the role of masters and on the best way of exercising their authority.[52] Mistresses, too, as a succession of commentators recognised, had vital day-to-day responsibilities in respect of household management and should share with their husbands the burdens of maintaining the spiritual welfare of the family.[53] The standard recommendation was that gender distinctions should be observed; mistresses should discipline maidservants only and leave erring menservants to be dealt with by their husbands. 'Those families wherein the service of God is performed are, as it were, *little churches*, yea, even a paradise upon earth.' Thus wrote William Perkins in his *Christian Oeconomie* (1590). Like many other writers of this kind of literature, Perkins underlined the fundamental value of the regular exercise of household religion in morning and evening prayers, catechising, blessings at mealtimes, fasting and zealous sabbatarianism:

The first or principal office of a master [Thomas Becon had pronounced in the dawning years of the Reformation] is to bring up his servants and family in virtue and in the true knowledge of God and to train them daily in the exercises of true godliness at certain hours appointed that by this means God may prosper their labours and travails and bless his household and enrich every corner of his house giving him abundance of all things.[54]

Each day, Becon continued, should begin and end with an act of worship for the whole family, servants included, with exhortations from the master about the need to 'fear God, avoid sin, embrace virtue, and in all points to frame their lives according to their vocation and calling'. The singing of psalms and hymns when working should be encouraged and the entire household should go together to church twice each Sunday, with catechising in between services. Negligent and forgetful servants who could not call to mind what they had heard in church were to be prodded to improve. The very regularity and intimacy of family worship, insisted Richard Baxter, a vigorous promoter of catechisms in the following century, provided obvious advantages and offered a firm religious foundation on which pastors could build in their public ministry.[55] Catechising was the key to success, Thomas Becon and others claimed. Ian Green's comprehensive study of *The Christian's ABC* (Oxford, 1996) documents the proliferation of catechisms and their centrality in early modern religious practice and education.[56]

Christopher Hill argued that, especially in times of persecution and crisis (as in the 1630s under Archbishop Laud), household religion might have to become the alternative to public worship. Later, in the very different circumstances of the revolutionary decades, fears of this imminently happening provided conservative opponents of religious toleration with one of their most powerful arguments.[57] The envisaged norm, however, was for household worship to function effectively as the preliminary to ministerial instruction provided in church services. Having prepared his household, servants included, for worship, the master's duty was to ensure that everyone attended church. What the master had to do, declared William Perkins in 1590, was to:

bring his family to the church . . . on the sabbath day, to look that they do religiously there behave themselves, and after the public exercise is ended, and the congregation is dismissed, to take account of that which they have heard, that they may profit in knowledge and obedience.

Thomas Carter in 1627 echoed these sentiments and urged masters not simply to bring their servants to church but to 'police' them during service time:

It is not enough that the master bring his servants unto the church and then let them give him the slip at the church door, or go out as soon as they come in, and so run to taverns or alehouses or as bad places, or else get into some corner of the church where either they may sit and talk all the time or else sleep it out.[58]

The whole sabbath day, these clergymen authors insisted, should be set aside for prayer and worship in the best biblical tradition. It was a sin for masters to expect servants to work on Sundays, and the Westminster Assembly's *Larger Catechism* in 1648 was one of many attempts to proscribe the malpractice:

Do not think the sabbath is ended when the sermon is done [declared Richard Mayo in 1693]. Call the sabbath a delight . . . Admire the kindness of God to poor servants in appointing a day on purpose for that which else you would hardly have found time for. Look upon it as the great Thanksgiving Day . . .[59]

It clearly strengthened the case of those writing on master–servant relations to be able to invoke specific instances of godly employers and godly families and to hold them up for imitation by others. Funeral sermons provided obvious opportunities of this kind, and examples abound. At the funeral service in 1614 of Thomas Dutton, of Dutton, in Cheshire, the preacher paid tribute to the tight godly discipline maintained in his household 'both for credit and his profit. He abhorred idleness in his servants . . . He appointed them such offices and employments that everyone in his house had either a sweating brow or a working brain.'[60] When Sir Thomas Lucy of Charlecote, Warwickshire, died in 1640 it was said that 'a houseful of servants have lost not a master but a physician who made their sickness his and his physic . . . theirs'.[61]

Biographies of godly masters provided an even more obvious channel for celebrating the achievement of individuals in setting up the godly discipline in their households and exerting a powerful influence in their own localities. A particularly notable example is William Hinde's *A Faithfull Remonstrance of the Holy Life and Happy Death of John Bruen of Bruen Stapleford in the County of Chester, Esquire* (1641). Bruen (1560–1625) was hailed by his biographer (who was related to him through marriage) as one of the beacon lights of the reformed religion in his county, one whose patronage was used to promote the spread of the gospel in a region where Catholicism still remained deeply entrenched. His godly household was depicted as one which became a shining example to others. Hand-picked godly servants, selected from a fertile supply of recruits magnetically attracted to his locally renowned home, were fully integrated into his family. Each had a particular calling, and idleness was a thing unknown. Bruen had indeed 'a church in his house . . . he was so well provided and furnished with honest and faithful, godly and gracious servants, both men and women'. Every Sunday, led by Bruen himself, the whole household walked the mile-long journey to the parish church of Tarvin, singing psalms as they went. Hinde commended Bruen as a model employer:

> He allotted [his servants] their places according to their skill and knowledge and proportioned their labour to their strength and their wages to their labour. He would often go abroad amongst them both to see the work and to encourage the workmen . . . There was not the meanest amongst them but he would labour to cheer him and to encourage him in his service.

Marriage portions were given to servants and those seeking employment elsewhere were helped to good places.

Bruen, said Hinde, classified his most faithful servants as those who were most devoted to God. One in particular stood out from all the others, Robert Pasfield, 'Old Robert', who had 'a good gift in prayer and praise, very willing and well able to confer of good things, careful to hear the word read or preached, and to help his own, and his friends' memories by repetitions [catechising]'. His greatest feat was to have committed the whole Bible to memory and by means of an extraordinary *aide-mémoire*, a belt marked with divisions and subdivisions, he was able to bring each book, chapter and verse to mind. Yet this valuable human encyclopaedia, Hinde made clear, was:

> a man utterly unlearned, being unable to read a sentence or write a syllable, yet he was so taught of God that by his own industry and God's blessing upon his mind and memory he grew in grace as he did in years and became . . . a very profitable *index* to the family to call to mind what they had learned and to recover what they had lost by slip of memory; and not only so but a godly instructor and teacher . . .

A special relationship developed between master and servant, with Bruen seeking out the faithful Robert so that they could confer together,

> the master never a whit the more abased because he did bow himself to the low condition of and company of a servant, nor the servant ever a jot more proud or presuming because of this his master's kind and christian dealing with him. They were both of them gainers and not losers.

Living to a ripe old age, and long past useful employment, the faithful 'Old Robert' was kept on and cared for by his godly master, nourished 'with some of the best morsels from his own table'.

A good example for rebuke [Hinde concluded] of many merciless and profane masters who deal no better oftentimes with their impotent and old servants than they do with their old dogs. First they grow weary of them and then they turn them off their land without any means or maintenance to live on a commons or die in a ditch.[62]

Hinde's biography of the Cheshire puritan is notable in more senses than one. It is a particularly eloquent example of its type – a top-down, idealising representation of the social order and the place of masters and servants within it. In this respect it bears some passing resemblance to all those guidebooks on the rearing of children which the early modern period in England spawned.[63] Neither biographies nor household manuals, of course, can be taken uncritically as literal descriptions of realities. Such writings tell historians more about the preoccupations, fears and phobias of those in authority, usually those of an older generation, and of the necessity which *they* perceived of social engineering and social control. The household manuals, which write *about* servants as a labour force, rarely, if ever, allow individual servants' own voices to be heard.

Hinde's biography clearly resonates in a very particular way, as some of the key dates in the story make clear. John Bruen himself died in 1625, William Hinde, his biographer, not long afterwards, in 1629. That this book – with its comforting testimony about the power of the godly discipline to bring about social harmony – was published years after its original protagonists were dead and in the troubled times of 1641, as England lurched on the brink of civil war, says much about its perceived value as religious and political propaganda.[64] It came into print at this critical juncture, most certainly, as an ideological tract for the troubled times, a pointedly didactic biography, with unambiguous lessons about the necessity of social harmony and interdependence. Nor, for the record, was that the end of Bruen's posthumous history. Rather astonishingly, a shortened version of Hinde's book was again reprinted no less than 150 years later, in the 1790s, as the English establishment struggled to come to terms with the effects of the French Revolution and popular radicalism at home. The soothing social message of an early seventeenth-century book about good relations between a master and servant seemed still relevant.

The ideal of the godly household, and the harmonious master–servant relations which formed part of it, had been insistently present in the household manuals since their inception in the previous century but they took on added urgency as the prospect of civil war loomed dangerously close. The mid-seventeenth-century upheavals in England challenged and tested the patriarchal family unit in all kinds of ways, master–servant relations included, and exposed the frailty of the idealism which lay behind conduct books, the paradoxes and inconsistencies in their logic, and the relative failure of their social engineering. A number of the writers discussed here had spoken openly about the spiritual equality of masters and servants. 'If the greatest man that ever was in the world,' declared William Gouge in 1622, 'should have a servant that were the meanest that ever was, and a case betwixt that master and that servant should come before God, God would not any whit at all lean to that master more than to the servant.' That said, however, neither Gouge nor any other of these writers entertained even for a moment the thought that democracy might be the natural corollary. But effective social *control* proved an unattainable vision. Strident and endlessly repeated claims about the natural superiority of masters and their God-given authority coexisted very uncomfortably with flashes of recognition that households, like society in general, were actually *dependent*, for better or worse, on the labour of servants. Pessimism sometimes gripped even the most pious of conduct book writers. 'There never were worse servants in an age than now,' cried Thomas Hilder in 1653. 'They will filch, pilfer and steal, waste and consume the estates of their masters.'[65] At no point in the century after the Reformation – or later, for that matter – did godly households constitute a majority, and those that did exist were intrinsically impermanent. Servants, one of the most mobile sections of society, came and went with unsettling regularity. Masters died. Widows remarried. Families disintegrated or died out. Implicitly, even the clergymen authors of these texts recognised the painful facts and took time out from their characteristic lofty moralising to denounce irreligious, ineffectual or tyrannical masters on the one hand and the natural depravity of servants on the other:

> The common complaint [lamented Lewis Bayly in 1613, in the light of the unedifying realities surrounding him] is that faithful and good servants are scarce to be found. True, but the reason is because there are so many profane and irreligious masters.[66]

John Bruen and 'Old Robert' – model master and model servant – were strategically paraded in 1641 for general imitation by masters and servants throughout the land. It was not to be. It was all too obvious that many servants boycotted known godly households altogether. 'They cannot endure to dwell in these families where the word of God and the worship of God [are] in use,' declared Philip Goodwin in 1655. 'A religious family is as a prison in which they are loath to live. If into any such unaware they fall they soon get out, and being once out they will come no more there.'[67]

An epitaph of a kind on the outpouring of literature on godly households and the social engineering which underpinned it was provided a century later by Oliver Grey, in his *An Apology for Servants* (1760). Presenting himself as a servant (though in reality, as we have seen earlier, Grey was the other *persona* of James Townley, whose successful play *High Life below Stairs* is discussed elsewhere in this book (see pp. 68, 85, 161–2), Grey deplored the readiness of masters to condemn servants for faults they themselves regularly committed. Servants, he lamented, were expected to endure so much without uttering the least complaint. They experienced a thankless, exhausting and frustrating life:

> Besides the bodily labours which we undergo it is incredible to think what a well disposed servant suffers in his mind in the space of twenty or thirty years from pride, insolence, moroseness, avarice, peevishness, hastiness, meanness, etc., not to mention the absurd messages, the long-winded compliments he is to carry every day and the confounded lies he is obliged to tell.

Significantly, Grey's self-portrait is of a godly servant who knew his duty – the very kind the earlier household manuals had recommended. Tellingly, however, he recalled that in forty-five years' service with fourteen masters (all Anglicans) 'I was never showed the way to church but by three of them.'[68]

The religion of some masters, it was clear, was superficial, undemanding and self-serving. Josiah Dare's *Counsellor Manners his last Legacy to his Son* (1710) is a curious example which illustrates the point. It belonged to a category of parental advice literature that had flourished since the sixteenth century and offered guidance on a familiar range of subjects. Religion had a place in the discussion, and indeed the text launched itself with the exhortation to 'more desire godliness than gold'. The religious advice on servant-keeping was also conventional. 'Take care that they be seasoned,' the author writes, 'with the fear of God ... He that admits a common swearer or a debauched person into the bowels of his family admits a Jonah that may sink his ship.' Religion, unquestionably, was good for servants. When Dare moved to the subject of wife-taking, however, he was much more cautious. Piety, he declared, was no bad thing in a wife as long as it was not allowed to dominate her character, 'for it is commonly found that those women are most heart hollow who are most lip holy . . . Beware of those that pretend to religion,' he continued, those 'who canonise themselves and call themselves the saints'. Inspiring religious leadership in the household from such a master and mistress was not to be expected in the family regime that Dare was recommending.[69]

By the time Dare and Grey were writing, of course, the original context of the puritan godly discipline had largely been superseded. Grey rather noticeably belonged to a society that differed in so many ways from that in which Bruen's 'Old Robert' had lived and died. Nonetheless Grey's frank criticism of his worldly masters provides a telling comment on the disjunction between the theory and practice of the godly ideal of the household in the early modern period. The social engineering discussed here took for granted that masters would take the lead in establishing and upholding a godly household regime. In reality there were too many negligent masters, as Defoe recognised, and they were directly to blame for some of the servant problems of which they themselves complained. Without their active support the law could not be expected to solve everything that was amiss; establishing and maintaining order required joint effort.

NOTES

An earlier version of this chapter appeared as an article: 'Social engineering in early modern England: masters, servants, and the godly discipline', *Clio*, 33:2 (2004), 163–87.

1 There were isolated earlier examples, however, such as William Tyndale's *The Obedience of a Christian Man* (London, 1528) and Robert Whitford's *A Work for Householders* (London, 1531).
2 *Oxford DNB*, s.v. Matthew Griffith.
3 *Oxford DNB*, s.v. Edmund Gibson.
4 L. B. Wright, *Middle Class Culture in Elizabethan England* (1935, 2nd edn. London, 1958), pp. 228–96; C. Hill, *Society and Puritanism in Pre-revolutionary England* (London, 1964), pp. 443–81. See also L. L. Schucking, *The Puritan Family* (1929, English trans. London, 1969) and E. S. Morgan, *The Puritan Family* (Boston, MA, 1944, new edn. New York, 1966).
5 Downame, *Guide to Godlynesse*, p. 329. John Downame, BD (d. 1652), had a London ministry, was one of those who petitioned against Archbishop Laud's canons in 1640, and was appointed a licenser of the press in 1643. Significantly, earlier publications of this kind such as Whitford's *A Work for Householders* (London, 1531) did not recognise the quasi-ministerial role of heads of households.

6 Bayly, *The Practice of Pietie* (London, 1613, 1627), pp. 340–1. Lewis Bayly, D.D. (d. 1631), was a pro-puritan Bishop of Bangor. His book cited here is his chief claim to fame.

7 Cleaver, *Godly Forme of Household Government*, p. 13.

8 Perkins, *Collected Works*, III, *Christian Oeconomie* (London, 1609), epistle dedicatory. William Perkins, M.A. (1558–1602), was a prolific author and one of the towering figures in Elizabethan puritanism.

9 Hilder, *Conjugall Counsell*, p. 135.

10 Perkins, *Christian Oeconomie*, epistle dedicatory; Downame, *Guide to Godlynesse*, p. 330; Swinnock, *The Christian Man's Calling* (London, 1668), p. 379. Children and servants were often spoken of in the same breath and were seen as having the same needs.

11 Cleaver, *Godly Forme of Household Government*, epistle dedicatory; Naomi Tadmor, *Family and Friends in Eighteenth-Century England* (Cambridge, 2001), is the latest in a long line of historians to emphasise this point.

12 Publications of this kind continued to appear long after the period at present under review. Thomas Broughton's *Serious Advice and Warning to Servants* reached its fifth edition in 1787. W. J. Irons's *The Christian Servant's Book* appeared as late as 1849.

13 Goodwin, *Domestic Religion Revived*, p. 461.

14 Lucas, *The Duty of Servants* (London, 1685), p. 24. Richard Lucas, M.A., D.D. (1648–1715), started his career as a schoolmaster in his native Wales but achieved fame through his later ministry in London and through his many publications. Later, John Wesley much admired him.

15 Cleaver, *Godly Forme of Household Government*, p. 391; Gouge, *Of Domesticall Duties*, p. 648. William Gouge, M.A., D.D. (1578–1653), ministered in London, served as one of the Feoffees for Impropriations in the early part of the reign of Charles I, and later in the revolutionary decades was an active promoter of the Presbyterian system. Much later in the seventeenth century, John Evelyn – no puritan – advised his grandson when hiring servants 'to entertain none that are swearers, quarrelsome, intemperate, lazy, unfaithful'. John Evelyn, *Memoirs for my Grandson* (London, 1926), p. 17.

16 Gouge, *Of Domesticall Duties*, p. 649; Cleaver, *Godly Forme of Household Government*, p. 391; Richard Bernard, *Joshua's Godly Resolution in Conference with Caleb touching Household Government for Well Ordering a Familie* (London, 1612), p. 28.

17 P. S. Seaver, *Wallington's World. A Puritan Artisan in Seventeenth-Century London* (London, 1985), p. 79.

18 Lucas, *The Duty of Servants*, pp. 203–4. The Marquess of Halifax described household servants as 'the wheels of your family; let your directions be never so faultless yet if these engines stop or move wrong the whole order of your house is either at a stand or discomposed'. (Halifax, *The Ladies New Year Gift or Advice to a Daughter*, London, 1688, p. 66.)

19 Fleetwood, *Relative Duties of Parents, Children, Husbands, Wives, Masters, Servants* (London, 1705), p. 386. William Fleetwood, B.A., D.D. (1656–1723), one of the most famous preachers of the day, and a prolific author, was successively Bishop of St Asaph and Bishop of Ely.

20 Ephesians 6:5–9, Colossians 3:22–5, I Timothy 6:1–2, Titus 2:9–10. I Peter 2:18–20 was also sometimes used as a text in sermons and treatises on household management; Gouge, *Of Domesticall Duties*, pp. 591, 639.

21 Janeway, *Duties of Masters and Servants* (2nd edn., London, 1726), 442–4.

22 For the context of political thought see G. J. Schochet, *Patriarchalism in Political Thought . . . in Seventeenth-Century England* (Oxford, 1975), *passim*.

23 Fosset, *The Servants Dutie* (London, 1613), 'To the reader'. His tract was designed 'to do good to the evil, to teach the ignorant, to reprove the stubborn, and to let all servants see and understand what is required of them and whereunto they be called'.

24 Cleaver, *Godly Forme of Household Government*, pp. 387, 90; Irons, *The Christian Servant's Book, passim*.

25 Carter, *Christian Commonwealth* (London, 1627), p. 246. These clergymen authors were less than crystal-clear in their advice about how servants should respond to masters' *unlawful* commands.

26 Whately, *Prototypes* (1640), sig. b7. William Whately, B.A. (1583–1639), ministered in Banbury, Oxfordshire. *Prototypes*, one of his most famous books, published (posthumously) in 1640, reached its second edition seven years later.

27 Mather, *Good Master well Served*, pp. 38, 42.

28 Hinde, *Faithfull Remonstrance*, p. 55. On Bruen, held up as a shining example to other masters, see pp. 135–7.

29 Darrell, *A Short Discourse of the Life of Servingmen* (London, 1578), 'To the reader'.

30 Floyd, *Picture of a Perfit Commonwealth*, pp. 239–40.

31 Dent, *Plain Man's Pathway to Heaven*, pp. 170–1. Arthur Dent, M.A. (d. 1607), was rector of South Shoebury, Essex, and the author of numerous published works.

32 Griffith, *Bethel, or, A Forme for Families*, p. 380. Matthew Griffith, M.A., D.D. (1599?–1665), had a London ministry and continued using the prescribed Anglican rites during the revolutionary decades. His royalism was rewarded after the Restoration with the rectory of Baydon, Oxfordshire, and the mastership of the Temple in London.

33 Whately, *Prototypes*, p. 63.

34 Cotton Mather, *Magnalia Christi Anglicana* (London, 1702), VI, p. 39.

35 Anon., *Instructions for Apprentices and Servants* (London, 1699), p. 36.

36 Goodwin, *Domestic Religion Revived*, (London, 1655), p. 491.

37 C. L. Martz (ed.), *George Herbert/Henry Vaughan*, Oxford Authors (Oxford, 1986), p. 168.

38 Dent, *Plain Man's Pathway*, p. 171.

39 Lucas, *Duty of Servants*, pp. 92–3.

40 Mather, *A Good Master Well Served*, p. 34.

41 Bunyan, *Christian Behaviour*, p. 86.

42 Anon., *An Earnest Exhortation to Housekeepers to set up the Worship of God in their Families* (5th edn., London, 1719), pp. 16–17. Other examples abound of published model prayers for servants. See, for instance, Baxter, *The Poor Man's Family Book*, p. 523, Lucas, *Duty of Servants*, pp. 77–78, and Anon., *A Short Prayer for Children and Servants* (London, 1700).

43 Baxter, *Poor Man's Family Book*, p. 213. Richard Baxter (1615–91), largely self-educated, ministered in Shropshire and Worcestershire, served as a chaplain in the New Model Army, and worked strenuously for religious unity during the Interregnum. Persecution under the Act of Uniformity in 1662 did not halt his steady stream of publications.

44 Mayo, *A Present for Servants* (London, 1693), pp. 45, 47.

45 Thomas Seaton, *The Conduct of Servants in Great Families* (London, 1700), p. 215.

46 See, for example, Cleaver, *Godly Forme of Household Government*, p. 364, and Mather, *A Good Master Well Served*, p. 10.

47 Carter, *Christian Commonwealth*, p. 234.

48 Thomas Hobbes, 'Of masters and servants', in F. O. Wolf (ed.), *Die Neue Wissenschaft des Thomas Hobbes* (Stuttgart, 1969), p. 149.

49 Perkins, *Christian Oeconomie*, p. 699; Gouge, *Of Domesticall Duties*, pp. 685, 671–2; Griffith, *Bethel*, p. 382.

50 Hilder, *Conjugall Counsell*, p. 127.

51 Baxter, *Poor Man's Family Book*, p. 311.

52 Hobbes, *Neue Wissenschaft*, pp. 149–53.

53 Thomas Hilder's *Conjugall Counsell* (London, 1653) is a clear example in which wifely duties are set out at great length.

54 Perkins, *Christian Oeconomie*, p. 670; Thomas Becon, *Catechism* (Parker Society, 2, 1844), p. 359.

55 Becon, *Catechism*, pp. 359, 361, 360; Baxter, *Poor Man's Family Book*, pp. 290–1.

56 In the late seventeenth century John Tillotson, later Archbishop of Canterbury, declared that 'catechising and the history of the martyrs [Foxe's *Acts and Monuments*] have been the two greatest pillars of the Protestant religion'. (Tillotson, *Six Sermons . . . preached in the Church of St Lawrence Jewry*, London, 1694, p. 162, cited in Green, *The Christian's ABC*, p. 1.)

57 Hill, *Society and Puritanism*, pp. 454, 479.

58 Perkins, *Christian Oeconomie*, p. 699; Carter, *Christian Commonwealth*, p. 268. See pp. 113, 199 for cases of servants' misbehaviour in church.

59 Westminster Assembly of Divines, *Larger Catechism* (1648; Edinburgh, 1865), p. 163. Whether servants ordered to work on Sundays shared in their master's sin was an issue frequently aired. (Schucking, *The Puritan Family*, p. 98; Mayo, *A Present for Servants*, p. 78.)

60 Richard Easton, *A Sermon preached at the Funeralls of that Worthie and Worshipfull Gentleman Thomas Dutton* (London, 1616), p. 23, cited in J. T. Cliffe, *The World of the Country House in Seventeenth-Century England* (London, 1999), p. 98.

61 R. Harris, *Abner's Funerall* (London, 1641), p. 25, cited in Cliffe, *World of the Country House*, p. 97. Other similar instances can be found there.

62 Hinde, *Faithfull Remonstrance*, pp. 55, 210, 63, 64, 65, 57, 60, 61; On Bruen and his biographer see R. C. Richardson, *Puritanism in North West England. A Regional Study of the Diocese of Chester to 1642* (Manchester, 1972). William Hinde, M.A. (1569?–1629), ministered in Cheshire and published other works besides his life of Bruen. On the plight of old servants see also Hilder, *Conjugall Counsell*, p. 156.

63 See R. C. Richardson, 'The generation gap: parental advice in early modern England', *Clio* 32:1 (2002), 1–26.

64 Hinde's book was seen through the press by his son Samuel, later to be a chaplain to King Charles II.

65 Gouge, *Of Domesticall Duties*, p. 693; Hilder, *Conjugall Counsell*, pp. 90–1. See also Durston, *The Family in the English Revolution*. Durston's book, insightful in many ways, curiously omitted household servants altogether from its coverage.

66 Bayly, *Practice of Pietie*, p. 341.

67 Goodwin, *Domestic Religion Revived*, p. 473.

68 Grey, *Apology for Servants*, pp. 20, 28.

69 Dare, *Counsellor Manners*, pp. 6, 66, 69, 101.

7

℮

ORDER AND DISORDER
IN THE HOUSEHOLD

For faithful servants are always servants and good men are always
poor; nor do they ever rise out of servitude unless they are unfaithful and
bold, nor out of poverty unless they are rapacious and fraudulent.
(Machiavelli, *Florentine Histories*, trans. Laura F. Banfield and H. C.
Mansfield, Princeton, NJ, 1988, III.13, p. 123)

Come here fellow servants and listen to me.
I'll show you how those of superior degree
Are only dependants no better than we.
(James Townley, *High Life below Stairs*, London, 1759, Act II, scene 1)

Uninterruptedly from the second half of the sixteenth century a steady
stream appeared of clergyman-written household manuals, tracts and
sermons, as the previous chapter has shown, in praise of the godly family,
its contribution to religious harmony in the state and to the well-being
of society at large; echoes of the message were still being heard in the
mid-nineteenth century. The model rested on sound leadership being
provided by the family head, harmonious marital relations, obedient and
receptive children and hard-working, docile, god-fearing servants who
accepted their lowly place in society and the 'calling' that was theirs. Not
surprisingly such godly, well integrated, households always represented
an ideal and they were constantly extolled precisely because the real world
was often very different. 'It were better for [a master] to wink at some
faults in his servants,' declared one realistic commentator in 1607, 'than
to disquiet himself in going about to reform them'. And if servants proved
obdurately bad, said William Penn in 1682, it was better just to get rid
of them rather than waste time attempting reform.[1]

Recognising the importance of good order in households and, by
extension, in the state, was not a godly monopoly, of course, and there
is plenty of evidence to show that it was no less appreciated and promoted

in the later seventeenth and eighteenth centuries by those of a more secular outlook. This was the stance of Caleb Trenchfield's *A Cap of Gray Hairs* (1671), directed chiefly at masters though it brimmed with conventional wisdom for servants (mainly menservants). It rehearsed traditional views on servants' duties and the benefits of industry, sobriety, modesty, frugality and truthfulness, and warned against the depraved nature of both maidservants and the stage. Masters were advised to avoid confiding in servants, placing themselves in any way in their debt, and showing too much kindness, which could easily be construed as weakness. Servants' private affairs should not be pried into; all that mattered in the end was the quality of their work. Idleness among both servants and the poor should never be countenanced or rewarded. Recognising a common cause of friction, Trenchfield insisted that apprentices, whose fathers had normally paid a premium for them to learn a trade, should not be treated as though they were simply another kind of servant and made to share household chores. A mistress should never be rebuked by her husband in front of servants; to do so would in the end undermine his authority as well as hers. Nor should a master trespass into the routine details of ordinary household management – 'peeping to find fault in the feminine jurisdictions' – which were best left to the good offices of a wife or housekeeper. Men had more important business to attend to.[2]

Order in the household with no mention made of household religion also characterised a later advice manual, Eliza Haywood's *A Present for a Servant Maid* (1744). Bad servants were the natural accompaniment, this writer declared, of a showy age dominated by luxury and pride. Knowing their place ought to be the first requisite of a servant, and their dress should be decently humble and plain. The self-evident benefits of thrift were extolled; something as apparently innocent as tea-drinking was denounced as an expensive evil which could all too easily progress to a partiality for alcohol. (Another writer of the time, Anne Barker, in *The Complete Servant Maid* (1770), mindful of another vice of conspicuous consumption, urged servants to 'divest themselves of the useless and obnoxious custom of taking snuff'.) Above all, said Haywood, servants ought to recognise that, relatively speaking, they had a carefree existence while employers shouldered all the burdens. For servants to complain was rank ingratitude.

> The exorbitant taxes and other severities of the times have for some years past reduced our middling gentry as well as tradesmen to very great straits; and the care of providing for you and paying your wages is much

more than an equivalent for your care of obliging them, and doing your
duty by them.

A letter writer to the *London Chronicle* in 1758 emphatically agreed. 'If
times are good or bad, the markets high or low, they of all people feel
no difference.'[3]

Clearly, secular no less than godly commentators had an ideal of
servants and service in mind and were distressed by the many contradictions of reality. A longish tract on *Domestic Management, or, The Art
of Conducting a Family* (1800) was still struggling to narrow the gap
between the two widely separated poles. So many commentators underlined the fact that servants, after all, if not actually children themselves
– and many of them, of course, were – were certainly *like* children and
were always best treated as such; it was common for religious tracts
which stressed the need for household catechising to treat children and
servants as an almost undifferentiated single category. But long service
was often valued; a London Society for the Encouragement of Honest
and Industrious Servants was proposed in 1752 to provide rewards. John
Huntingford at the end of the century described another metropolitan
society with a similar agenda resting on a well regulated system of character references and register offices.[4]

A well ordered household was one which was led from the top by
experienced, just and caring employers. 'It is impossible the servant should
be diligent if the master be negligent,' stated one household manual in
1607. 'It is the master's fault if an evil and dishonest servant serve him
long,' declared Henry Percy, ninth Earl of Northumberland in 1609. 'Good
men make good servants,' echoed John Fielding in 1763. 'Profligate and
extravagant masters corrupt the morals of the best servants.' Evenhanded
firmness was always preferable to tyranny. Favouritism was always best
avoided; it produced dissension in the household and rebounded on the
giver:

> He that affordeth his servant raiment too costly or nourishment too
> dainty [Swinnock warned in *The Christian Man's Calling* (1668)] or
> carrieth himself towards him too familiarly will find him at last a young
> master in his house, so malapert as to equalise with the children, and to
> tyrannise over his fellow servants.

The model of the ideal employer was often paraded by both godly and
more secular commentators, and good masters, as previously noted, were
memorialised in funeral sermons. Sir Robert Harley of Brampton Bryan
in Herefordshire was one such model in the 1630s with his hand-picked

godly household. The mother of Margaret, later Duchess of Newcastle, was held up as another paragon. Though she was careful always to maintain a proper social distance between employer and servant, nonetheless:

> my mother was a good mistress to her servants, taking care of her servants in their sickness, not sparing any cost she was able to bestow for their recovery: neither did she exact more from them in their health than what they with ease . . . could do. She would freely pardon a fault, and forget an injury . . .

Parliamentarian lawyer, ambassador, author Bulstrode Whitelocke (1605–75) was similarly inclined, if his own self-portrait can be believed:

> Whitelocke's charge was to be loving and kind to his servants, not awfully magisterial and harsh to them; to treat them with a fitting familiarity, rather than too great a distance, and to take care that they should want nothing fit for them. This caused his servants to return love again to their master and the service of love is the best service . . .

Edmund Verney (1636–88), by contrast, was a benevolent, but inept, master who kept a somewhat disordered household in which servants trespassed on his good nature. His financial affairs were very confused and he died heavily in debt. He stands in marked contrast to the ideal master personified by Richard Steele in early eighteenth-century fiction, Sir Roger de Coverley, a man truly loved and respected by his servants. 'His orders are received as favours rather than duties; and the distinction of approaching him is part of the reward for executing what is commanded by him.'[5]

An ineffectual master who could not exert authority over his servants was a danger not only to his own household but also, potentially, to society. Keeping servants at arm's length was always advisable and overfamiliarity should be avoided at all costs. Such, for instance, was the advice of a household manual of 1607. 'Being "hail fellow well met" with his servants [the master] should show himself too low minded and not fit to command and to be as it were a servant with servants which would redound to his reproach.' Richard Vaughan, second Earl of Carbery, four decades later said much the same:

> Converse not with the inferior servants of the family [he warned his son] nor with any notoriously vicious. For besides the danger of their discourse you make yourself cheap . . . Take therefore a special heed of familiarity with them and suspect their humouring your vices. For if once they serve you in base unworthy offices from that time they become your masters . . .

In New England in the seventeenth century, where family and the social order were inextricably connected and on the defensive, such failures in domestic management drew a stern rebuke from the courts. In a Plymouth colony case of 1658 a shamefaced master was obliged to seek a legal ruling to obtain the cancellation of a servant's indentures, confessing that the servant 'ran up and down like unto a runaway and he could have no command over him'. In a Virginia court case of 1663 a maidservant was twice punished by the court for insolent behaviour towards her master, Robert Bruce, but so too was he on the second occasion. 'The said Bruce hath degenerated so much from a man as neither to bear rule over his woman servant nor govern his house, but made [all] one in that scolding society, wherefore the said Bruce is [sentenced] to be ducked' – the ultimate humiliation.[6]

A household manual author of 1669 advised young married couples to delay setting up their own separate establishment until they were confident they had sufficient management skills, 'for otherwise they will be like freshwater soldiers going to a military command before they are fitted with arms and understand the use of them'. A century later Hester Chapone advised young ladies to study their mother's household management practice and urged caring mothers to give their daughters some helpful practical training in the household arts and the superintending of servants. Constant criticism of servants, barbed sarcasm and insults without any show of encouragement or gratitude would have predictable consequences. 'Nothing so much weakens authority as frequent chiding ... When once a servant can say, "I cannot do anything to please my mistress today," all authority is lost.' (John Gabriel Stedman quickly discovered in 1785 that 'dear Adriana', his foreign-born wife, was out of her depth when trying to run a Devon household, she being not 'acquainted with the customs of England and finds not a method to keep the peace between she and the servant maids.') Similarly, a master who proceeded on the assumption that all servants were thieves and traitors would sink in their esteem to 'one whose money only gives him power over them and who uses that power without the least regard to their welfare'.

> Those who continually change their servants [Chapone continued] and complain of perpetual ill usage have good reason to believe that the fault is in themselves and that they do not know how to govern.

Governance of a household required skill and experience. The larger the household the greater the need for delegation of particular responsibilities and a sensible division of labour among servants. No task should be delegated, however, insisted Lady Sarah Pennington in an advice memoir of 1761, without the mistress having a secure grasp of what was involved, advice that was later echoed in nineteenth-century manuals, including the great classic, many times reprinted, by Mrs Isabella Beeton. And once a proper household regime had been established a mistress should avoid 'the ridiculous drudgery of following your servants at the heels and meanly peeping into every obscure corner of your house . . .' A housekeeper should be trusted but should be regularly instructed by, and report back to, the mistress of the house. Too severe punishment of servants was also unlikely to produce the ordered state in the household that was intended. Richard Braithwait in 1641 had earlier observed that 'Masters who cannot govern effectively make their servants either dissolute or desperate . . . The like may be spoken of domineering mistresses who make the correction of their maids their sole recreation.'

> Through excessive severity [a New England domestic handbook of 1755 declared] you are in danger of begetting a lasting hatred and ill will in your children and servants against you and of making them secretly despise all your instructions, counsels and admonitions.[7]

Similar censure of inept management by employers and its direct contribution to the wider 'servant problem' continued half a century later. *Hints to Masters and Mistresses respecting Female Servants* (1800) frankly criticised bad employers and pointedly reminded them that the loyalty of servants, on which household order ultimately depended, had to be earned. It could never be arbitrarily imposed by force.[8]

Larger households had detailed ordinances drawn up for their better regulation which were either read out periodically to the whole body of servants or displayed prominently in the servants' hall. It was common practice for fines to be levied for any breaches of the published rules. The household regulations initially drawn up by John Harrington in 1566 and renewed by his son in 1592 when High Sheriff of Somerset provide a good example. Hours of early morning rising and going to bed were carefully set out for both summer and winter, with a 2*d* fine for any failures. Rules for observing mealtimes and waiting at table were again precisely defined, with a heavy fine (6*d*) for breach. Rules for cleaning the rooms and staircases were to be unfailingly followed. Personal cleanliness was insisted on and also decency in dress. Swearing was forbidden and a 4*d* fine specified for any servant found guilty of teaching children 'any dishonest speech or bawdy word or oath'. A manservant found dallying with any of the maids faced a similar fine. Any act of violence by one servant against another incurred a fine of 12*d* or loss of his place. Much later, the Lancashire squire Nicholas Blundell, certainly not a harsh master, fined servants for offences. 'Robert Weedow, Thomas Marrow and Edward Pinington begged my pardon for a misdemeanour [reads a journal entry for 20 March 1727]. I made them pay some money which was this day distributed to the poor.'⁹

Enormously detailed regulations were compiled for the household of Lionel Cranfield, Earl of Middlesex, in 1621–22, with the responsibilities of each officer in this large establishment precisely laid out. The long document containing all this detail was prefaced by general orders about duties and demeanour which applied equally to all servants. Unauthorised absence from the household was strictly forbidden, as was blasphemy, uncivil behaviour, sexual immorality, drunkenness, quarrelling and gambling. Personal cleanliness and decency in dress were to be observed. Attendance at morning and evening prayers was obligatory. General orders having been set forth, the list proceeded to enumerate the rules for each individual office holder, starting with the steward, lynchpin of the establishment. Cranfield's steward was delegated with full authority for the management and governance of the household and was required to conduct himself at all times with the gravity which his office demanded. The steward was to keep an exact check roll of all servants in the household hierarchy 'and who recommended them' and their particular functions. No hangers-on of any kind were to be harboured 'whereby unnecessary charges be increased besides much disorder which may ensue thereby'. The steward was to keep an exact inventory of all household furnishings, keep a regular check on the expense of provisioning, and ensure that proper decorum at mealtimes was observed. The duties of gentlemen ushers were rehearsed, as were those of the yeoman usher in respect of domestic security, heating and lighting. The yeoman of the wardrobe was to ensure that 'all hangings, beds, curtains, counterpanes, carpets, cushions, tables, chairs and stools . . . be kept very fair and clean, viewing them often and causing them to be beaten, brushed, repaired, amended and supplied, so often as cause shall require'. New acquisitions of furnishings were to be carefully inventoried. The cleaning duties of the groom of the great chamber – washing floors, dusting furniture, brushing carpets, strewing flowers – were carefully prescribed, as were detailed safety precautions. A daily tally of wood, coal and candles used the previous day was to be presented. Several paragraphs were devoted to the duties required of the clerk of the kitchen, the yeoman of the larder, the yeoman of the pantry and the yeoman of the buttery. Wastefulness was to be avoided at all costs and a delicate balance struck between 'honour and frugality'. The yeoman of the hall was to regulate access to the house and ensure that only those who were properly authorised gained admission. The groom of the hall, responsible to the usher, was to be constantly on his guard for 'unfit or suspected' intruders 'lurking in the entries . . . and must always have a bell and a whip for dogs'. One of the allocated tasks of the groom or almoner was to see to it that left-over meat, bread and beer was passed on to the poor at the gatehouse each day. These provisions would be supplemented periodically with other charitable hand-outs to the poor of the parish.[10]

A similar concern for 'honour and frugality' lay behind many other sets of household ordinances of this period; maintaining order and due economy went hand in hand. Such convictions clearly informed the rules drawn up in 1673 for the Earl of Bridgewater's house at Ashridge, Hertfordshire, during his absences in London. Things had clearly got out of hand. Henceforth unauthorised visitors were not to be hosted and servants themselves were not to expect to enjoy the fat of the land while their master was away from his country seat. They would face discharge if in future they were found to have spent 'their time at alehouses, making themselves drunk and so becoming incapable to follow their business'. Sundays, it seems, had witnessed the worst excesses committed at Ashridge, 'the days not only of the greatest expense but of the greatest disorder'. In future, it was forcefully stipulated, the day would be observed 'in service to God and not debauchery abroad'.[11]

A much more copious set of household instructions was provided by James Brydges, first Duke of Chandos, in 1721, an even more necessary task than usual since his 'family' consisted of no fewer than ninety-three persons in all. The steward was to keep a watchful eye on expenditure and the prices paid for the household's provisions. Prompt payment of bills was to be attended to and servants' wages were to be paid twice a year. He was to ensure that no servants absented themselves without leave and that they regularly attended divine worship. Due decorum in the household was to be observed, with no tippling, let alone drunkenness. After evening prayers in the household all domestic staff were to 'repair to their respective rooms and none be suffered to sit up in their chambers afterwards and the groom of the chambers go about and see that all candles be put out in due time'. The Usher of the Hall was to judge whether visitors to the house were 'persons fit to be invited to stay for dinner and to what table it will be proper to bring them . . . He is not to suffer any dogs to come into the hall.' Dignity must be allowed to prevail at all costs. Later in the eighteenth century the Duchess of Buckingham, always a stickler for detail, exacted a promise from her personal servants as they surrounded her when she lay dying that they would not sit until she had been certified dead.[12]

Order in the household was subverted by a variety of circumstances, some external, some internal. Many external factors could be cited, some long-standing or recurrent and others quite specific in their chronology. One of these, which historians of servants, like other components of early modern society, must take account of is the many-sided impact of the English Revolution. The mid-seventeenth century upheavals undoubtedly brought challenges and dislocation to the social, religious and political order. Local economies were disrupted, taxation went up, disposable income went down. London, chief centre of servant-keeping, as of so much else, was destabilised.[13] Families – the normal setting of household service – in many cases divided or their menfolk were scattered; the family unit itself faced its most severe testing time.[14] Royalist and Parliamentarian armies were on the move, demanding horses, waggons, food, lodging and (sometimes) sexual solace. Heavy military casualty rates were experienced.[15] Jobs, including those of servants, were lost as towns and cities were besieged and as some great houses fell.[16] Most fundamentally, traditional forms of authority – indeed, patriarchy itself – were called into question. 'Everyone did that which was good in his own eyes,' bemoaned the Royalist historian Edward Hyde, overtaken by the course of events and the attendant cultural shifts. The social and religious commentator Thomas Fuller felt compelled to observe in 1662 that in earlier decades servants were 'in far greater subjection than nowadays, especially since our Civil Wars hath lately dislocated all relations'. 'In a commonwealth,' the even more extreme conservative John Nalson later ranted, 'Joan is as good as my lady even by daylight.' A man of very different opinions, heresiographer Thomas Edwards, famous for his sprawling tract *Gangraena* (1646) in which he denounced the excesses of the Civil War sects, denounced religious toleration, since it meant masters 'have no command of their servants, no quiet in their families'.[17]

Servants, like others, got caught up in the maelstrom of the English Revolution, became politicised, and felt the impact of the upheavals. In the 1640s household servants in London were to be found taking to the streets in noisy demonstrations (as they did later in the eighteenth century in the Sacheverell riots and the Gordon riots), fighting in the rival armies (conscripts or volunteers as the case might be), taking up radical religious and political causes, actively helping to shape and express public opinion, or simply suffering the human cost of the coming of war and its many burdens. Servants joined their masters in Edinburgh in 1637 in agitating against the imposition of the English prayer book. In Aberdeen sixty-five servant maids were made pregnant by Lord Sinclair's troops between 1640 and 1642, only to be punished by the city authorities, who did not distinguish between rape and consensual sex. A Staffordshire servant, co-opted as a waggoner to move ammunition north against the Scots, was lamed in the course of his duties and petitioned for compensation. Katherine Hadley, servant maid to the irrepressible John Lilburne, was sentenced to seven months' imprisonment in 1640 for distributing 'A Cry for Justice', one of his rousing pamphlets. London apprentices and servants played a noisy part in the agitation against bishops at the end of 1641 and were eventually placed under restraining orders in their attempts to canvass signatures for the second Root and Branch petition. During the trial of the hated Earl of Strafford the authorities attempted to impose a curfew in London to keep apprentices and servants from spilling out on to the streets.[18]

A Devonshire servant was prosecuted in August 1642 in connection with the circulation of a scandalous song about the attempted arrest of the targeted Five Members of the House of the Commons by Charles I. As conditions all around deteriorated in 1643 the embattled puritan Lady Brilliana Harley repeatedly expressed concern about her servants. London servant maids took part in a women's peace petition to the House of Commons in August 1643. Some time later in the same decade a London servant maid remonstrated with the prophetess Anna Trapnel:

> You confine yourself to your chamber and take no notice of what is done abroad. We are commanded to shut up our shops and there are great fears among the citizens. What will be the issue they know not.

Royalists in exile like Sir Ralph Verney found it very difficult to recruit good servants, such were their straitened circumstances. Charles I, under intense pressure to raise as much money as he could from the population of Oxford while it served as his temporary capital in the 1640s, was obliged to turn for money even to college servants, who had been previously exempt from taxation. Poignantly, it was in disguise as a servant that the King eventually quitted Oxford in April 1646. Taking advantage of the teeming religious freedom of the 1640s, servants joined the proliferating separatist sects and some, like William Kiffin, the Particular Baptist, became preachers, to the undisguised horror of Thomas Edwards, who reserved a place for him in the libertarian hell of *Gangraena*.

Servants became Ranters or found a welcome among the early Quakers. The Levellers, favouring a more broadly based, but still property-owning, democracy, held back from advocating the extension of the franchise to servants (and to women of all classes). But some servants joined the proto-communist Diggers, of whom shocked newsbook writers claimed that 'they would have none to work for hire or be servants to other men'. Captured Scots in 1648 who had voluntarily enlisted earlier in the now defeated army faced either indentured service in the colonies or slavery in Venice.[19]

Much later, in 1659, as the republic collapsed and another civil war seemed a distinct possibility, the single sheet *A Declaration of the Maids of the City of London* (1659) claimed to speak for servants by vehemently opposing 'this armyfied Parliament' and all those 'upstart preachers' and sectaries, and stood up for the bringing back of the monarchy, 'the right proprietor which alone can settle us against all fictions and factions'. Popular conservatism certainly existed alongside popular radicalism at this time, as it was to be at the end of the next century across the Channel during the French Revolution, which, by eliminating many elite employers, caused much unemployment among servants, especially in Paris. However, in England, reactions against all kinds of plebeian vocalising and activity, it has been argued, helped bring about the Restoration of 1660. The property-owning classes closed ranks. The prevailing view was that servants and others among the meaner sort were best kept out of politics. Looking back on the Civil War period encouraged employers and the governing classes to make increased efforts to keep servants under control. Charles II issued a proclamation in 1660 forbidding menservants within London and Westminster to carry swords and other weapons. But servant engagement in politics continued and re-emerged in periods of instability or, in individual cases, due to personal rancour. A much rankled eighteenth-century Yorkshire servant maid, dismissed at election time by Lord Malton, vowed to go up and down the streets of the town shouting 'Stapleton for ever' to promote his rival.[20]

The actual immediacy of Civil War upheavals was relatively short-lived, though memories of it, and lessons derived from it, were long-lasting. However, external factors of other, less dramatic, kinds impacted on the maintenance of order in the household. One, in particular, was frequently invoked as a part-explanation of the 'servant problem'. As Defoe and other hostile commentators frequently observed, the distractions and licence of town life, especially London, often proved too much for impressionable young country folk drawn there in search of employment.

London is so much the sink of vice [declared John Trusler in 1786] that the lower class of people are very corrupted. Those brought from the country are soon infected with the dissolute manners of town servants and become equally bad with them.

The contagion of London in this respect, however, was geographical as well as social. 'The . . . vices of the servants of the metropolis soon spread into the country whither they are always going,' opined John Huntingford in 1790.[21]

London – magnet, dynamo and threat rolled into one – was in a class of its own and loomed large in wearied, pessimistic analyses of the 'servant problem'. It was satirised as well as openly denigrated. *Hell upon Earth, or, The Town in an Uproar* (1729) depicted one day (Sunday) in the social life of the capital, starting at 6.00 a.m. with 'lascivious gentlemen and tradesmen stealing from their maidservants' garrets to their own bed-chambers'. By 7.00 a.m., before others were stirring, 'servant wenches [were] pilfering their mistresses' tea and sugar to entertain their visitors in the afternoon'. By 8.00 a.m. out-of-work servants had gained access to the houses of former employers to help themselves to the same free, loosely guarded supplies. In the lull of the late afternoon, at 4.00 p.m., 'footmen, journeymen and apprentices [were] engaged in low amours in gentlemen's and shopkeepers' kitchens'. By 6.00 p.m. a favourite servant sport had started. 'Hired servants got together railing at and reviling the families that entertain them and advancing the old doctrine of their being more places [jobs] than parish churches.'[22]

London and the horror stories to which it gave rise were unique. Alehouses, however, and the threat they constituted to the good management of servants, were everywhere. Research by Peter Clark and others has shown that servants were among their most regular users. They went to alehouses sometimes on errands for their employers and lingered there while picking up household supplies of ale and beer. But they often visited them on their own account to find an escape, to enter neutral ground, and to enjoy a more democratic, informal setting. In early modern Westminster alehouses tended to become hubs of servant networks. In keeping with these social realities by the eighteenth century keeping an alehouse or an inn had become an occupation of choice for many ex-servants, as evidence from Norwich, Stamford as well as London clearly shows.[23]

Because they were a favourite destination of servants and others of the meaner sort – often indeed a competing focal point to churches – alehouses, both licensed and unlicensed, were resented and opposed by many employers, high-minded clerics and those in authority. Apart from the moral objection to alehouses there was the lurking anxiety that a craving for drink in alehouses could encourage hard-up servants to steal from their masters. Additionally, inebriated servants were by nature known to be truculent, less governable and sometimes prone to violent outbursts. Many writers of tracts were absolutely convinced that drunkenness led to the undoing of large numbers of servants. 'They become incapable to govern themselves or to attend their master [so one tract observed in the mid-eighteenth century] and spend their money, ruin their character, neglect their business, leave open doors or windows, and neglect putting out candles.'[24]

Innholders and alehouse-keepers in Banbury, Oxfordshire, faced fines of 6s 8d under restrictions introduced in 1564 if they allowed servants and apprentices 'to play at any unlawful games or other ways to spend their masters' or parents' goods'. An unlicensed alehouse-keeper from Richmond, Yorkshire, was disciplined in October 1607 'for suffering men's servants to sit drinking in her house all the night through', while a few months later Roger Robinson, who kept an alehouse in Northallerton, appeared at the quarter sessions charged with 'receiving men's servants and others and suffering them to use drinking and disorder'. The better-off inhabitants of Bayton, Worcestershire, in 1621 petitioned the JPs against the excessive number of unlicensed alehouses in their district which 'constantly harbour vagrant and lewd persons in their houses during divine service and also harbour men's servants and children in the night time'. JPs in Cheshire received a similar petition in 1638 from parishioners of Bunbury against alehouse-keepers who harboured 'men's children and servants in the night season whereby much evil riseth and God's creatures abused and consumed'. Parishioners from Little Bedwyn in Wiltshire complained in the late 1620s that they could not 'keep [their] servants at home but they go and abide in alehouses profaning the Lord's Day and . . . consuming their money and neglecting their masters' business'. A victualler from Defford, Worcestershire, was presented as one who 'entertaineth men's servants out of due season' and for keeping a disorderly house'.[25]

Individual employers took up cudgels against particular alehouses and alehouse-keepers for wrongs allegedly inflicted in alehouses on their servants; not to do so would have involved failure to recognise an undermining of the utility and value of their own personal property. A Gray's Inn gentleman complained that his servant's modest savings had been purloined by a victualler and two women lodgers. A London bookseller who had made use of his servant as a debt collector in 1654 discovered that women of the town had exhausted the money he had raised (£36) by keeping him drinking and spending in an alehouse 'night and day'. Richard Mayo in *A Present for Servants* (1693) went out of his way to warn servants 'to take heed of alehouses, places of drunkenness or uncleanness, of loving cards and dice, or sitting up to unseasonable hours at such vanities'. John Scott in the following century went further in his denunciation, stressing the all-too-common link between alehouses and poverty:

> The alehouse is indeed the infernal mansion where the demons of avarice, extravagance, fury and prophaneness hold their perpetual residence; and whence the demons of famine and disease issue, like strong men armed, to desolate the cottages of the hamlet or the streets of the city . . . a nuisance so flagrantly pernicious to the community . . . Alehouses debauch the people . . .

So did gambling, a related theme which commentators often coupled with alehouses.[26]

Tract writers and others, though they never failed to grasp how destructive of good order in the household these external threats were, were equally quick to see how the family unit and employer–servant relations could be undermined by forces and developments operating entirely from within. One of these, undoubtedly, was the propensity of many servants to gossip about or slander the private life of the family in which they served, a practice which employers rightly recognised as not simply a bad habit but as a source of power used to discredit those they were currently serving or those whose service they had recently left. Dudley Ryder in October 1716 found himself in a coach with a maid-servant from Hackney who launched herself into open criticisms of her over-censorious mistress whose strict household regime she held to be as confining as a nunnery. 'I began to think,' said Ryder, 'it was not proper of me to give attention to or encourage servants talking of their masters and therefore would not encourage it.'[27]

Warnings about, and denunciations of, this widespread servant vice were a recurring motif in household manuals throughout the early modern period. Never to confide in a servant ought to be the unswerving practice of all employers, it was insisted, 'for every man's house is his castle and should be as his cabinet'. Thus declared Caleb Trenchfield in 1671. 'Lodge nothing with a servant . . . than you would be willing to hear if proclaimed from the house top,' said another pessimistic commentator much later. But even the routine details of the personal life and household practice of employers – embellished for maximum effect – were commonly broadcast. The author of *The Court of Good Counsell* (1607) held it to be a fact that:

> when a servant departeth from his master in what sort soever it be, whether contented or discontented, he cannot refrain from reporting wheresoever he go the life and behaviour of his former master. And though with one truth he mingle a hundred lies yet there be enough that will believe him . . .

Countless other writers in the next two centuries echoed the same sentiments:

> It is ordinary for servants to be tattling to others of their master's and mistress's infirmities [said one commentator in 1668] . . . They are spies in a house to discover its weakness and may expect the punishment of a spy from God for their wickedness.[28]

Servants' gossipmongering and slandering could be downright malicious in intent. A 1622 case in London centred on Joan Knipe, dismissed maidservant of an apothecary, who did everything she could to damage her former employer's good name. She gave out that her master and his son were whoremongers, his daughters whores and his wife a witch. A pregnant unmarried friend of Knipe was prevailed upon to broadcast that the master's son was the father of her unborn child. A century later, long-suffering spinster employer Gertrude Savile, whose unending 'servant problem' filled the pages of her diaries, discovered in January 1728 that her Swiss servant Michael had been spreading malicious rumours about her mother and herself. 'He has been a swearing, quarrelsome fellow below ever since he came.' Robert Dodsley, ex-servant poet, could not fail to include the gossiping habit in his collected verse *The Muse in Livery* (1732):

> But here among us the chief trade is
> To rail against our lords and ladies,
> To aggravate their smallest failings
> T' expose their faults with saucy railings.

Even Samuel Richardson's virtuous, but incessantly letter-writing, Pamela had to be warned, 'you ought to be wary what tales you send out of a family'. The Rev. William Cole and other neighbours in 1767 were regaled with slanderous gossip about the matrimonial problems of the Rev. and Mrs Goodwin. These people were 'in great affliction on account of their late maidservant who went away about a fortnight ago and has reported that Mr G. offered five guineas to lie with her'. But there was more. The manservant in the house, it was said, 'was familiar with Mrs Goodwin', declaring to all who would listen that 'he was sure his mistress loved not her husband'. Not surprisingly, employers often declined to employ servants from the immediate locality of the house – where they would already have social networks based on family and friends hungry for the latest news – as an attempt to combat the likelihood of gossip. This was one of a number of security measures advised by Henry Best of Elmswell in 1642. 'Never hire such as are too near their friends,' he said. Such networks could also function in the disposal of stolen goods.[29]

Gossip and slander could easily become sources of power – indeed, weapons – in servants' hands. Another servant power resided in the way, for better or worse, they could influence their master's children. 'What deadly poison may wicked servants be to our children,' declared Matthew Griffith in a publication of 1633. Accordingly the Duchess of Newcastle's ever vigilant mother

> never suffered the vulgar serving men to be in the nursery among the nursemaids lest their rude love making might do unseemly actions or speak unhandsome words in the presence of her children, knowing that youth is apt to take infection by ill examples having not the reason of distinguishing good from bad.

In the late 1660s another writer underlined the same anxieties, even more forcibly. A bad servant, he insisted, was like 'an usher to instruct the children in the black art of Hell. Believe it, thy children will catch sins as soon as vermin from those that are of Satan's ragged regiment.'[30] Children should be kept as much as possible in the company of their parents, advised John Locke, a thoughtful educationalist, away from the corrupting influence of servants. Children 'frequently learn from unbred or debauched servants such language, untowardly tricks and vices as otherwise they possibly would be ignorant of all their lives'. No less destabilising to a household was the common experience of children, censured for some offence by their parents, finding solace among well-meaning but misguided servants, 'foolish flatterers who thereby undo whatever their parents endeavour to establish'.[31]

Generalisations about disordered families are, of course, impossible, since the social chemistry and dynamics of a household depended on its particular characteristics, size and personnel. Large households especially were sometimes plagued with 'eye service' and idleness, inter-servant rivalries and hierarchical, managerial and division-of-labour problems. An eighteenth-century pamphlet complained about the snobbery of upper servants in large households endeavouring 'to imprint the strongest idea they possibly can of their own consequence and authority on the minds of every menial servant'. Gentlemen's valets were notoriously full of self-importance. Precedence disputes came to the surface. Established housekeepers sometimes resented the arrival of a new mistress with novel ideas or different priorities. The jealously defended jurisdictions of stewards and housekeepers in great houses sometimes collided. John Potts, steward to Sir Marmaduke Constable, in Yorkshire, complained of the new housekeeper there in 1726. 'She pretends to much but I see her do nothing but sew and open and shut the windows . . . She never appears before seven' in the mornings.[32] 'A long retinue may make thy state the greater,' quipped another commentator in 1710, 'but will make thy estate the less; the length of the peacock's train makes his wings the shorter.'[33]

Elderly employers sometimes risked exploitation by their household staff; Hannah More in her declining years certainly suffered in this way. Bachelor and widower establishments, it seems, were sometimes badly managed and out of control, since the men supposedly in charge often had no interest in, or grasp of, domestic details. Lancashire tradesman William Stout always preferred to have a female relative – sister or niece – keeping house for him. Generally his experiences of relying on a servant housekeeper were unsuccessful, and when his available supply of relatives eventually ran out he gave up housekeeping altogether and took lodgings. In 1748 the Lancashire businessman Robert Parker was advised to marry once he no longer had any surviving female relative who could keep house for him. 'Don't think of keeping house [only] with servants,' he was sternly warned. 'In my opinion there's few to be trusted.' At Sir Joshua Reynolds's dinner parties hopelessly mismanaged servants stood 'in idle clusters gaping upon the guests, and seem as unfit to attend a company as to steer a man of war'. Thus opined Samuel Johnson, a widower not a bachelor. Dr Johnson's own experience of the running of his own household was more fortunate but he made much use of coffee houses, frequently dined out, and stayed with friends. A servant perspective on bachelor households was expressed by the footman John MacDonald: 'servants that live with single gentlemen are not good family servants'. The servant shenanigans depicted in James Townley's farce *High Life below Stairs* (1759) take place in the home of a London bachelor, oblivious to what is going on behind his back until he is alerted by a friend's manservant. A Yorkshire widower, Thomas Wright, of Birkenshaw, came to the view in the 1770s that he had no choice but to remarry to fill the managerial void which his late wife had left behind:

> I found that servants and housekeepers were not to be trusted . . . I had no grandmother, no mother, no sister upon whom I might rely . . . During the state of my widowhood for want of a wife in the house when I was absent I had already suffered to my own knowledge to the amount of forty or fifty pounds at least by downright thievery, so that, continuing as I was, I had no prospect before me but ruin.[34]

The role of the mistress in a household of any size was always critical and sometimes difficult. 'Power sharing' in his household was not something that came easily to Henry Percy, ninth Earl of Northumberland:

> Wives will have their own wills [he advised his son] and will believe better of their own ways than of yours. They will have the command of all your servants, who, for the most part, will be apt out of inclination to lean that way. For women's humours are steps nearer their reaches than wise men's can be. [But a mistress's authority, once established, was more easily subverted than a man's.] More ways there be to cut the grass under a woman's foot to overthrow her than under a man's.

Marital discord, unsurprisingly, had a tendency to disrupt and divide households. Godly commentators urged masters never to ride roughshod over their wives; a household ought to be run as a true partnership. The mistress of the house was 'her husband's shadow', insisted Richard Bernard in 1612. 'As the moon doth from the sun so she is to receive her light from him.' But such celestial harmony did not always prevail. Sir Ralph Verney's sister quarrelled with her husband about the hiring of a particular maid. Since she did not get her way, at dinner 'she seated herself at the lower end of the table . . . saying it was fit for him that was mistress to sit at the upper end'. Lancashire squire Nicholas Blundell in the early eighteenth century had to cope as best he could with his wife's impetuous and peremptory dealings with their household staff. A generation later Thomas Turner, Sussex shopkeeper, had to endure similar outbursts against servants from his first wife; his second wife, significantly perhaps, was herself a former servant. 'I take care never to come into a married family,' says Archer in his servant guise in Farquar's *The Beaux' Stratagem* (1707). 'The commands of the master and mistress are always so contrary that 'tis impossible to please both.' Elizabeth Foyster has documented many eighteenth-century cases of fractured households and marital violence, with servants being drawn in to help protect at-risk mistresses in the home and then later in lawsuits and divorce cases as witnesses. Maidservant Ann Davis, for example, rallied to the defence of her threatened mistress when she was faced with a violent assault from her husband, George Whitmore. The would-be aggressor, it seems, was 'quite thunderstruck by her denunciation of him and by what she threatened to do and so much confounded that he had not one word to say for himself'. Injured wives sometimes solicited servant support by showing them their bruises. Servants in the marital battleground contained in the Prescott household in London in the early 1780s could find 'no peace or happiness' on account of what was taking place there and many quit. Later in the same decade Mary Eleanor Bowes, Countess of Strathmore, owed her eventual deliverance from her brutal second husband and her success in the bold divorce suit which followed to loyal servants, especially Mary Morgan, her maid, whose 'matchless, persevering friendship' was duly celebrated in a memorial.[35]

Domestic order was undermined by the psychological as well as physical abuse by employers of their wives. It caused a local scandal when it came to light that an early seventeenth-century small farmer from Somerset 'trusteth his [maid]servant with the keys of most of his doors and will not suffer his wife to keep them'. Anne Kugler has carefully documented the unhappy marriage of Lady Sarah Cowper (1644–1720) and its impact on employer–servant relations. Husband and wife in this case were equally strong-willed and their domestic life witnessed endless sniping about their personal differences and about their completely different models of household management. Sir William refused to allow his wife/competitor to hire, discipline or dismiss household servants and openly criticised her in front of relatives, guests and indeed servants themselves. Flagrant acts of servants' unsatisfactory conduct and disobedience (drunkenness and embezzlement included) went unpunished and all Lady Sarah's protests and demands for remedial action went unheeded. Though her widowhood in the early years of the eighteenth century no doubt initially opened up an exhilarating prospect, she never recovered the high ground and lived on into an embittered old age, failing to cope with the incessant servant problem which engulfed her life. Managing servants was also hardly one of the strong points of Lady Fermanagh, one of the Verney family. She wrote despairingly to her husband in December 1710 complaining of a drunken keeper and gardener and, indeed, most of her household:

I will take care of all things that lie in my power but some of our servants are more beasts than christians . . . They have drunk up all the small beer which would have lasted till four or five days after I was gone but I shall starve them in their kind.[36]

The Ettrick marriage dispute of 1778 brought into the open how Catherine Ettrick, well educated and from a good family, and who had brought her husband a £2,000 dowry, endured sustained ill treatment after her marriage. Her unfeeling husband 'used her as a servant by frequently obliging her to go and sit with the servants in the kitchen, not suffering her to sit in the dining room with him . . . and by frequently obliging her to run after his cows and horses in the fields'. Mrs Shackleton, of Alkincoats, Lancashire, in the same period fought a losing battle against inept, dishonest and ungovernable servants, since her authority in the household was so frequently undermined by her brutish husband.

Mr S. is quite cruel, ungenerous [she exclaimed], takes the servants' parts against me. He lets them abuse me scandalously and never contradicts them. All wrong I do, all right they do. God Almighty bless, preserve and be with me.

Emotionally draining though they were, however, Mrs Shackleton's trials scarcely compare with those revealed in the tortured pages of the journal of the continually depressed and neurotic spinster Gertrude Savile (1697–1758). Her whole life, it seems, was a long-drawn-out encounter with the 'servant problem' and it provides many insights into its components – management inadequacies and tensions, recruitment difficulties in the London labour market, servant mobility and servant 'power'. For that reason the unhappy story of the Savile household is perhaps best left until a later chapter, where it can receive more notice and be placed in its proper context.[37] (See pp. 177–9.)

Some of these destabilising marital tensions referred to above, it is clear, involved a sexual dimension in employer–servant relations and exposed servant vulnerability. It is perhaps not altogether surprising that servants on occasion seem to have taken a prominent part in skimmington rides, shaming exercises in local communities which brought employers' adulterous transgressions and marital breakdowns into the open. As vigilant domestic observers, and as victims of the lust of their social superiors, servants were doubly qualified to pass judgement. Masters and servants lived, worked and slept in close proximity. Privacy, even in larger establishments, was difficult or impossible to secure. In 1608 two servants in Colchester even had sexual intercourse at the foot of their employers' own bed while they were sleeping. At Everingham Hall, Yorkshire, in the eighteenth century the housekeeper (and sometimes her lover) shared the same bedroom with two maids. As historians – Bridget Hill, Laura Gowing and others – have long recognised, maidservants of this period were sexually vulnerable, playthings of their masters, masters' sons, lodgers, menservants and apprentices, though some, it is no doubt true, exploited their sexuality as a bargaining counter to gain advantage. A Somerset maid who was obviously flattered when she attracted the advances of her employer 'did not tell her dame because her master promised her new clothes'.[38]

Church court records are filled with cases involving master–servant sexual relations. A moralist warned parents in the late eighteenth century, 'you had better turn your daughter into the street at once than place her out to service. For ten to one her master shall seduce her or she shall be made the confidante of her mistress's intrigues.' John Trusler in 1786 took it for an incontestable fact that 'there are few servant maids in London ... but what are whores'.[39] At the beginning of the previous century Edward Glascocke, from Enfield, Middlesex, found himself in court, since he had been discovered in bed with his maidservant as well as his wife. In the same period churchwardens in Stoke St Mary, Somerset, were scandalised by an employer's open preference for his maidservant rather than his wife. When they went to work in the fields the maid rode on horseback while the mistress was made to walk. The master and maid slept in the same room while the unhappy mistress was consigned to another. In Nottinghamshire in 1600 John Drayton sent his maidservant away to Worksop after having had an adulterous relationship with her. In a similar case from Essex in the same year, involving a servant maid forced to have sex with both the master and his son, it was the mistress of the house who on this occasion intervened and dealt with Susan Lay, the maid, when she became pregnant, packing her off to the anonymous sink of London to prevent shame falling on the family. A Somerset mistress in 1618 shielded her son from being named as the father of her servant maid's bastard to defend the reputation of the household.[40]

It was made clear to a London servant maid in 1605 that providing the master with sexual favours on demand was part of her job. 'Thou art my servant and I may do with thee what I please.' Martha Bevers, a late seventeenth-century servant maid, also from London, received a similar response when she protested against the unwanted advances being made by her employer. 'What was it to her,' he was reported as saying, 'if he found her meat and paid her wages for nothing else but to [play] with him?' Civil servant and famous diarist Samuel Pepys frequently took sexual liberties with the servant maids employed in his modest household – over a third of them were molested – and he found himself repeatedly on the receiving end of the wrath of his ever alert and affronted wife for so doing. He resented her calculated counter-attack of starting to employ maids who were 'very ugly'. A Cheshire maidservant in 1669, made pregnant by her master, was forced to name another man as the father in the face of her employer's threat to have her put in the house of correction or driven out of the county. In 1693 Agnes Hunter, servant maid to a brewer in York, was seduced by her master during his wife's lying-in period and when she became pregnant was told not to worry since such things had often happened before in his house. In the same year the newspaper *The Athenian Mercury* carried the story of a man-servant who, with his master's active encouragement, married a servant maid in the same household only to find that she had been made pregnant by the employer in question, who was only too grateful to have 'such cracked ware [taken] off his hands'. There were financial compensations, however, which enabled the manservant for a time 'to live handsomely and save money'. A 1716 case which came before the London Consistory Court centred on a widower employer in St Giles in the Fields and his determination to enjoy sexual favours from two of his maidservants. One, offered 5s as a down payment, defiantly refused, 'asking him if he took her to be a common whore'. The other succumbed and became pregnant and was then offered £10 to lay the paternity charge at someone else's door. She firmly refused but bargained for a higher price of £15 to enable her to withdraw to the country to give birth to her illegitimate child. Prosperous gentleman William Byrd II (1674–1744), of Westover, in colonial Virginia, regularly made use of a maidservant for casual sex. At Loughton in Bedfordshire in 1767, the Rev. Thomas Goodwin and his wife, at loggerheads with each other, were under suspicion of seeking sexual solace with maidservant and manservant respectively.[41]

Throwing caution to the winds, and risking all the consequences of a male-dominated and enforced double standard of sexual morality, mistresses, too, sometimes destabilised their households by having clandestine relationships with menservants. In an early seventeenth-century adultery case a mistress had enlisted her maid's help in concealing her liaison; she kept watch for the lovers and warned of her master's impending return. (Representations of such mistress–maidservant complicity were later a commonplace in Restoration comedies.) A Cheshire employer in

1620 had a manservant imprisoned on a charge of disorderly behaviour since he suspected him of having an illicit affair with his wife. Dorothy Skelton, daughter of Charles II's physician, when accused of having an adulterous relationship with a footman, tried to defend herself by denouncing the man as 'a loose, scandalous and lascivious person' and protesting (too much, one suspects) that she 'would not prostitute herself to the lust of so base a fellow'. A scandal erupted in 1715 when Diana Dormer, mistress in a London household, was convicted of adultery with one or more of her male servants. Other servants in the house, aggrieved by the social destabilisation which the liaisons caused, testified against the guilty parties and gave the aggrieved husband their support. Thomas Jones, one of the convicted footmen, emboldened by his favoured position in his employers' household, flouted all the usual conventions by making use of the main staircase – normally off limits to servants – to gain access to his mistress's bedroom. Dismissed in 1711, Jones nonetheless was reunited with his mistress in Bath in 1713. The young footman John MacDonald acquired a notorious reputation as a ladies' man in Scotland. 'No family here [in Edinburgh] will hire you for fear of their women,' he was advised. A groom to the Duke and Duchess of Beaufort was handsomely bribed in 1740 after witnessing his mistress's adulterous indiscretions. Even more scandalous, and tragic in its consequences for all parties, was the Middleton *v*. Middleton divorce case of the 1790s which destroyed the household in which the mistress and a young groom committed adultery.[42]

There were occasional examples – notorious in their day – of infatuations which led to actual marriages bridging the employer–servant divide. The headstrong Elizabeth Aston scandalised her well-to-do Warwickshire family in 1600 by marrying one Sambach, 'a mean, mercenary serving man without other means to live'. Clergyman's son Azariah Pinney in the 1680s married a servant girl whose mother had been a recipient of poor relief; his own son, by contrast, married the heiress to a West India fortune. In the following century, Betty, third daughter of Sir Hugh Stewkley (d. 1719), married William Blake, her father's groom. The wife of textile master Jedediah Strutt was a former servant, experience which clearly assisted her in her knowledgeable management of household affairs. Later still, in 1825, Sir Harry Fetherstonhaugh, of Uppark, in Sussex, aged over seventy, wed his head dairymaid. The well kept secret of the marriage in the Victorian period between respectable professional man Arthur Munby and the maid-of-all-work Hannah Cullwick was an anomaly that both parties struggled to come to terms with, ultimately unsuccessfully; Munby remained essentially a bachelor husband, with Hannah no more than a very intermittent, ill at ease, lady.[43] In other cases involving employer–servant sexual relations hard bargaining occurred before marriage eventually took place. A Hampshire clergyman in 1571, having had sexual relations with his maid, made it clear that he was disposed to marry her only if her father and brother could come up with a suitable dowry. An early seventeenth-century Somerset master, John Goodins, having got his maidservant pregnant, fought hard for the best settlement he could get from her friends and neighbours before he would marry her; they offered £20, he wanted £30.[44]

Often, however, though promises of marriage had been made to servant maids by predatory masters, nuptials conspicuously failed to materialise. G. R. Quaife in his study of the sex lives of Somerset peasants has several examples of gullible or ambitious servant maids providing favours to masters who promised marriage when their spouse died. One such master told an incredulous neighbour that 'he had leave of his wife to beget a maid with child and would marry her when his wife was dead – and she should bear no shame'. Another deluded servant maid who had been seduced and then ditched by her randy employer told her sad story. 'I yielded to his adulterous ungodly desire . . . he having no child . . . And his wife dying he [promised me] would not only marry me but give me all the goods . . . he had.' Later in the seventeenth century a Yorkshire master persuaded his maidservant 'to lie with him . . . on pretence that his wife was an old woman and could not live long and then he would marry her'.[45]

For its lurid details of marital breakdown and the involvement of servants in what amounted to a household sexual circus, and for the publicity it received, the trial in 1631 of Mervin Touchet, second Earl of Castlehaven, had no equal. Cynthia Herrup has carefully investigated the whole sordid story and its significance for early modern patriarchalism. The subtitle of her book – *Sex, Law and the Second Earl of Castlehaven* – provides the specificity, but it is the chosen title (printed on the dust jacket in larger font), *A House in Gross Disorder*, that highlights the circumstances which gave rise to the whole affair. Castlehaven, an Irish peer of no great fortune, had sought to stabilise his finances through two successive marriages, the second of them to the widow of the fifth Baron Chandos, a daughter of the Earl of Derby. His principal seat was at Fonthill Gifford, Wiltshire, where he lived with his wife, son and daughter-in-law, and a household of at least twenty servants. What became a *cause célèbre* originated in 1630 with complaints to the Privy Council from

Castlehaven's son, fearful of his inheritance being squandered, about his father's lavish generosity to favourite servants and to his encouragement of their sexual improprieties. The son insisted that he himself had been cuckolded by one of these out-of-control servants and that Castlehaven's own wife had been ravished. Investigations were instigated by a commission of inquiry (whose members included the future Archbishop William Laud) set up by the Council. It was shocked by its findings, which exposed a completely dysfunctional household in which disorder and vice were openly countenanced: the complaints first made by Castlehaven's aggrieved son were completely corroborated. But much more came to light. Castlehaven himself, as well as apparently allowing the rape of his wife and daughter-in-law, now himself stood accused of sodomy with two of his menservants.[46] Not just his own honour but the good name of the peerage itself was thus impugned.

Castlehaven was quickly brought to trial, and his defence that he was unable to control the actions of his unruly household or, indeed, his immediate family was quickly set aside. Men of his rank were invariably expected to be able to exert authority. Inside information provided by some of the Earl's servants, it seems, may have earned them immunity from prosecution, since their names ceased to figure in the proceedings. Found guilty, Castlehaven – protesting his innocence to the last and insisting that much of the evidence used against him was insubstantial or fabricated and that family members simply wanted to get rid of him – was beheaded on Tower Hill in the early summer of 1631. Broadway and Fitzpatrick, the two menservants accused in the case, were also condemned and hanged at Tyburn five weeks later. There were, in truth, no winners in this extraordinary case. Castlehaven's whole disordered household came crashing down with him. The Fonthill estate was confiscated to the Crown – and (irony of ironies!) ended up after 1650 in the possession of John Bradshaw, who presided at the trial of Charles I. Castlehaven's son, who made the first accusations against his father, thus lost his inheritance and struggled to make ends meet as a soldier of fortune. His semi-estranged wife lived off her wits. Castlehaven's widow went into total eclipse and her marriage to the condemned peer was expunged from the Derby family records. Nor was that the end of the Fonthill story. The house acquired more notoriety in the early nineteenth century on account of its exuberant rebuilding by William Beckford (1759–1844), a man who, in his own fashion, was no less colourful and dissipated than the Earl of Castlehaven.[47]

The Castlehaven case, in its uniquely grotesque way, underlines many of the points explored in this chapter about patriarchalism, the importance attached in early modern society to good order in the household as a foundation for the well-being of the state, to harmony between husbands and wives and parents and children, and to the evenhanded exercise of authority and discipline over servants. The case also exhibited the insidious threats – drunkenness, gossiping and sexuality, especially – which were always at hand to destabilise or even destroy the idealised family unit. The loss of authority and control, even self-control, which the Castlehaven case exposed was telling. But even the resolution of the case was in no sense edifying. It was a compelling story, however, that continued to be retold in later generations, not only on account of its own sordid fascinations but as a dire warning to others.

NOTES

1 See, for example, Irons, *The Christian Servants' Book* (London, 1849); *The Court of Good Counsell* (London, 1607), chapter 24 (unpaginated); quoted in E. Strutt, *Practical Wisdom, or, The Manual of Life. The Counsels of Eminent Men to their Children* (London, 1824), p. 272.

2 Caleb Trenchfield, *A Cap of Gray Hairs* (London, 1671), pp. 38, 17, 21, 33, 13, 57–8, 70, 101–2, 104, 103, 144, 105, 139–40.

3 Eliza Haywood, *A Present for a Serving Maid* (London, 1744), pp. 24, 10, 6, 32.

4 Eliza Haywood, *A Present for a Serving Maid* (London, 1744); quoted in Hecht, *Domestic Servant Class*, p. 124; *A Proposal for the Amendment and Encouragement of Servants* (London, 1752), p. 6; Huntingford, *The Laws of Masters and Servants Considered . . . to which is added an account of a society formed for the increase and encouragement of good servants* (London, 1790).

5 *The Court of Good Counsell* (London, 1607), unpaginated, chapter 27; G. B. Harrison (ed.), *Advice to his Son by Henry Percy, ninth Earl of Northumberland* (1609, repr. London, 1930), p. 77; Fielding, *The Universal Mentor* (Dublin, 1763), p. 191; Swinnock, *The Christian Man's Calling* (London, 1668), p. 117; Jacqueline Eales, *Puritans and Roundheads. The Harleys of Brampton Bryan and the Outbreak of the English Civil War* (Cambridge, 1990), p. 60; C. H. Firth (ed.), *The Life of William Cavendish, Duke of Newcastle* (London, 1886), pp. 157, 165; Whitelocke, Journal, I, p. 39, extracted in Godfrey Davies, research notes, Huntington Library, box 61; *Memoirs of the Verney Family*, III, pp. 168, 214, 436–37; Steele, *The Spectator*, I, 327, quoted in Turner, *What the Butler Saw*, p. 25.

6 *Court of Good Counsell* (1607), unpaginated, chapter 26; V. B. Heltzel (ed.), 'Richard Earl of Carbery's advice to his son', *Huntington Library Bulletin*, 11 (1937), 102; J. Demos, *A Little Commonwealth. Family Life in Plymouth Colony* (New York, 1970), p. 112, cited in Mary Beth Norton, *Founding Mothers and*

Fathers. Gendered Power and the Forming of American Society (New York, 1996), p. 136.

7 *Observations and Advices Oeconomical*, p. 97; Chapone, *Letters on the Improvement of the Mind addressed to a young Lady* (Dublin, 1773), pp. 148, 165, 163, 94–5; *Journal of John Gabriel Stedman*, p. 263; Pennington, *An Unfortunate Mother's Advice to her Absent Daughters* (London, 1761), pp. 28–9. See, for example, Kitchiner, *The Housekeeper's Oracle*, (London, 1829) p. 16, and Isabella Beeton, *The Book of Household Management* (London, 1861), p. 2; Braithwait, *The Turtles Triumph* (London, 1641), p. 32; *Family Religion Revived, or, An Attempt to Promote Religion and Virtue in Families* (New Haven, CT, 1755), p. 94.

8 For a telling example from the end of the nineteenth century see J. Burnett (ed.), *Useful Toil. Autobiographies of Working People from the 1820s to the 1920s* (London, 1974), p. 207.

9 H. Harrington, *Nugae Antiguae* (London, 1775), II, pp. 86–8. I am indebted to Professor P. H. Hardacre for drawing my attention to this reference; *Blundell Diaries*, III, p. 209.

10 Huntington Library, HM 66348 L9 G2, 'Orders and Duties for the Better Ordering and Direction of the House of Lionel Cranfield, Earl of Middlesex' [compiled by Morgan Coleman].

11 Huntington Library, Ellesmere 8139, 'Rules for the Household of the Earl of Bridgewater at Ashridge, Hertfordshire during his Absence', 17 November 1673.

12 Huntington Library, Stowe. ST 44, James Brydges, first Duke of Chandos, instructions to his servants, 1721; Turner, *What the Butler Saw*, p. 16.

13 See S. Porter (ed.), *London and the Civil War* (London, 1996), and B. Coates, *The Impact of the English Civil War on the Economy of London, 1642–1650* (Aldershot, 2004).

14 See Durston, *The Family in the English Revolution, passim.*

15 See C. Carlton, *Going to the Wars. The Experience of the British Civil Wars, 1638–1651* (London, 1992).

16 S. Porter, *Destruction in the English Civil Wars* (Stroud, 1994).

17 Quoted in Durston, *Family in the English Revolution*, p. 130; T. Fuller, *History of the Worthies of England* (London, 1662), p. 85; *Nalson, The Character of a Rebellion* (London, 1681), p. 11, quoted in Ann Hughes, *Gangraena and the Struggle for the English Revolution* (Oxford, 2004), p. 114.

18 J. Rushworth, *Historical Collections* (London, 1659), pp. 405–6; Dennison, *Aberdeen before 1800*, p. 256; D. Cressy, *England on Edge. Crisis and Revolution, 1640–1642* (Oxford, 2006), p. 105; Diane Purkiss, *The English Civil War. A People's History* (London, 2006), p. 410; K. Lindley, *Popular Politics and Religion in Civil War London* (Aldershot, 1997), pp. 106, 151, 154; Cressy, *England on Edge*, p. 43.

19 Cressy, *England on Edge*, p. 332; Purkiss, *English Civil War*, pp. 154, 217, 220, 348; *ibid.*, p. 280; *ibid.*, p. 474; *ibid.*, p. 269; M. Braddick, *God's Fury England's*

Fire. A New History of the English Civil Wars (London, 2008), p. xxi; Verney, *Memoirs of the Verney Family during the Civil War*, II, pp. 222–5; quoted in Purkiss, *English Civil War*, p. 521; Braddick, *God's Fury*, p. 545.

20 B. Reay, *The Quakers and the English Revolution* (London, 1985), pp. 98–100; R. Cobb, *The French and their Revolution*, ed. D. Gilmour (London, 1998), pp. 8–9; [Proclamation of 29 September 1660] *For the Suppressing of Disorderly and Unseasonable Meetings in Taverns and Tippling Houses and also forbidding Footmen to wear Swords or other Weapons within London, Westminster and their Liberties*; Holmes, 'Domestic Service in Yorkshire', p. 118.

21 Trusler, *London Adviser*, p. 47; Huntingford, *The Laws of Masters and Servants Considered*, p. 100.

22 *Hell upon Earth*, pp. 2, 3, 8, 9.

23 P. Clark, *The English Alehouse. A Social History, 1200–1830* (Harlow, 1983), pp. 126, 148; Flather, *Gender and Space*, p. 113; Merritt, *The Social World of Early Modern Westminster*, p. 175; Clark, *English Alehouse*, pp. 76, 282.

24 *The Footman's Looking Glass* (London, 1747), p. 9.

25 Helen Berry and Elizabeth Foyster (eds.), *The Family in Early Modern England* (Cambridge, 2007), p. 58; J. S. W. Gibson and E. R. C. Brinkworth (eds.), *Banbury Corporation Records*, Banbury Historical Society, 15 (1977), p. 40; Atkinson, *Quarter Sessions Records* (North Riding), pp. 99, 112; J. W. Willis Bund (ed.), *Worcestershire County Records. Calendar of Quarter Sessions Papers, 1591–1643* (Worcester, 1900), II, pp. 345, 524; Bennett and Dewhurst, *Quarter Sessions Records. County Palatine of Chester, 1559–1760*, p. 94; Clark, *English Alehouse*, p. 127; Willis Bund, *Worcestershire County Records*, II, p. 524.

26 Berry and Foyster, *Family in Early Modern England*, p. 58; Mayo, *Present for Servants*, p. 31; Scott, *Observations on the Present State of the Parochial and Vagrant Poor* (London, 1773), p. 59.

27 W. Matthews (ed.), *The Diary of Dudley Ryder, 1715–1716* (London, 1939), p. 352.

28 Trenchfield, *A Cap of Gray Hairs*, p. 25; H. G. Watkins, *Hints and Observations seriously addressed to Heads of Families in reference chiefly to Female Domestic Servants* (London, 1816), p. 25; *Court of Good Counsell*, unpaginated, chapter 23; G. Swinnock, *The Christian Man's Calling* (London, 1668), p. 139.

29 P. Griffiths, A. Fox and S. Hindle (eds.), *The Experience of Authority in Early Modern England* (London, 1996), p. 117; Saville (ed.), *Secret Comment. The Diaries of Gertrude Savile, 1721–1757*, p. 98; Dodsley, *Muse in Livery*, p. 21; Richardson, *Pamela*, p. 44; Stokes, *The Blechley Diary of the Rev William Cole*, pp. 270–71; *Farming and Memorandum Books of Henry Best*, p. 140.

30 Griffiths, *Bethel*, p. 379; *Memoirs of the Duke of Newcastle*, p. 157; Swinnock, *Christian Man's Calling*, p. 387.

31 Locke, *Some Thoughts concerning Education* (London, 1693), pp. 70, 58.

32 Quoted in Hecht, *Domestic Servant Class*, p. 36; Jones, *The Man of Manners, or, The Plebeian Polished*, p. 23; quoted in Holmes, 'Domestic Service in Yorkshire, p. 70.

33 Dare, *Counsellor Manners his last Legacy to his Son*, p. 67.

34 Turner, *What the Butler Saw*, pp. 104–7; J. D. Marshall (ed.), *The Autobiography of William Stout of Lancaster, 1665–1752*, Chetham Society, 3rd ser., 14 (1967), *passim*; quoted in Vickery, *The Gentleman's Daughter*, p. 128; quoted in Horn, *Flunkies and Scullions*, p. 143; R. B. Schwartz, *Daily Life in Johnson's London* (Madison, WI, 1983), p. 109; MacDonald, *Travels in Various Parts of Europe, Asia and Africa*, p. 169; on Townley's play see pp. 85, 161–2; Vickery, *Gentleman's Daughter*, p. 128.

35 *Advice to his Son*, pp. 100, 102; Gataker, *Marriage Duties . . .* , p. 42, Bernard, *Joshua's Godly Resolution in Conference with Caleb touching Household Government for well ordering a Family* (London, 1612), p. 32; *Memoirs of the Verney Family*, III, pp. 126–27; on Blundell see Hill, *Servants*, pp. 150–71; Vaisey, *The Diary of Thomas Turner, passim*; *Beaux' Stratagem*, Act III, scene 3, p. 342; Elizabeth Foyster, *Marital Violence. An English Family History* (Cambridge, 2005), pp. 186–7; Wendy Moore, *Wedlock* (London, 2009), pp. 193, 218, 232, 268, 306.

36 Quoted in Quaife, *Wanton Wenches*, p. 155; Anne Kugler, *Errant Plagiary. The Life and Writing of Lady Sarah Cowper, 1644–1720* (Stanford, CA, 2002), pp. 47, 48, 69, 149, 151, 190; See below, pp. 176–7. Lady Verney, *Verney Letters of the Eighteenth Century from the Mss at Claydon House* (2 vols., London, 1930), I, pp. 284–6.

37 Foyster, *Marital Violence*, p. 76; Vickery, *Gentleman's Daughter*, p. 159; Saville, *Secret Comment. The Diaries of Gertrude Savile, passim*.

38 M. Ingram, 'Ridings, rough music and mocking rhymes in early modern England', in B. Reay, *Popular Culture in Seventeenth-Century England* (London, 1985), pp. 166–7; Flather, *Gender and Space*, p. 72; Holmes, 'Domestic Service in Yorkshire', p. 96; Quaife, *Wanton Wenches*, p. 71.

39 J. Moir, *Female Tuition* (London, 1787), p. 182, quoted in D. Jarrett, *England in the Age of Hogarth* (London, 1974, 1986), p. 86; Trusler, *London Adviser*, p. 48.

40 Flather, *Gender and Space*, p. 72; P. Hair (ed.), *Before the Bawdy Court* (London, 1972), p. 143; Quaife, *Wanton Wenches*, pp. 154–5; D. Marcombe, *English Small Town Life. Retford, 1520–1642* (Nottingham, 1993), p. 141; Flather, *Gender and Space*, p. 50; Quaife, *Wanton Wenches*, p. 187.

41 Gowing, *Common Bodies*, p. 61; P. Earle, *The Making of the English Middle Class, 1660–1730* (London, 1989), pp. 224–5; Garthine Walker, *Crime, Gender and Social Order in Early Modern England* (Cambridge, 2003), p. 217; D. M. Turner, *Fashioning Adultery. Gender, Sex and Civility in England, 1660–1740* (Cambridge, 2002), pp. 69–70; Joanne Bailey, *Unquiet Lives. Marriage and Marriage Breakdown in England, 1660–1800* (Cambridge, 2003), p. 146;

Hitchcock, *Chronicling Poverty*, pp. 54–5; K. Berland *et al.* (eds.), *The Commonplace Book of William Byrd II of Westover* (Chapel Hill, NC, 2001), p. 5; *Blechley Diary of the Rev. William Cole*, pp. 9, 270–3, 279.

42 Hitchcock, *Chronicling Poverty*, pp. 55, 58–9; Walker, *Crime, Gender and Social Order*, p. 217; Turner, *Fashioning Adultery*, pp. 149, 160–3; MacDonald, *Travels*, pp. 91–2; Horn, *Flunkies and Scullions*, p. 202; L. Stone, *Broken Lives. Separation and Divorce in England, 1660–1857* (Oxford, 1993), pp. 162–247.

43 Fairfax-Lucy, *Charlecote and the Lucys*, pp. 95–6; Pamela Sharpe, *Population and Society in an East Devon Parish. Reproducing Colyton, 1540–1840* (Exeter, 2002), p. 250; R. Dutton, *A Hampshire Manor. Hinton Ampner* (London, 1968, 1988), pp. 42–3; *Uppark, Sussex* (National Trust guide, 1985), p. 55; Horn, *Flunkies and Scullions*, p. 2. For comparative purposes it is worth noting that an ordinance of 1673 in Zeeland declared null and void any marriage between a servant and the child of the servant's master. (S. Schama, *The Embarrassment of Riches. An Interpretation of Dutch Culture in the Golden Age* (New York and London, 1987), p. 458; Hudson, *Munby, Man of two Worlds*, esp. pp. 329, 347, 367, 380.

44 A. J. Willis (ed.), *Winchester Consistory Depositions, 1561–1602* (Winchester, 1960), p. 7; Quaife, *Wanton Wenches*, pp. 93–4.

45 Quaife, *Wanton Wenches*, p. 51; Holmes, 'Domestic Service in Yorkshire', p. 256.

46 Francis Bacon, often over-indulgent to his servants, reputedly had a homosexual relationship with one of his household staff, 'one Godrick, a very effeminate-faced youth'. (I. McCormick, ed., *Secret Sexualities. A Sourcebook of Seventeenth and Eighteenth-Century Writing*, London, 1997, p. 53.) Much later, evidence was uncovered of servant involvement in a homosexual network in nineteenth-century Lancashire. (H. G. Cocks, 'Safeguarding civility: sodomy, class and moral reform in early nineteenth-century England,' *Past & Present*, 190 (2006), 126, 133.

47 Herrup, *House in Gross Disorder, passim*, esp. pp. 12–13, 38, 39, 94–5, 100, 103, 109.

8

THE 'SERVANT PROBLEM'

[Servants are] an order of our species that we can't well do without but there are few of us who have not reason to complain of them.
(D. Gibson, ed., *A Parson in the Vale of White Horse. George Woodward's Letters from East Hendred, 1753–1761*, Stroud, 1982, p. 110)

I wish that I was to live here all my days! This is life indeed! A servant lives up to his eyes in clover. They have wages and board wages and nothing to do but to grow fat and saucy. They are as happy as their master; they play for ever at cards, swear like emperors, drink like fishes, and go a-wenching with as much ease and tranquillity as if they were going to a sermon.
(Davy, a country servant, on the joys of London, in David Garrick, *Bon Ton, or, High Life above Stairs*, Dublin, 1776, p. 29)

The 'servant problem', it has already been stressed, was not an intrinsically new development of the eighteenth century. Complaints about servants' idleness, unreliability, 'eye service', insolence, not serving their full term, drunkenness and debauchery had been heard since the Elizabethan Age and underpinned the great tide of godly literature calling for the reform of households and the recognition of duties by both men and masters:

> It is as hard a matter to find servants without faults as dropsy patients without thirst [bemoaned the anonymous author of *The Court of Good Counsell* in 1607] . . . Though their faults be innumerable their chiefest ornaments are the three properties of a dog, to wit the gullet (for that they are gluttons), barking (for that the master can do nothing but they will presently report it abroad), biting (which is so natural unto them that let their master do never so well by them yet they will not stick to call him ungrateful) . . .[1]

The 'servant problem' also featured as an ingredient in Restoration drama, as Congreve's *The Way of the World* (1700) amply demonstrated.

Man-about-town Witwoud can think of no more telling insult to apply to Petulant than to compare him with servants. Lady Wishfort's opinion of Peg, her chambermaid, is beneath contempt. Even Foible, her once trusted lady's maid, falls completely and irredeemably from favour.[2] (See pp. 29–31.)

But complaints about servants reached new heights in the Augustan Age as the practice of servant-keeping and competition for servants both spread, as London continued its staggeringly relentless growth, as the national economy boomed, and as new sensibilities and new standards of decorum blossomed. Court records and family papers abound with individual case histories of dysfunctional households and the exercise of servant 'power'. The Hampshire gentleman Sir Thomas Jervoise meticulously kept an account book in the two decades after 1690, not only listing servants' wages but their periods of service and the reasons for their dismissal. No fewer than twenty-four of the sixty-four servants whose names are recorded (37.5 per cent) were turned away, often after only a relatively brief period of employment. Anthony Saunders, groom, appointed in February 1690, was dismissed in February 1696 'for his laziness, folly and sauciness'. Charles, an elderly retainer, was finally sent away in January 1697 for being 'perpetually drunk'. In August the same year Alexander Constant was cast out for unspecified 'vices'. His immediate successor, Robert Pitt, did not last long, either, being despatched in June 1699 'for cheating'. William Izard, coachman, taken on in June 1701, was sent packing only nine months later as 'a great lazy fellow'. Joseph Stubbs, a footman arriving in January 1702, was thrown out in less than a month, having been caught wearing his master's linen.[3]

The experience of Lady Sarah Cowper (1644–1720) in Hertfordshire was no better, partly because servants in this household were able to take advantage of the fragile state of their employers' marital relations. The house became a domestic battleground, with servant discipline falling apart and cases of insubordination, immorality, drunkenness, violence and embezzlement going largely unpunished by a master chiefly devoted to humbling his wife. After her husband's death in 1706 Sarah vainly tried to retrieve the situation and claim the high ground, dismissing many unsatisfactory members of the household staff:

> It is deplorable that human creatures living under the instruction of christian religion should be so brutified ... Before I was a widow I used to think that were I in power I should manage servants to my content. But so wicked and profligate is this age that I find it impracticable by any means or method.[4]

An aloof silence or unemotionally delivered insults became standard practice in her household management strategies, along with practical measures like padlocking doors and barring windows as an attempt to force menservants to keep regular hours. But her 'stupid, lying servants' proved quite ungovernable and in her final years she concluded that the best option was simply to give up housekeeping on her own account altogether and go to live with her son and daughter-in-law.[5]

The story of Elizabeth Freke (1671–1714), a lawyer's daughter unhappily married to a spendthrift tyrant and surviving into a no less unhappy and cantankerous widowhood, was similar in many respects to Lady Cowper's and was carefully documented in her self-serving *Remembrances*. Arriving in London from Ireland on 17 July 1696, baggage containing all her clothes was lost through her maid's carelessness. More negligence by two other maids on 2 May 1712 led to the disappearance of six weeks' washing left hanging overnight in the yard outside the house. The previous year another maid was dismissed for theft and a manservant and maid absconded 'after they had cheated me of above a hundred pounds and above seven dozen bottles of cordial water and wine in half a year beside a great trunk of linen'. Intended arson, even her own murder, Freke was convinced, were narrowly prevented on this occasion. The manservant, it transpired, 'was a rogue burnt in the hand and . . . had got into my service under a false certificate contrived with my own maid Sarah Fiennes who had lived with me above three years and was privy to it'. Good servants, whose deaths were lamented by their mistress, did from time to time enter her household but they appear to have been few and far between. Some mistresses, their eyesight sharpened by long and painful experience, claimed to be able to spot a good servant as soon as they saw one. Lady Rockingham in eighteenth-century Yorkshire quickly reached a judgement on Betty Hankin, one of her maidservants, one who was 'unlikely to turn out a very steady servant as she passes for a beauty'. Molly Vicars, by contrast, had 'more the look of a servant than any in the house and I fancy is a solid, sober woman and always about her business'.[6]

Few heads of household can have had a more prolonged and desperately unhappy experience of the 'servant problem' than Gertrude Savile (1697–1758), a well connected Yorkshire clergyman's daughter and sister of an affluent MP. Savile was the epitome of the insecure, neurotic spinster. Her personal life, starved of affection by her domineering mother and largely ignored by her brother, was deeply unhappy. But Savile's misery was always made worse by her frustrating and soul-destroying experience with servants. Part of the problem was sharing a household with her mother (and additionally for a time her aunt) which produced constant line-management problems with menservants and maids. That said, however, Gertrude Savile constantly mismanaged those servants directly responsible to her, was always interfering with, and prying into, their work, and imprudently confused favouritism with kindness. Servants formed a staple ingredient in her meticulously kept diaries from the 1720s to the 1750s. More space was devoted to them than to any other single subject; for several years indeed she compiled an end-of-year review of servants' misconduct and their comings and goings and indulged her phobias, prejudices and festering grievances. Foreign servants she despaired of. 'He is quite useless to me,' she said in January 1728 of Michael, her Swiss footman, who could hardly speak a word of English. Irish servants, as well as being 'stiff and sulky' and 'sad rubbish' were likely to have the additional disadvantage of being papists. Welsh servants also did not score high marks in this difficult household. Mary Morgan lasted for only a few months in 1751, 'she having Welsh pride and boldness (as well as blood) it made her above her business [and] unable to bear reproof'. Sarah, a stubborn, obstinate Welsh cookmaid who departed abruptly in February 1757 'confirmed my dislike of that country'. But hardly any of her servants – wherever they came from – were considered satisfactory for any length of time; initial hopes of finding 'jewels' always seemed to be cruelly dashed. Savile's narrative of the 'servant problem' she experienced, indeed, makes depressing reading.[7]

The year 1727 saw five footmen come and go in Gertrude Savile's household. One proved 'a perfect fool', another 'grew mad, I thought; his behaviour was so intolerable and unaccountable'. William, another, on 22 August 1727 'went out early in the morning and did not return till night. Made no excuse nor seemed to think he had done wrong. He has been too violently officious to hold. I think there is something in the air of this place that infects servants!'[8] But her maidservant, Ellen Rixley, 'from the first [was] good for nothing [and] grew so intolerable bad she was not to be endured. Giving her very handsome mourning for the King [George I] I think blew her quite up.' (With cruel irony Savile noted that in December 1727 she was reading the text of a play, *The Grateful Servant*, consoling herself with the optimistic thought, presumably, that such characters could at least be found in fiction, if not in real life.) Things showed not the slightest improvement in 1728. In January Mary Grey, a housemaid, was accused of stealing a silver spoon. 'There have been several ugly, suspicious things which laid together made it not safe for her to continue in the house.' A new maid, Mary Cooper, taken on at the end of the year, was (revealingly) 'too new yet to find many faults in'.[9] William, the unsatisfactory manservant complained of the previous year, went on from bad to worse and was finally dismissed on 19 August. 'He is grown as hardened in all sorts of wickedness as if he had been a practitioner of many years: ungrateful, unpersuadable. No usage, kind or severe, has any effect.' Frank, a new footman, quickly fell from grace when it became clear that he dawdled on errands, had a cheeky, defiant manner and was pert in his answers. Michael, the dismissed Swiss footman, took classic servant-style revenge on the Savile household by spreading hard-hitting gossip about it. 'He said that mother and me were devils; that no servant ever stayed more than a week or a fortnight with abominable strange lies' about Gertrude's brother and his wife.[10]

October 1729 saw the Saviles' cook involved in a street fight with the wife of a sedan chair man, whose whore she had been for some years. It took Savile two days to summon sufficient courage to confront and dismiss the offending woman. 'We had reason to fear she might fire the house or murder the maid ... It seems she is scandalous in the whole neighbourhood for a whore and a drunkard.' And so, we can be sure, it went on, despite an unfortunate gap of about a decade in the surviving diaries. The entry of 10 May 1741 recorded the departure of the Henry Ellers 'the best servant I ever had, but according to custom, spoiled with too much encouragement and liberty ...' A maidservant, Anne Dickson, was turned out on 23 April 1743: 'she proved the vilest hussy, impudent whore, drunkard, liar, slut and, I believe, thief'. Dorothy Robinson came and went very quickly in 1747. 'She was a proud, conceited, lousy, sluttish, sturdy and unfaithful servant.' Betty Weally, who had been 'a favourite of mine', was discharged in March 1751 when her numerous faults came to light: 'falsehood, whorishness, cheating, cruelty to my dogs and cats ... I never was so grossly deceived as in this last ignorant, silly girl. If half what I heard of her was true there never was a real or poetical character that exceeded her in artful hypocrisy.' Six changes of servants, some of them having been well recommended, took place in 1755. Character references, the exhausted and impotent Savile lamented, 'signify nothing at all'. That there was a 'mistress problem' in this household as well as a 'servant problem', of course, went unrecognised by Gertrude Savile herself. Having become firmly convinced that servants were invariably a bad lot this mistress expected to find inadequacies in her household staff, and always did![11]

The 'servant problem', as we have seen, was constantly discussed and complained of by early eighteenth-century employers. In the light of this experience, not surprisingly, a new literature appeared underlining the rapidly deteriorating seriousness of the situation, the reasons behind it, and the desperate need to stem the swelling tide. New genres of satire and farce joined conventional prose and verse as vehicles of denunciation.

Daniel Defoe (c. 1661–1731), economic conservative, inveterate moraliser and one of the most prolific of Augustan writers, turned frequently to the subject of the 'servant problem' in a succession of tracts and books on society and the economy in the second and third decades of the eighteenth century. Non-fiction now preoccupied him in a steady stream of publications; *Roxana* (1724) – with an enterprising, and then criminal, mistress and maid at its heart – was his last, and only moderately successful, novel. *The Family Instructor* (1715, 1727) was his initial venture into the world of household manuals and displayed strong transitional features. It was firmly connected to an older tradition in exalting 'the value of a religious family' (as was its distinctly clerical tone), but it was fictional in its characterisation and story line (though both were offered as echoes of recognisable realities), and in its use of dialogue format it closely resembled a series of plays. A servant character enters the first part of Defoe's book, concerned chiefly with parents and children, but it is in the five dialogues contained in the second part, dealing expressly with masters and servants, that they occupy centre stage. Throughout this part of the book, at considerable length, godly and ungodly masters and servants and their relationships with, and effects on, each other are constantly contrasted. A tearaway apprentice complains at one point that 'our house is like a monastery instead of a shop or workhouse . . . We have such a world of ceremonies and religious doings among us 'tis enough to weary a body off their legs.' His godly friend, placed in a very different kind of family, however, bemoans the fact that 'as to religion I never heard a word of it in [our] house since I came to it'.[12] Unsurprisingly, since Defoe had a fixed moralising agenda, the ungodly master and ungodly servant are made to see the error of their ways and to recognise their respective responsibilities. The erring master is brought to accept that he had 'the whole duty of a parent' devolved upon him and that this extended to the oversight of servants' souls as well as their bodies. The reformed apprentice becomes a blessing to others. In a different way the central character – a godly servant maid – in the first of Defoe's dialogues in Vol. II, dealing with a master, mistress, servants and a negro slave boy from Barbados, becomes a shining example to others. The moral was blindingly obvious. 'If all servants in such places did their duty like her it would spread religion through the world in a secret and imperceptible manner for ought I know equal to all the other means that God has appointed for it.'[13]

Defoe's *Religious Courtship* (1722) addressed a number of the same issues in a lengthy appendix devoted to servants and servant-keeping. Taking as its starting point that 'irreligious servants 'are the plague of families', its author reflects at some length on the reasons for their intrusive presence even in godly households and on the harm they can do. 'Turn them all away that pretend to behave irreverently or pretend to mock or scoff at it,' says one of his mistress characters in one of the dialogues in this book. Ill considered, glibly dispensed testimonials were one major cause of irreligious servants being preferred to other households. 'It is all our own fault; we recommend sluts and thieves and drones and saucy, insolent fellows and wenches. I say we recommend them to one another without any concern for our neighbours' safety or peace.' Irreligious masters and mistresses paid no heed to the religious well-being of their servants. 'There are mistresses enough in the world,' a servant character is made to say in another of the dialogues included here, 'that never . . . care whether their servants serve God or the Devil . . . Religion is so much made a jest of among masters that it is hard to find any servants that do not jest at it too . . .' Even some of those servants professing to be good Christians were in fact downright hypocrites, using religion as a cloak to hide their base motives and to gain advantage.[14]

Defoe returned to some of these same themes, but at greater length and with even greater vehemence, in his book *The Great Law of Subordination Considered* (1724), 'a black history of the degeneracy of English servants' written not in dialogue form but in hard-hitting continuous prose. Apprentices and outdoor servants came under attack but the rampant insubordination and idleness of liberty-seeking indoor servants had escalated so much that they were now truly a national problem calling out for remedy. 'If it goes on,' Defoe trumpeted,

> the poor will be rulers over the rich, and the servants be governors of their
> masters . . . the canaille of this nation impose laws upon their superiors,
> and begin not only to be troublesome but, in time, may be dangerous; in
> a word, order is inverted, subordination ceases, and the world seems to
> stand with the bottom upward.[15]

In general a believer in high wages (as a stimulus to the economy) Defoe was convinced that due to an imbalance between supply and demand servants' wages had doubled or even trebled in recent times and that servants were largely dictating their own terms. Even good servants, he claimed, became corrupted by being over-rewarded and by their unchecked, false pride. The servant problem in London, not surprisingly, was in a class of its own and Defoe, a Londoner himself (the son of a Dissenting tallow chandler) was well placed to observe it.

As in earlier publications on the same subjects Defoe blamed masters as much as servants for this deplorable state of affairs:

> It is since family discipline decayed in England and the good example of masters ceased that servants have got the head and mastership over us, and until something of an orderly and virtuous governing of families comes in fashion again among us I fear that no laws, Acts of Parliament, or public regulations will be effectual to this purpose . . . Drunken and disorderly families will be filled with drunken and disorderly servants; nay indeed, they are seminaries of such.

Only the sternest of remedies could stem the tidal wave of such problems. Masters, Defoe insisted, should be fined for giving a character reference to a dismissed servant and made financially responsible for any losses a new master incurred from a dishonest servant who had been knowingly recommended by another. Reasons for dismissal must always be included in testimonials for servants. Masters, he went on, should also be fined for not bringing a profanely swearing servant before a JP. Servants themselves, of course, felt his lashes. Those rightly dismissed for misconduct or insolence should be required to remain unemployed for at least six months. A servant who threatened his master should be transported for a twenty-one-year term.

> Now is the time [Defoe roundly concluded] for the people of England to rescue themselves out of the hands of the worst slavery they were ever yet in . . . I mean a bondage to their own servants . . . Insolent servants are the worst masters.[16]

Defoe must surely have thought that with *The Great Law of Subordination* he had written something which was pointedly relevant to his troubled times and which the employing classes would immediately appreciate. It was not to be. By his own usual standards *The Great Law* was a resounding commercial failure, Defoe's characteristically trenchant style notwithstanding. The reasons are, perhaps, not hard to find. The chosen *persona* of the author – a Frenchman in England writing to his brother at home – was a strategic error; Englishmen, Defoe discovered to his cost, did not take lightly to be being lectured and reprimanded by an arrogant foreigner. There was too much pointed criticism of masters for comfort. The 'servant problem' was widely recognised by England's elite but masters would have been happier with an analysis that exonerated them from any share of the blame. Moreover Defoe's book was far too long (more than 300 pages), prolix in its argument and expensive to become a best-seller.

The undaunted and indefatigable Defoe attempted to put things to rights almost immediately by bringing out in the following year *Everybody's Business is Nobody's Business*. This, in contrast to the book-length diatribe of 1724, was a longish but lively *tract*, on sale for only 6*d*. Moreover the new author *persona* – Andrew Moreton – was unmistakably English and the archetype grumpy old man who saw servants themselves (especially maidservants) as the sole creators of the 'servant problem'. Employers were the aggrieved party. This tract has a defiantly misogynist, as well as haughtily top-down, stance. Such had been their scarcity value that maidservants' wages, Defoe lamented, had trebled or quadrupled 'of late', putting them beyond the reach of hard-pressed tradesmen whose wives now found that they no longer had time to help in the shop since they had been personally obliged to take on an unremitting routine of household drudgery. A well paid maidservant dressed too finely to want to engage in dirty and exhausting manual labour:

> Her neat's-leathern shoes are now transformed into laced ones with high heels, her yarn stockings are turned into fine worsted ones ... Plain country Joan is now turned into fine London-madam [who] can take tea, take snuff, and carry herself as high as the best.

Worse followed. No male was safe, Defoe declared, from the lewd machinations of these 'pert sluts'. Naive and impressionable young men, all too often, were lured into fornication or shotgun marriages. Bastards abounded.

> Thus many of them rove from place to place, from bawdy house to service and from service to bawdy house again . . . The greatest abuse of all is, these creatures have become their own lawgivers; nay, I think they are ours too though nobody would imagine that such a set of slatterns should bamboozle a whole nation . . .

And they were causing a mutiny among menservants, who, seeing the high wages and luxurious lifestyle of the maids, understandably were starting to agitate for even higher wage increases themselves. It was essential, Defoe urged, that wage reductions should be imposed through the agency of the law and that wage levels should be properly calculated and controlled according to length of service. Servants' dress should also be regulated, 'that we may know the mistress from the maid', and what better way of doing this than to require maids to wear a livery or at least wear 'a dress suitable to their station . . . [This] would teach her humility and put her in mind of her duty . . .'[17]

All this was music to middling and upper-class readers' ears. Whereas *The Great Law of Subordination*, Defoe's book of the previous year, had failed to find a market, *Everybody's Business* went through four printings with relative ease in the space of a few months in 1725. It unashamedly cashed in, too, on the backlash provoked by Bernard Mandeville's *The Fable of the Bees*, which had originated as a pamphlet, 'The Grumbling Hive', in 1705. Going through successive enlargements, it culminated in a book-length offering first published in 1714 and was substantially expanded again in later editions. Even the subtitle of Defoe's tract – *Private Benefits, Public Abuses* – locked horns with Mandeville's *Private Vices, Public Benefits*. Mandeville (1670–1733), a Dutch doctor of medicine who settled in London within a few years of graduating from the University of Leyden, saw fraud, luxury and pride as the major 'vices' of the day. Lawyers, politicians, stock jobbers and clergymen were as notable fraudsters as any professional criminals, Mandeville maintained, while luxury and pride had been embraced (usefully in his view) by the whole nation. Full employment and prosperity were the resultant outcome, whereas frugality, often praised as a virtue by others, had no economic benefit whatever. Poverty and ignorance among the lower orders, however, Mandeville insisted, were the necessary foundation of national prosperity, and for this reason – to the horror of leading churchmen like Isaac Watts and John Wesley and conventional moralists like Defoe – he lambasted charity schools and their promoters for their misguided attempts to eradicate what they wrongly diagnosed as social evils and for providing avenues of social mobility. Attempts to eradicate poverty were foolish, in Mandeville's view. Encouraging a stoical and socially valuable acceptance of it among those at the bottom of society made much more sense.

> In a free nation . . . the surest wealth consists in a multitude of laborious poor . . . To make the society happy and people easy under the meanest circumstances it is requisite that great numbers of them should be ignorant as well as poor . . . The knowledge of the working poor should be confined within the verge of their occupations . . . Every hour those of poor people spend at their book is so much time lost to the society . . .'[18]

All this directly related to servants, of course, the principal products of charity schools. The 'servant problem', in Mandeville's view, was to a large extent the direct consequence of their over-education which made them discontented with their lot in life, insolent, avaricious and ambitious. 'People of the meanest rank know too much to be serviceable to us.'[19] Education, in Mandeville's view, easily undermined that bond between men and their masters. 'A servant can have no unfeigned respect for his master,' Mandeville admitted in a cynical aside, 'as soon as he has sense enough to find out that he serves a fool.' Servants' wages in a sellers' market had become punishingly high for employers, and vails – now audaciously claimed as a right – were an added infliction. 'A housekeeper who cannot afford to make many entertainments and does not often invite people to his table can have no creditable man servant'; if there were no household guests then the prospect of supplementary income from vails ceased to exist. For footmen in particular Mandeville had undisguised contempt, and he was alarmed to see those in London forming an 'association' or proto-trade union to 'protect' themselves and keep both wages and vails high.'[20] '. . . 'Tis too much money, excessive wages and unreasonable vails that spoil servants in England.' Mandeville went on, 'The greatest part of [footmen] are rogues and not to be trusted; and if they are honest half of them are sots . . . Many of them are guilty of all these vices, whoring, drinking and quarrelling.' No maidservant was safe from their lust. Compulsory attendance at church, where duties and the need for subservience could be regularly proclaimed, and the abolition of vails were Mandeville's prescriptions for improvement. Workers of all kinds, servants included, had to be made to work uncomplainingly for the wages offered to them; that was their lot in life. Ignorance was bliss.

> Abundance of hard and dirty labour is to be done and coarse living is to be complied with. Where shall we find a better nursery for these necessities than the children of the poor? None certainly are nearer to it or fitter for it. Besides that the things which I have called hardships neither seem nor are such to those who have been brought up to 'em and know no better. There is not a more contented people among us than those who work the hardest and are the least acquainted with the pomp and delicacies of the world.[21]

The 'servant problem' was no less a preoccupation with Defoe's and Mandeville's contemporary Jonathan Swift (1667–1745), though he wrote on the subject rather later than the other two and in a very different way. Swift had limited, though direct, inside experience of household service, since his first employment around 1690 had been as an amanuensis to the recently retired Sir William Temple. His own household in Dublin, when he was a well established, high-ranking churchman, was run according to strict routines. Laws drawn up in December 1733 listed the duties of different servants and the fines to be imposed for acts of neg-ligence, drunkenness and absence without leave. Swift also knew from personal experience that, though rare, good servants were sometimes to be found; his own faithful manservant was in due course gratefully cele-brated in a memorial tablet in Dublin cathedral.[22] Nonetheless Swift's views on large numbers of the servant class in general were every bit as pessimistic as those of Defoe and Mandeville. His highly distinctive approach to the problem of servant failings and vices, however, was not simply to criticise or denounce them but to pillory them in biting satire. It was a strategy which obviously relied on the fact that what was being treated with black humour was at bottom a depressing reality all too famil-iar to his readers. Swift's *Directions to Servants*, written in the late 1730s and published in 1745, deservedly ranks as a minor classic, a satire in which Swift in the form of apparently solemn advice exposed 'the villainies and frauds of servants to their masters and mistresses . . . The reader may draw from what is here exhibited means to detect the many vices and faults which people in that kind of low life are subject to.'[23]

Swift's satire consists of a general section in which characteristic fail-ings of all servants are rehearsed before he moves on to look at those specific to each different kind of household officer, from butler down to housemaid. The general section covers all manner of issues relating to conduct and decorum within the household, to the receiving of visitors, and to interactions with other servants and with tradesmen in the out-side community. Tardiness in obeying a master or mistress's summons, it is stressed, ought to be standard practice. 'Never come until you have been called three or four times, for none but dogs will come at the first whistle. And when the master calls "Who's there?" no servant is bound to answer for "Who's there" is nobody's name.' It was best to leave inter-nal doors constantly open to avoid the unnecessary effort of opening and closing. But if their closing was perversely insisted on by an inconsiderate master, 'then give the door such a clap as you go out and make every-thing rattle in it to put your master and mistress in mind that you observe their directions'. Remembering the names of callers to the house was a practice best avoided, 'for indeed you have too many other things to remember . . . And you will certainly mistake them and you can neither read nor write.' Other helpful tips followed about introducing servants' own guests to the household without the employers' knowledge and about general cleanliness. 'Wipe your shoes for want of a clout with the bottom of a curtain or damask napkin. Strip your livery lace for garters. If the butler wants a jordan in case of need he may use the great silver cup.' Accidents, breakages and acts of negligence, of course, should never be confessed. 'When you have done a fault be always pert and insolent and behave yourself as if you were the injured person. This will immediately put your master or lady off their mettle.' Similar discretion was no less necessary where the faults of fellow servants were concerned, except in the case of a servant who basked in the special favour of the master or mistress and who, therefore, surely deserved to be undermined. Enjoying the best possible diet in the household should be the *sine qua non* of service. 'If your master can afford it don't stint what you spend on provision at his expense.'[24]

Going on errands, naturally, should be taken as an opportunity for leisure; 'spend as much time as you want and always have a rich assortment of excuses ready'. When sent out to buy household provisions hard bargaining with shopkeepers should be avoided at all costs. 'You are to consider, if your master hath paid too much he can better afford the loss than a poor tradesman.' The master's guests should always be intimidated to pay the highest vails on departure and if they don't oblige then take revenge on them when they next enter, or attempt to enter, the house. And when you have a mind to leave your master's service

> your best way is to grow rude and saucy of a sudden and beyond your usual behaviour till he finds it necessary to turn you off, and when you are gone, to revenge yourself. Give him and his lady such a character to all your brother servants who are out of place that none will venture to offer them service.[25]

Gossiping, always pleasurable, also conferred power.

Eighteen separate sets of detailed advice followed for particular servants in the household hierarchy to ensure that the overall ethos and *modus vivendi* of the domestic establishment was properly understood by the entire staff. The butler, for instance, was given prudent advice about not washing glasses so as to save time and about part-filling wine bottles with water to conceal what he himself had taken the liberty of consuming.

> Clean your plate, wipe your knives [he went on] and rub the foul table with the napkins and tablecloth used that day, for it is but one washing ... In reward of which good husbandry my judgement is that you make use of the finest damask napkins to be night-caps for yourself.

Storing fine china dinner and tea services, naturally, ought to be a special priority. 'Always lock up a cat in the closet where you keep your china plates for fear the mice may steal in and break them.' Similarly 'do all in the dark (as clean glasses, etc.) to save your master's candles'. When bottling wine for the master's use a good practice was to use corks flavoured with tobacco 'which will give to the wine the true taste of the weed, so delightful to all good judges in drinking'. Making tea ought also to be treated with no less seriousness and required those special touches which made the English tea ceremony a hallmark of civilised society:

> When you are to get water on for tea after dinner . . . to save firing and to make more haste pour it into the tea kettle from the pot where cabbage or fish have been boiling, which will make it much wholesomer by curing the acid corroding quality of the tea.[26]

The cook, similarly, scarcely needed reminders about the good practice expected of that particular household office. For example, it was simply common sense 'when you have plenty of fowl in the larder [to] leave the door open in pity to the poor cat, if she be a good mouser'. Soot falling into the soup pan should, naturally, be stirred in thoroughly to 'give the soup a high French taste'. Another obvious culinary tip 'to save time and trouble [was to] cut your apples and onions with the same knife, for well-bred gentry love the taste of an onion in everything they eat'.[27]

Advice running to nine pages was given to footmen, stalwarts of any well run household. Anything which made their dreary, monotonous, labour-intensive life more bearable and exciting ought to be eagerly grasped:

> When dinner is done carry down a great heap of plates to the kitchen and when you come to the head of the stairs trundle them all before you. There is not a more agreeable sight or sound, especially if they be silver, besides the trouble they save you and there they will lie ready near the scullery door for the scullion to wash them.

Every possible economy, of course, should be made to keep heating bills down. 'In winter time light the dining room fire but two minutes before dinner is served up that your master may see how saving you are of his coals.' Dress code was no less important:

> Never wear socks when you wait at meals on the account of your own health as well as of them who sit at table, because most ladies like the smell of young men's toes as it is a sovereign remedy against the vapours.

And what better way to end the advice to footmen than some helpful tips on facing the inevitable grand finale of death by hanging! The good news was that 'the surgeon shall not touch a limb of you and your fame shall continue until a successor of equal renown succeeds in your place'.[28]

The catalogue of advice continued with the recommendation that coachmen should always feel free to be drunk on duty 'and then show your skill by driving to an inch by a precipice'. Grooms, since they were never in charge of driving a coach, could enjoy the licence of being perpetually drunk:

> In long journeys ask your master leave to give ale to the horses. Carry two quarts full to the stable, pour half a pint into a bowl, and if they do not drink it, you and the ostler must do the best you can. Perhaps they may be in a better humour at the next inn, for I would have you never fail to make the experiment.[29]

Chambermaids were advised to have a good stock of excuses ready when anything got broken; breaking a mirror, for instance, could easily be blamed on a flash of lightning coming through the window. Fastidiousness was needed with the preparation of bread and butter. 'Let the mark of your thumb be seen only upon one end of every slice to show your cleanliness.' Similar niceties should be observed when clearing chamber pots from bedrooms:

> Do not carry down the necessary vessels for the fellows to see but empty them out of the window for your lady's credit. It is highly improper for men servants to know that fine ladies have occasion for such utensils. And do not scour the chamber pot because the smell is wholesome.[30]

The same refrain was continued when Swift's advice catalogue reached housemaids:

> Never empty the chamber pots until they are quite full. If that happens in the night empty them in the street, if in the morning in the garden . . . Never wash them in any other liquor except their own. What cleanly girl would be dabbing in other folks' urine? . . . Leave your lady's chamber pot in the bed chamber window all day to air.

No less attention to detail was needed when it came to wiping walls and scrubbing floors in any of the rooms in the house. 'Throw the foul water out of the street door but be sure not to look before you for fear those on whom the water lights might think you uncivil and that you did it on purpose . . .' This simple and effective method, of course, had the additional benefit of humorous consequences. 'The latter practice will be very diverting to you and the family on a frosty night to see a hundred people falling on their noses or backsides before your door when the water is frozen.' Housework, clearly, by such means could easily become a source of much fun! Swift's deepest sympathies were extended to waiting maids when they found inconsiderately locked cabinets containing much needed supplies of tea and sugar. And he gave detailed advice on striking the best bargain when their sexual favours were sought by the master. At all costs, however, the eldest son of the house should be avoided, since 'you will get nothing from him but a big belly or a clap and probably both together'. As for their role as facilitator of their mistress's amours, Swift conceded that no advice at all was needed, since 'your whole sisterhood is already so expert and deeply learned . . .'[31] And what better way to round off this satirical handbook on servants and servant life – obviously the outcome of careful observation and wearied experience – than with a sample character reference for a discarded member of the household staff?

> Whereas the bearer served me the space of one year during which time he was an idler and a drunkard. I then discharged him as such. But how far his having been five years at sea may have mended his manners I leave to the penetration of those who may hereafter choose to employ him.[32]

In Swift's hands satire was an effective instrument to attack the 'servant problem'. But in choosing this sharply pointed weapon the Dean of Dublin found few, if any, followers except among dramatists. Direct, heavy-handed frontal assaults in the manner of Defoe continued unabated. Henry Fielding in his *Enquiry into the late Increase of Robbers* (1751) denounced 'the rude behaviour and insolence of servants of all kinds' and lamented the profusion of forged character references which helped make this possible by quickly allowing dismissed servants to gain new employment.[33] 'The insolence of household servants' also found a central place among the public nuisances denounced in a lengthy tract of that name which appeared in 1754. Though its author chose to remain anonymous it is clear that he was a Londoner and wrote chiefly of conditions prevailing in the metropolis as, echoing Defoe, Mandeville and Swift, he catalogued the vices and deficiencies of servants of his day:

> Neglect of duty, absenting themselves from service without leave, insolence in behaviour, wilful wasting and destroying of goods, running in debt in the master's name, leaving their service abruptly or with short warning and before the master or mistress is provided with another, defaming and slandering the families they serve, and refusing to serve but under extravagant wages and conditions.

The law, this despairing author continued, was a blunt instrument so far as servants were concerned. Too often they had the upper hand. They chose their master, not vice versa, and increasingly they regarded service as a way of life which existed chiefly for *their* convenience and benefit.[34]

It was all so outrageously unjustified. Servant life, after all, said this author, was hardly onerous. 'They have nothing but a very easy duty to perform and all that is required of them beyond that is but to behave with humility and obedience to their superiors as becomes their station.' Instead even new recruits to service from the countryside were quickly corrupted by the degeneracy of London, were lured into drunkenness, gambling, vice, keeping bad company, and ended up as fodder for Tyburn. So, for example, claimed Thomas Broughton in his deeply pessimistic *A Serious Advice and Warning to Servants* (4th edn., 1763). (See p. 213.) Charles Jones, footman author, agreed in 1797. 'How many young fellows have I known who lived honestly and happily in their native place,' he wrote in his autobiographical sketch, 'come up to London in the hope of higher wages and there forfeit their integrity, their peace of mind, their health, their character and souls.' Nor was any improvement in prospect. Some thought that the supply of good servants was simply drying up, a fact which they connected with the decline of small farms.

> Small farmers were the people that used to stock the country with the best of servants [opined one social commentator of the time]; 'these were the nurseries for breeding up industrious and virtuous young men and women. Whereas the generality of servants nowadays are such as have had but little opportunity of learning how to do business so as to befit to make good servants ...

Household servants of the present time, Sarah Trimmer agreed a little later, in 1801, were in 'a very corrupt state'. Gripped by an apparently uncontrollable 'spirit of independence' among household servants the 'problem' they presented was now without any doubt 'a national concern'.[35]

And so, in the eyes of employers and social commentators, it continued. Augustus Mayhew published his satire *The Greatest Plague of Life, or, The Adventures of a Lady in Search of a Servant* in 1847 as a tract for the times:

> What with their breakages and their impudence and their quarrelling among themselves ... and their followers and their dirt and filth, and their turning up their noses at the best of food and their wilful waste and goings on, and their neglect and ill treatment of the dear children, and their pride,

their airs, and ill tempers . . . I'm sure it was enough to turn the head of ten Christians.[36]

Shrewd social commentator Harriet Martineau felt obliged to discuss the continuing 'servant problem' in a leading periodical in 1862, underlining as a cause of it the lack of proper training.[37] America, evidently, was no better in this respect, if the subtitle of C. Chamberlain's *The Servant Girl of the Period, or, The Greatest Plague of Life* (New York, 1873) can be believed. So common had the 'servant problem' become in England that a music hall song with this title burst on the scene in 1912 with music by Henry E. Pether and words by Percy Edgar. A printed version, in solo and duet versions, quickly became available and demonstrated the distance travelled over two centuries of complaining about this on-going issue. What had started with Defoe and his contemporaries as a call for drastic, emergency action in the national interest was now, at the beginning of the twentieth century, a widespread, and apparently permanent, sick joke which was guaranteed to produce laughter.

NOTES

1 *Court of Good Counsell*, chapter 24, unpaginated.
2 Gosse, *Restoration Plays from Dryden to Farquar*, pp. 176, 221–2.
3 HRO, 44 M69 E8/4/22, Small Account Book relating to Britford compiled by Thomas Jervoise.
4 Anne Kugler, *Errant Plagiary. The Life and Writing of Lady Sarah Cowper, 1644–1720* (Stanford, CA, 2002), pp. 47–8, 90, 149, 151.
5 *Ibid.*, p. 190.
6 R. A. Anselment (ed.), *Remembrances of Elizabeth Freke, 1671–1714*, Camden Soc., 5th ser., 18 (2001), pp. 65, 194, 274, 159, 272, 57; Holmes, 'Domestic Service in Yorkshire', p. 66.
7 Saville, *Secret Comment*, pp. 95, 293, 214, 291, 328. Grosley's *A Tour to London* (3 vols., London, 1772), I, p. 81, spoke very disparagingly of a 'fat Welsh girl who has just come out of the country, scarce understood a word of English, was capable of nothing but washing, scouring and sweeping the rooms and had no inclination to learn anything more'.
8 Saville, *Secret Comment*, pp. 88, 89, 54–5.
9 *Ibid.*, pp. 89, 97, 154.
10 *Ibid.*, pp. 130, 153.
11 *Ibid.*, pp. 187–8, 244, 250, 281, 295, 308, 313.
12 *Family Instructor* (15th edn., 1761), I, pp. 168, 178.
13 *Ibid.*, II, p. 252. See also II, p. 351, for another tribute to the same maidservant.

14 *Religious Courtship* (10th edn., 1796), p. iv, 288, p. v, 250–1.
15 *Great Law of Subordination Considered*, pp. 13, 17.
16 *Ibid.*, pp. 293–4, 295–6, 302.
17 *Everybody's Business* (4th edn., 1725), pp. 7, 9, 13, 16, 17, 18.
18 *Fable of the Bees* (1729, repr. 1981), I, p. 294.
19 *Ibid.*, p. 307. Others, of course, sprang to the defence of the charity schools, a favourite social investment of the time, claiming that by inculcating obedience and humility, as well as imparting some basic knowledge, they made the children of the poor more, not less, serviceable to society. (See, for example, W. Hendley, *A Defence of the Charity Schools* (London, 1725).
20 *Ibid.*, pp. 296, 308. 'I'll stand your friend as much as one servant can to another,' declared a servant character in Richard Steele's play *The Lying Lover* (1705), 'against all masters and mistresses whatever'. (Quoted in Hecht, *Domestic Service Class*, p. 85.)
21 Mandeville, *Bees*, pp. 309, 307, 315.
22 Turner, *What the Butler Saw*, p. 23.
23 Swift, *Directions to Servants* (1745), publisher's preface.
24 *Ibid.*, pp. 10, 9, 12, 14, 7.
25 *Ibid.*, pp. 8, 9, 12–13. See pp. 155–60, 228–9 for more on servant gossiping.
26 *Ibid.*, pp. 17–19, 24, 27, 22, 23.
27 *Ibid.*, pp. 30, 32.
28 *Ibid.*, pp. 36, 42, 41, 45. An earlier publication – *The Wit's Cabinet* (8th edn., London, 1698, p. 93) – had also held forth on the good manners expected of servants when waiting at table and outlawed all spitting, coughing, sneezing, chiding and brawling.
29 *Ibid.*, pp. 45, 49.
30 *Ibid.*, pp. 56, 53.
31 *Ibid.*, pp. 61, 62, 56–58, 60.
32 *Ibid.*, appendix.
33 Fielding, quoted in Elizabeth W. Gilboy, *Wages in Eighteenth-Century England* (Cambridge, MA, 1934), p. 34.
34 *Public Nusance considered under the Several Heads* (London, 1754), pp. 39, 46. The title page describes the author as a 'Gentleman of the Middle Temple'. The miscellany of other nuisances examined here included bad pavements, butchers and the enforced billeting of foot guard. In the course of the eighteenth century, however, increasing attention was paid to the law relating to masters and servants. See pp. 194–7.
35 *Ibid.*, p. 39; *History of Charles Jones*, p. 9; *An Address to the Parliament on behalf of the Starving Multitude* (London, 1766), p. 39, quoted in Hecht, *Domestic Servant Class*, p. 9; Sarah Trimmer, *The Oeconomy of Charity* (London, 1801), I, pp. 3–4.
36 Mayhew, *The Greatest Plague of Life*, p. 4.
37 Martineau, 'Modern domestic service,' *Edinburgh Review*, 115 (1862), 409–39.

9

℘

SERVANTS AND THE LAW

In process of time that precious thing called liberty of the people gained
so much ground in our laws as now a master cannot sufficiently chastise
his servant or put any restraints on him within limits of his house without
incurring a complaint to the magistrate for breach of the peace or false
imprisonment which giveth much presumption to servants . . .
(*Observations and Advices Oeconomical*, London, 1669, pp. 45–6)

English law in its different branches variously encircled, impinged on,
threatened, and potentially protected household servants in a vast
number of ways. At one extreme it prescribed draconian penalties for
servants violating either their master's property or person, as some of
the individual maids or menservants discussed later in this chapter
discovered to their personal cost. Arson and murder committed by a
servant against a master were defined under the law as petty treason.[1]
The law upheld the contractual relations between masters and servants
– a complex area in itself which by the end of the eighteenth century had
been helpfully summarised in legal manuals produced by Blackstone
and others.[2]

Blackstone went over the generally standard, time-honoured practice of annual contracts for servants as well the statutory provision for
conscripting into service those children and single men and women
between the ages of twelve and sixty and forty respectively who had no
visible alternative means of support. Wage entitlement was rehearsed,
making it clear, however, that magistrates' brief to set wage rates applied
only to servants in husbandry and not to household servants. Masters'
right to impose due punishment on servants was covered as well as their
right under the law to take action against any third party assaulting or
injuring their servants and to claim damages for any loss of service which
ensued. In this as in other respects, service from domestics counted as

part of their masters' property. Blackstone emphasised, however, that masters were answerable for servants' acts done under their command and that they could not shelter from blame by attributing responsibility to the agent. J. B. Bird's manual, published later in the century, continued in the same vein.[3] Once made, Blackstone and Bird emphasised, a contract of employment between master and man could not be broken by either party with impunity; a defaulting master was liable to a fine of 40s, a defaulting servant to a year's imprisonment. A master could legitimately assault a third party in defence of his servant, as could a servant in defence of his master. A servant assaulting his master, however, was liable to a year's imprisonment. *Reasonable* – imprecisely defined – punishment of a servant by a master was allowed under the law, even if it unintentionally led to a servant's death. A charge of manslaughter against a master would be brought only if a fatal punishment of one of his servants was inflicted 'passionately and without deliberation', and a murder charge would stick only if it could be proved beyond all reasonable doubt that over-severe punishment was 'done with deliberation or forethought' and resulted in death.

By the time Bird was writing his legal manual at the end of the eighteenth century the law also stretched out to masters and servants in a different way in the form of enforced taxation. Taxing foreign servants – unpopular, unwanted, troublemaking intruders to some – had been a subject aired by their critics in the 1750s and 1760s. But even such advocates were no doubt taken aback when a general tax on all menservants, initially to help pay for the war against the American colonies, was introduced in 1777. In 1785 a sliding scale was added to take account of household size, and the imposition of the tax was extended to cover maidservants as well as men and servants in inns and coffee houses. Henceforth households with one or two menservants paid £1 5s a year for each, while for those with three or four the rate went up to £1 10s. Large households with more than eleven menservants were taxed at the heavy rate of £3 each. Those menservants with powdered hair such as footmen in elite households, judged to be chiefly ornamental in their function, were liable to another tax supplement. Bachelor masters – presumably judged to have less genuine need of servants – paid a supplement in all cases of £1 5s a year per manservant. Female servants were taxed at a much lower rate. A maid-of-all-work cost only 2s 6d in tax. Where there were two maidservants the rate went up to 5s and for households with three or more maidservants the higher rate of 10s each was charged. Serving officers in the army and navy were given an entitlement of one tax-free servant. A serving-maid 'allowance' was given for families with young children. The universities, public schools and the London hospitals were exempt. Servant taxes were collected, not by separate officers, but (for convenience) by those already responsible for bringing in the window tax. London, not surprisingly, bore the brunt of the servant taxes. though both in the capital and elsewhere evasion was probably common. In rural households there was much wrangling before magistrates and in the courts about the status of farm servants conscripted for occasional household duties. J. J. Hecht long ago warned historians that servant tax returns were statistically unreliable; under-recording of servants was endemic. The tax on female servants, much wider and socially burdensome in its incidence, was withdrawn in 1792 and contributed to the increasing feminisation of household service which had already begun in the previous century. The levy on menservants, however, remained in force until 1937 – not quite so long-lasting as income tax, that other 'temporary' wartime fiscal expedient.[4]

Quarter sessions records are replete with cases concerning servants' terms of employment. Those for the North Riding of Yorkshire in the early seventeenth century abound with instances of servants being brought to book for leaving their job before the expiry of the due term, masters for withholding wages or dismissing servants before the agreed end date of their contract or taking on without testimonials servants who were already contracted to someone else. So, later, do the cases recorded in the post-Restoration notebook of the Norfolk justice Robert Doughty. A Cheshire husbandman from Darnhall successfully petitioned the JPs in July 1611 for the return of his maidservant, who had quit before the end of her term. 'Your petitioner hath his harvest to get and is destitute of a servant, neither at this time can be furnished with any but is like to sustain great loss unless your worships' aid be extended to his relief.' Considerably later a different kind of contractual case was heard at the borough sessions in Portsmouth in 1679. The incident involved a mistress who had given her maid temporary leave of absence to care for a sick relative but then, evidently relieved to be rid of her, refused to take her back.[5]

Pauper servants, young or old, were governed by the terms of the Poor Law and the stipulations relating to apprenticeship and settlement which it included. Pauper children could be directed into service and poor relief withheld from parents resisting the provision. In 1732 in St Budeaux, Devon, a pauper girl was apprenticed 'in housewifery' to a husbandman until she reached the age of twenty-one or until she married, the employer being enjoined that 'she be not in any way a charge to the said parish or parishioners'. Jane Yarmouth, about six years old, was bound in 1769 to Elizabeth Peck, of Adbury, in Berkshire, who 'would take her apprentice till she is twenty-one years of age and would teach her to sew and instruct her to make a good servant'. A Hertfordshire yeoman who challenged the pauper apprenticeship system was hauled before the Privy Council and imprisoned. In 1701 Widow Dickson, of Aldenham, Hertfordshire, similarly resisting, was duly warned that if she 'doth not forthwith put her daughter to service [she would] be stricken out of the monthly collection and be wholly excluded from any further relief'. By the end of the eighteenth century reformers like Mrs Cappe of the Grey Court School in York had risen in opposition to pauper apprenticeship in housewifery for girls, branding it as often little more than a sentence to slavery. But it was not until 1844 that the system of pauper apprenticeship, much exploited, and ultimately discredited, during the early Factory Age, was finally laid to rest.[6]

For others for whom after childbirth or in old age poverty became an issue, working for a year or more in the same place gave them a 'settlement' and entitlement to poor relief in the parish in question. All too aware of this, some parishes exerted pressure on employers to contract servants for less – sometimes only just less – than one-year terms. Richard Burn in his *History of the Poor Laws* (London, 1764) wryly observed that it was becoming more common to hire servants 'half-yearly, or by the month, or by the week or by the day, rather than by any way that shall give them a settlement; or if they do hire them for a year to endeavour to pick a quarrel with them before the year's end and so to get rid of them'. And so it continued into the early nineteenth century. 'No man will hire either a labourer or a servant for a year from another parish.' So wrote a Norfolk clergyman in 1817. The overlap, in fact, between Poor Law and labour law was substantial, as Carolyn Steedman has demonstrated in her examination of settlement cases involving women, some of them servants, in which Lord Chief Justice Mansfield intervened between the 1760s and 1780s. Another ramification of the Poor Law for household service is revealed in countless letters from parents of would-be or actual young servants of both sexes, or directly from the young people themselves, asking for grants of money to buy more respectable clothing or for financial assistance during periods of illness.[7]

Servants made frequent appearances before JPs and in the courts – quarter sessions, assizes, the courts of higher jurisdiction in London (especially Equity), and diocesan church courts for moral offences. They entered into court proceedings in very many cases as witnesses; in the intimate worlds of household and community life few things escaped their notice or prying gaze. Elite families especially in this period, it has been observed, lived in 'goldfish bowls', constantly on view to their servants. Laura Gowing's work on church court records relating to early modern London revealed that servants and apprentices made up 16 per cent of the witnesses who were summoned. A servant to Sir John Acton in Worcestershire in 1619 testified in the quarter sessions that a local tailor had stolen goods from his master. A Cheshire maidservant launched a joint prosecution alongside her master in 1645 in a case of theft, items of missing clothing, a remnant of new cloth, and a pair of scissors 'being her goods'. Another maidservant from the same county in 1668 was threatened and injured when she intervened to prevent fellow servants from making off with some of her master's goods. No less intrepid was the fictional 'valiant cookmaid' depicted in a 1680 ballad (*A Leicestershire Frolick*) who, armed only with a black pudding, terrorised her master's two journeymen into handing back wages received from their master.[8] A servant from Egham, Surrey, deponed before a JP in 1769 that two men (both named by him) had stolen bundles of wood from his master.[9]

Servants were commonly called upon to help settle cases involving neighbourly or matrimonial disputes. Though scarcely on high moral ground herself, the Duchess of Norfolk in her divorce case of 1700 deplored the fact that the evidence against her was frequently being supplied by bribed ex-servants.

> Masters are already too much in the power of their servants, and if they charge their masters with adultery, felony, or even treason, it is not easily in the power of the master to defend himself against downright swearing. Servants have those opportunities of the knowledge of times and places and company which cannot easily be denied or avoided and which others have not, whereupon they may frame and build false evidence. Many times they are of ill principles and desperate fortunes and of tempers very revengeful so that whoever turns away a servant he is in his power for his estate, honour and even life itself.

In the Calvert divorce case of 1709 nineteen servants were brought in to testify in court. Even more – twenty-three in total, many of them long-serving – gave evidence in the notorious Cadogan divorce case in 1794 painstakingly unravelled by Lawrence Stone.[10]

Household servants appeared frequently as defendants accused of a variety of petty and more serious offences, ranging from quitting their employment, theft of money and goods, drunkenness, sexual licence, assault, arson, infanticide and murder. In church court proceedings they sometimes figured in defamation cases and were occasionally accused of acting as bawds for their mistresses. A Westminster maidservant, Ann Baynham, charged in 1610 with railing against her mistress as a 'whore', was required to do public penance in front of the original witnesses and in the same place where the offence occurred. She was warned that a repeat performance of her ill judged outburst would incur a whipping. Some cases involved servants straying from their allocated space in church during service time. Two servants were charged in Norwich in the 1560s, one for shooting arrows in the cathedral and the other for defaming the bishop as a whoremaster. Cases concerning servant promiscuity abound in the church court records of Banbury in the 1620s and 1630s. Sixty-two servants were hanged in London between 1703 and 1772, twenty-one of them for robbing their masters. A third of the prisoners tried at the Old Bailey in 1789 were servants accused of stealing from their employers. There is even one case (1775) on record of a London servant maid being enlisted by her master into helping him counterfeit coin. The sentence of burning alive, as allowed under the law, was imposed on the unfortunate wretch but was subsequently commuted to transportation.[11]

Exceptionally servants were themselves cited in adultery and divorce cases. A scandalous case from Harefield, Middlesex, in 1619–20 involved a manservant and the mistress of the house and the child which allegedly resulted from their adulterous relationship. In the celebrated early eighteenth-century Dormer case Jones, a footman in the household, was taken to court for having a sexual liaison with his master's wife. With incredible bravado, however, he escaped from the courtroom and took refuge in the Mint. Probably the most notorious eighteenth-century legal case of this kind was the long-running matrimonial dispute of Middleton *v.* Middleton in the 1790s in which the mistress of the house became infatuated with a young groom and conducted a clandestine sexual relationship with him which, when discovered by the husband, led to divorce proceedings against the wife and a lawsuit against the young man.[12]

Servants were often referred to or drawn in as third parties in cases begun by their employers. In a Winchester diocesan case of 1577 a Portsmouth woman, Alice Trenell, was alleged to have said to her neighbour Joan Gay, 'I do vehemently suspect that thou art a witch. If my maid do not well who presently fell lame after thou didst go out of my house I will make thee burn a stake.' More mundanely two centuries later a Chertsey master launched a suit in 1774 on behalf of his servant, William

Wood, who had been assaulted by two labourers. Others were charged for leading servants astray. At the quarter sessions held in Malton, Yorkshire, in January 1608 Agnes Wilkinson was charged for unlicensed brewing 'and also for suffering men's servants to sit drinking in her house all the night through'. Three years later, at Richmond, Matthew Wilkinson was accused of 'suffering his neighbours' servants to play at his house at unlawful games and at times unlawful'.[13]

But with increasing frequency emboldened servants (with large numbers of women among them, it should be noted) went to law on their own account as petitioners and plaintiffs seeking redress (usually from employers) for physical mistreatment, sexual abuse, unpaid wages and other contractual irregularities. Records of the Norfolk quarter sessions in the 1650s, for example, abound with cases of servants successfully suing for unpaid wages. In the 1530s Joan Turner, former servant to a London haberdasher, petitioned the Court of Equity – a popular destination for redress of plebeian grievances – for the return of a chest containing her clothes worth £10 which had been unlawfully detained by her erstwhile employer. Margaret Gardner, maidservant, lodged a paternity suit in 1620 against a fellow servant in the household of Sir Samuel Sandys of Ombersley, Worcestershire. A seventeenth-century Somerset maid sought protection from the local JPs against her master's neighbour, a would-be rapist. In 1642 a Devon vicar and his wife were bound over at the assizes for 'abusing and wronging Elizabeth Gale their servant', while in the same year at the assizes held at Launceton, Cornwall, a contractual dispute between an employer and his manservant was referred to the investigation of two JPs 'who are to hear both parties and order punishment of the servant or payment of wages due'. A Coventry manservant assaulted by a constable was awarded redress by the mayor of the city in January 1656. A Yorkshire yeoman was fined £10 in 1661 for beating and attempting to strangle Anna Trimingham, his maid. In 1665 the sad case of an employer, Charles Jackson, Esq., of Rothwell, came before the Yorkshire assizes. In a fit of anger provoked by a servant's drunken return from a day of unofficial absence, Jackson had killed the man by hitting him over the head with a shovel. 'Browne had been his servant long and he loved him very well because they frequently took tobacco together.' A Norfolk husbandman convicted of excessively beating his maidservant in 1662 was made by the JP hearing the case to pay 5s compensation, return her clothes and release her from her term of service. A Surrey servant maid, Millicent Corick, complained to the magistrates in 1703 about being routinely overworked and beaten, saying that she was 'as great slave as any in Turkey'. Elizabeth Bussell, a maidservant in St Clement Dane's London, successfully brought a suit against her button-seller master and his father-in-law in 1750 for 'their base and unkind treatment'. At a case at the Buckingham assizes ten years later a servant maid was awarded £10 damages after a successful suit against a master who had beaten her unmercifully. In 1774 Sarah Hopkins of Egham, Surrey, complained against her master John Harcourt, Esq., 'for his uncontrolled and violent behaviour'. Another maidservant from the same village sued before the same JP for unpaid wages the following year.[14]

That servants were prepared to exercise their 'rights' is made clear in an example concerning one of his neighbours mentioned by the Rev. William Cole of Bletchley, Buckinghamshire:

> Dr Pettigal calling on his maid and her not coming as soon as he expected, went out and beat her very severely and on applying to Mr Hammer [a magistrate] for a warrant – who civilly refused it to a neighbour – the maid is gone to London and is supposed with a design to put him in the Crown office.

The law, a hostile observer had sighed as early as 1669, was all too often toothless when applied to servants' transgressions. Punishment of a servant or even an attempt to impose discipline or restraint was likely to lead to a formal complaint or legal action. 'All Europe affordeth no country where they have more freedom.' By the 1750s another commentator (apparently a lawyer) on public nuisances in England could state categorically that 'there is no servant hardly but is quick and knowing enough to put the law in execution'. D'Archenholz, a foreign visitor in the 1790s, believed that in England 'the first man in the kingdom is cautious of striking his domestics; for they may not only defend themselves but also commence an action in a court of justice'. Even in the 1820s in hearings before Thomas Allen, JP, in Macclesfield, Cheshire, a servant bringing an action against his master stood more or less the same chance of success as in cases which originated the other way round.[15] The Marquess of Paleotti and Earl Ferrers were executed in 1718 and 1760 respectively, the first for killing his valet in a fit of anger and the second his steward.[16]

Defoe and other pessimists had argued earlier in the eighteenth century that one of the most obvious remedies for the 'servant problem' lay in a rigorous tightening of the legal code and its enforcement. Such was the obvious intention which lay behind Christopher Tancred's *Scheme for an Act of Parliament for the better regulating Servants and ascertaining their Wages* (London, 1724). The author's starting point was the conviction that 'the laws now in force relating to the subject here treated of are now obsolete and not well adapted to the conveniences of the present age'. It was for him a fundamental defect of the system that the provisions of the Elizabethan Statute of Artificers related only to servants in husbandry and not to household servants. A fundamental review of employment law and Poor Law entitlement, therefore, was long overdue. In particular Tancred considered it was rashly generous that settlement entitlement should be given after only one year of employment in the same place. Far better, in his view, to give settlement rights only after a lifetime of service or, in exceptional cases, on account of a servant's physical disability. The present practice, he considered, simply encouraged mobility and idleness and rewarded the mere fact of unemployment. The law as it stood was far too lax about those who could be compelled into service, about the length of service they should complete, about maximum wages and about disciplining servants' irregular practices.

What Tancred proposed was nothing less than the compilation of a servant domesday with accurate registers kept in each county of all servants and their periods of employment based on information assembled by petty constables and high constables. Employers and others failing to supply the requisite information would face a heavy fine and distraint of goods. Schedules listing maximum wage levels would be issued, based on length of service and occupational status, from which no exceptions would be allowed. A 'certificate of service', updated annually, would be kept for every single servant in the land. Master and servants deviating from agreed wage rates would be severely punished. A rigorously enforced system of compulsory testimonials for all servant hirings would be put in place. The envisaged Act of Parliament setting out Tancred's provisions was to be read out monthly in all places of Anglican worship. And in every locality on a set day each month two JPs would sit to hear master–servant complaints and reach their judgements. Blissfully setting aside all issues concerning the administrative burdens and Leviathan state his scheme necessitated, and insisting that what was being proposed was 'absolutely free from the least tincture of bondage' and completely compatible with the nation's liberty, Tancred was no doubt baffled when Parliament failed to adopt his convoluted plan for legal reform and national improvement. It was only much later, chiefly between 1830 and 1850, that such tightening of the law governing masters and servants took place. From then on servants of all kinds found it increasingly difficult to achieve remedies for their grievances and the penalties inflicted on them became harsher.[17]

Jane Holmes in her D.Phil. thesis on Yorkshire servants analyses carefully the offences for which domestics were indicted in quarter sessions and assizes. The largest category by far (40 per cent) in cases heard at quarter sessions was absconding before completing their agreed term. Fornication offences (19 per cent) came second, with theft cases (18 per cent) closely following in third place. At the higher legal level of the assizes theft cases (52 per cent) notably topped the league, with a small number of cases involving money loss in excess of £100; stealing petty amounts of money or items of clothing was considerably more common. Thefts of goods or clothing in elite households with their larger stocks of supplies and more numerous personnel were often more difficult to detect and servants' inside knowledge could itself be a defence mechanism. Clemency could be shown, however, even after conviction. A fifteen-year-old Cheshire servant maid, found guilty of stealing several items of clothing from her mistress in 1678, was spared branding or hanging and got off lightly with a whipping, the girl being 'young enough to be taught more honesty'. In 1723 Yorkshire employer John Scott was advised by a solicitous aunt not to prosecute John Pinkney, a menial, for the long-undetected theft of a waistcoat 'for the sake of the peace and to prevent expenses as Scott was only a poor servant'. Jonathan Stubbs, a master in Hackney, lodged a complaint in January 1738 against his manservant for embezzling money and running away. A few months later the same master charged another servant with the theft of milk and other goods. Additionally a small number of cases involved servants being enticed by others, including employers, into thieving. Violent assaults on employers by servants were relatively rare. Holmes's research, however, unearthed one case of the premeditated murder of a former mistress by a maid-servant and another of an obviously provoked-beyond-endurance man-servant in 1730 threatening his master with a pitchfork. In this case the threat did not become a deed, since the servant in question wisely decided that he 'scorned to be hanged for him and called him [the master] old knave'. It was much more common in these records, Holmes finds, for servants to be on the receiving end of intimidation and violence from their masters and mistresses; one out-of-control employer beat her maid to death for allegedly supping a quart of cream.[18]

Bastardy cases involving servant maids were common in early modern England, as they were in other parts of Europe, and demonstrated a sexual vulnerability which was widely recognised both by contemporaries and by later historians. Such servant maids were also often, as has been pointed out earlier, very young, most of them in the fifteen to twenty-four age group. Hostile male commentators, however, bemoaned the loose morals of maidservants:

> [London's] being overstocked with harlots is entirely owing to those numbers of women-servants incessantly pouring into it from all corners of the universe [droned an anonymous observer in 1749]. Many of them are . . . running from place to place, from bawdy house to service and from service to bawdy house again . . . so that, in effect, they make neither good whores, good wives, nor good servants.

Sixteenth-century Ludlow saw many maidservant bastardy cases. Seven out of twelve servant cases in the Portsmouth borough sessions papers between 1653 and 1688 involved bastardy. In New Aberdeen in the second half of the seventeenth century about twenty-five maidservant bastardy cases occurred each year.[19] Bastardy cases involving maidservants abounded in eighteenth and early nineteenth-century London. Seventy per cent of the children admitted to the Foundling Hospital between 1801 and 1810 had unmarried maidservants as their mothers.[20] Of the very large number of individual maidservant case histories found in the edited volume of *Chelsea Settlement and Bastardy Examinations, 1733–1766* the majority listed other servants, often in the same household, as the father. In early modern Essex and Lancashire it has been found that about 23 per cent and 14 per cent respectively of those responsible for maidservant pregnancies were employers. A Banbury master in 1629 was alleged to have made his maidservant pregnant and then 'hired another to father it'. So also in the eighteenth-century Chelsea evidence there was a not insignificant subtotal of cases where the man named as father was either the maid's employer or in a few cases one of his relatives (son or nephew) or a lodger. By rank and occupation these included a gentleman, an attorney's son, a wig maker, an innkeeper and a button seller.[21]

All these Chelsea cases involved the women in question losing their employment, applying for poor relief and giving birth in the inhospitable surroundings of a parish workhouse. Indeed, in the previous century much heavier penalties – whipping and/or confinement in a house of correction – were common. But the law could sometimes show a more humane face. Much earlier than the cases immediately referred to above, at the Richmond quarter sessions in October 1607, it was enjoined that:

> Leonard Simpson of Middleton Tyas [be] fined 40s for putting away of Dorothy Cornforth his servant out of his service without case showed and for that she is now with child and in open court chargeth the said

Simpson to be father thereof. She is therefore committed to the keeping of William Wilson of Middleton Tyas until she be delivered and the said Simpson to be bound.[22]

At parochial level the mid-eighteenth-century Sussex shopkeeper and parish overseer Thomas Turner spent much time patiently and humanely investigating paternity cases involving servants and, sometimes, masters, prompted admittedly by his concern to indemnify the parish from financial responsibility for maintenance. No amount of sustained effort, however, from master, magistrates, neighbours and the man's own family could prevail in 1802 to make George Thorp in Yorkshire marry Phoebe Beatson, the maidservant of the Rev. John Murgatroyd, whose bastard daughter he had fathered. Sometimes, as this case showed, the law proved too cumbersome or powerless to work effectively, especially in 'raw, industrialising frontier country' like the West Riding.[23]

The close correlation between unmarried servant maids and bastardy cases was notorious in early modern England. Less common, though still noticeable, was the tragic extension in some such cases to infanticide by unmarried servant mothers to conceal the births and to shield themselves from the likely consequence of dismissal from their employment or more severe penalties. By so doing, however, they exposed themselves to a worse fate. An Act of 1624 'to prevent the Destroying and Murthering of Bastard Children' (which remained in force until 1803) imposed the death penalty for the crime.[24] A case in early seventeenth-century Somerset involved an anxious, and probably guilty, master offering his maidservant 20s to destroy her unborn child. Jane Holmes found ten infanticide cases involving maidservants in the Yorkshire assize records she examined, one involving a master in 1659 who had got his maidservant pregnant and then attempted to force her 'to take physick for to destroy the said child'. A Norfolk servant maid was accused in 1665 of 'murdering her bastard child and burying it in Plumstead churchyard'. In the seventy cases of infanticide found by Laura Gowing in the northern assize circuit records of the 1642–80 period the vast majority of women accused were maidservants, giving birth in secret isolation in lofts, outhouses and privies – 'narratives of traumatic maternity' – and forced to carry on with their work routines, almost immediately, as best they could. A Yorkshire servant, Grace Ward, one of these unfortunate women, confessed under examination in 1678:

> she did not apprehend herself in labour till the child fell from her as she was standing by her bedside and . . . she said she knew not whether it had

life in it or not but that so soon as she was delivered she laid it upon some straw and threw a coverlet over it and did not look after it till the morning her master called her down to her work and then the child was dead.

The overwhelming majority (85 per cent) of the sixty-five infanticide cases dealt with on the northern assize circuit between 1720 and 1799 involved maidservants. It was the same in Scotland in the same period. Simon Schama found exactly the same high correlation between infanticide cases and servant maids in early modern Amsterdam. Mary Ellenor, a gentleman's servant in London 'debauched by an apprentice coachmaker' and found guilty of infanticide was hanged in 1708. Sarah Allen, a maidservant in a Westminster public house, dismissed for her pregnancy, forced to apply for poor relief, suffocated her baby in the workhouse, was charged, found guilty and executed in 1738. All too rarely were the desperate circumstances which lay behind infanticide taken into account. The crime, so commonly associated with maidservants, was simply viewed as a brutal and extreme exposure of their natural depravity and was taken as an affront to the values and security of the wider community. Murdering mothers deserved the severe penalty which the law provided.[25]

An infanticide case like no other occurred in 1651 and centred on an Oxfordshire maidservant. Such were its extraordinary details that it very quickly became broadcast and celebrated. Two tracts rehearsing the story – *Newes from the Dead* (Oxford, 1651) and *A Wonder of Wonders* (Oxford, 1651) – appeared in rapid succession. Who wrote them is not at all clear; the tone at times is rather different from that of other 'last dying speeches' clergyman-penned publications. Visitors flocked to see for themselves the young woman in question, Anne Greene. It was indeed a story which, in its denouement, appeared to verge on the miraculous. Locally born Greene, about twenty-two years old, had worked as a servant maid for Sir Thomas Read at Duns Tew, Oxfordshire, where she was seduced by the young grandson, only sixteen or seventeen years old, of her master. She became pregnant (though she later claimed not to know of this), and months later was taken ill, went into labour and, in a privy, had a miscarriage. She concealed the dead baby (a boy) in a corner, covered it with dust and rubbish, where it was later discovered. The circumstances were brought to the notice of her employer, who passed Greene on to a local JP – presumably well known to the grandfather of the dead baby's natural father – who charged her with the crime of infanticide and referred her case to the next assizes held in Oxford. There Greene was expeditiously tried, convicted and sentenced to death. No clemency could be expected and the sentence – death by hanging – was duly imposed. Greene made a short, conventional speech before going up the ladder to the scaffold, asking her young cousin, who was present, to help her die quickly, which he did by pulling on her feet 'with all the weight and force of his body on them' as she swung by the neck on the rope. A soldier on guard at the execution beat her breast four or five times with his musket to further hasten the end and she was then left suspended for half an hour until there could be no reasonable doubt that she was dead. Finally she was cut down and her body placed in a coffin which was then carted off to the physicians (this being Oxford) to await dissection. As the medical men assembled and the coffin was opened, to the amazement of those present Anne Greene displayed signs of life. No less a figure than William Petty, Fellow of Brasenose College and Professor of Anatomy in the University, was present 'and perceiving life declared that there was a great hand of God in the business'. Under his direction hot cordials and oils were administered. Greene was bled, heated plasters were applied to her body, and her hands and feet were rubbed vigorously. A warm bed was prepared for her and a woman found who was brave enough to lie with her. After fourteen hours she regained consciousness and uttered her first words: 'Behold God's providence . . . Behold his miraculous and loving kindness.' Some, it seems, pressed for her to be taken back to the place of execution a second time to be properly despatched but physicians and soldiers – 'co-operating with Divine providence' – intervened to keep her safe. Petty's prescribed treatment was continued and by the following day Greene was much improved and, swollen neck, throat and stomach pains notwithstanding, she was able to drink a little and respond to questioning. Her recovery continued – it was complete within the space of a month – and she withdrew from the city to be cared for by friends in the countryside, taking her prison coffin with her as 'a trophy of her wonderful preservation'. Multitudes flocked to visit the Oxford miracle woman and the better sort of people, the prison governor included, contributed to a fund set up to relieve her wants. Divine judgement of a different kind crashed down on Sir Thomas Read, her employer and initial prosecutor, since he died three days after her miraculous 'resurrection'.[26]

'Wonderful' events of all kinds attracted popular attention in the early modern period, they were written up in eye-catching, moralising ways, and became favourite reading matter. The dividing line between fact and fantasy was easily lost. But that Greene's case and execution took place on the public stage and that leading scientists of the day were present places the record of these events on a more secure footing. The events of 1651 in Oxford certainly underline a number of the points already made in this chapter: the sexual vulnerability of servant maids at the hands of predatory male employers or their kin and the death warrant attached to a conviction for infanticide. Medical opinion in Greene's case in the event confirmed that it was a case of miscarriage, not infanticide. Greene freely confessed to Petty and others everything about her seduction and dated her giving birth to seventeen weeks later. The medical men, therefore, confirmed that the half formed dead child to which she gave birth was 'consequently not capable of being murdered'. Poems, some of them in Latin, from Oxford dons rounded off the first of the two commemorative publications on a high note by dwelling on the miraculous nature of the events in question. But it was a double-standard-laden men's world, and at least two of these little verses could not resist having a cynical dig:

> 'Tis more easy to recall the Dead
> Than to restore a once-lost maidenhead,

quipped one of them. Another droned,

> Hocus pocus, fast and loose, dead and gone,
> Here again: women have more tricks than one.

But her memory lived on. In his *History of the Worthies of England* (London, 1662) Thomas Fuller found a place for her story in his section on Oxfordshire, adding an afterword telling his readers that Greene 'is since married and liveth in the country in good reputation'.[27]

Moralising in a sense the accounts of Anne Greene's resurrection certainly were – divine intervention could overcome any circumstances, however desperate – and this was even more obviously the case in the narration of the events leading to the execution for arson in London in 1680 of Margaret Clark, another servant maid. Margaret, born in Croydon, was employed as a servant by a prosperous London dyer who had a house and business premises in Southwark and a country house in Lee in Kent, then only a village. She had worked for her master for only about a year in 1680 but as 'a wench of a competent understanding' she had evidently become sufficiently trusted to be left in charge, with only one other servant, of the Southwark property while the master's family was away in Lee. Late on the night of 1 February 1680 neighbours were awakened by the smell, sight and sound of burning, and rushed to investigate. They found fire raging in two places – the dyehouse and buttery – and while they were trying to bring them under control, another fire was noticed in a garret. Eventually the flames were extinguished and in due course an investigation took place which resulted in Margaret Clark being accused of starting the conflagration, an offence which – like infanticide – carried the death penalty. Under cross-examination a bizarre and complex story emerged. Clark confessed that she had been repeatedly importuned by a mysterious visitor to give him access to the master's premises in return for a substantial bribe which would be paid to her after the event at the Fleece Tavern in Holborn. The man charged her that 'I should not divulge it to any person in the world living, for if I did I should certainly die for it, and that quickly, in this world and be damned in the other.' Finally she capitulated to his wheedling and threats and an appointed time was agreed for the day in question when she would unlock the door to admit him to the dyer's property. Two separate fires were started and the mysterious arsonist took advantage of the confusion while crowds of neighbours were trying to put them out to start another fire in a garret before spiriting himself away. All this made Margaret at least an accessory to the crime but the man she accused and named was duly found and the two of them were brought to trial at nearby Kingston. However, the man successfully established an alibi, corroborated by others, had his character vouched for, and was acquitted. Margaret, now facing the arson charge wholly on her own account and admitting that she had done some pilfering while the fires were being brought under control by the posse of neighbours, was found guilty and sentenced to death.

The story line remained incomplete and raises tantalisingly unanswered questions, not least about why the stranger was allegedly targeting the dyer's premises. But in the event it was what the authorities and public opinion chose to make of the case that renders it particularly interesting and gives it a special importance. In the first place Margaret Clark was found to be not simply an arsonist, or an accessory to arson, but a lapsed Protestant who had been consorting with Roman Catholics. The mysterious stranger, Clark insisted, was a papist and he had tried (unsuccessfully) to take Margaret to a priest to be granted absolution before the arson attack took place. With the Great Fire of London – often attributed to papists – a fairly recent memory, and with the hysteria surrounding the Popish Plot of the previous year obviously still very much alive, Margaret had placed herself in exceedingly dangerous territory. (Her case closely resembled another, also from London, which took place the previous year centring on another servant maid, Elizabeth Oxley, accused of being bribed by papists to set fire to her master's house and absolved in advance by a Roman Catholic priest who had given her the assurance that 'it was no sin to fire all the houses of heretics'.) Secondly, in a way which did not, and could not, happen in the Anne Greene case (which remained locked in its remarkable uniqueness), Margaret Clark's own personal story was converted into an exemplar, a terrible warning to others in the same occupation. The very title of one of the two tracts published in 1680 covering the events in Southwark – *A Warning for Servants and a Caution to Protestants* – ardently proclaimed this general purpose for all to see. Written by clergymen, though incorporating some of Margaret's own words, these tracts were expressly designed 'to caution all others, and particularly those of her condition as servants . . . to beware of harking to . . . destructive insinuations suggested either immediately by Satan or mediately by any of his Popish imps'. Though Margaret unswervingly continued to the end to accuse the acquitted male stranger as the arsonist, her full confession of her part in the proceedings – vouched for by the High Sheriff of Surrey – was incorporated in the tracts. She praised her master and mistress, asked their forgiveness, and declared religious backsliding was the root of her present predicament. 'Pride and sabbath-breaking have been my downfall.' Truly penitent, said the clergyman author of one of the tracts, Clark was ready to face her end and rejoiced in her execution. 'This is my wedding day . . . I desire this downfall of mine may be a warning to all young men and maids. Let them be content . . . and not covet after great things as I have done.'[28] Margaret Clark's personal plight, clearly, had been rendered quite secondary to the wider socio-religious purposes it was being made to serve.

Murder cases involving servants, as Jane Holmes and others have found, were very rare. The historian William Dugdale, not chiefly renowned for racy anecdotes, included in his *Antiquities of Warwickshire* two sixteenth-century instances of servants being enlisted by a master or mistress to help them commit murder. In other situations, however, the law prescribed that servants should defend their employer against attack and protected servants from the charge of murder if they killed an assailant making the attempt.[29] When servants were arraigned on a charge of murdering a master it was the rarity of the crime as well as the deed itself – a more than capital offence, since murder represented the ultimate betrayal of a servant's duties and the trust residing in the office – which ensured they were well publicised and milked for their moral lessons. Thomas Savage, a London boy of only sixteen, apprenticed to an East End vintner, achieved unlooked-for notoriety at his execution in 1668. His youth notwithstanding he was, according to the clergyman author who wrote Savage's farewell pamphlet biography, 'a mere monster in sin' who dissipated his time in alehouses and brothels. To finance his vices he stole from his master and in a drunken rage murdered a fellow maidservant who got in his way. He took flight but was quickly apprehended, imprisoned, brought to trial and condemned to death. Visited by clergymen while awaiting execution, Savage confessed – like Margaret Clark – that Sabbath-breaking was the beginning of his downfall and that in the course of his apprenticeship 'he never knew what it was to hear one whole sermon'. Sentenced to be hanged at Ratcliff in Stepney, the scene of his crime, the execution and the condemned youth's repentance speech which preceded it produced 'a great moving upon the affections of those who stood by and many tears were drawn from their eyes by his melting speeches'. The execution, in fact, was doubly memorable, since in the event it took *two* hangings to finish him off: he had to be strung up a second time after starting to survive the first, botched attempt.[30] No Anne Greene type miracle was allowed to happen in this case.

Moral lessons were also drawn out of the case of Thomas Hellier, executed aged twenty-eight in 1678, though there are significant differences in his life story, not least since the final phase of his career took place in the American colonies, in Virginia, where he was employed as an indentured servant. It was there that he finally cracked and on a plantation near Charles City with an axe murdered his master, mistress and a maidservant who attempted to come to the rescue. But the different stages of his earlier life were all played out in England: it was there that the seeds of his ruin were sown, and it was in London that a graphic account of his downfall was published. Hellier was born near Lyme, in Dorset, of respectable parents, and served six of the seven years of a term of apprenticeship to a barber surgeon. His master dying, Hellier, having inherited a small farm from his grandfather, quit his apprenticeship, set himself up on his own account, married a wife worth £50 a year and had a daughter. Farming life, alas, was not to his liking and, having embezzled a sum of money due to his father, he absconded to London, where, with borrowed capital, he launched into business as a stationer. 'I was all on fire to set up in the world, to make a bustle abroad to and fro, and be doing that I might seem somebody.' That venture also failing, he left unpaid debts behind and relocated to Crewkerne, Dorset, where he led an abandoned life, swearing, drinking and getting ever deeper into debt.

His creditors in due course demanded satisfaction and he was forced to sell his small farm. He kept a tippling house for a short time before once more returning to London, the scene of some of his earlier misfortunes. But again having no money he decided to go to sea, serving as a ship's surgeon. That venture, too, was quickly added to his catalogue of failures and, in the face of mounting financial difficulties, a desperate Thomas Hellier eventually left for Virginia as an indentured servant.

He arrived at a time when master–servant tensions were on the increase in the colony. In Virginia, on a plantation appropriately called 'Hard Labour', he found a 'Hell upon earth' and a brutal mistress who constantly railed at him and made his life unbearable. The three murders he committed were the outcome of his desperation. He fled with stolen provisions on a stolen horse but was apprehended, tried at Jamestown, sentenced and, such was his monstrous crime, hanged in chains. The unknown writer – almost certainly a clergyman, as was common with such publications – drew out from the tragic particulars of this one man's life moral lessons for others to follow in the future. Parents and other relatives should learn from this case, he said, not to over-indulge their offspring. Young people themselves, however, should shun the kind of self-love displayed by this unfortunate man in his earlier years and the same kind of over-ambitious dabbling in affairs above their station. 'His monstrous, wonder-working brain built castles in the air of his lofty high-flown imagination.' Specifically, indentured service should never be entered into casually, as Hellier had done, without cast-iron guarantees about the kind of work to be undertaken. However, there were vital lessons here, too, for masters. Those who exercised a cruel tyranny over their subordinates might well find themselves its victims. It was unwise as well as unchristian to treat servants like dogs.[31]

London maidservant Sarah Malcolm was hanged in 1733 for taking part with three others in the robbery and murder of an old lady, Mrs Duncomb, who lodged in the same house as her master, Mr Kerrol, in Doctors' Commons. Although to the last she denied complicity in anything other than the robbery, Malcolm was convicted; what happened to the three accomplices she named, at least one of whom was another servant, is unclear.[32] More notice was attracted in 1746 by another London murder case centring on a servant, this time nineteen-year-old Matthew Henderson. His execution was accompanied by the usual clergyman-compiled publication. Henderson, it was made clear, had been a relatively blameless young man and did not go in for drinking, gambling or whoring, though he had neglected religious observance. His crime was unpremeditated and he had no accomplice. Harsh words and a blow from his mistress suddenly kindled his resentment and provoked his retaliatory attack on Mrs Dalrymple, the employer in question. Robbery followed the murder as an attempt to divert suspicion from himself, but he was apprehended, brought to trial and condemned to death. Duly penitent, devout at his end, 'the crowd [at his execution] was moved to compassion'. As in other publications of this kind the essential moral purpose rushed to the fore. 'Last, dying speeches' often took on a quasi-formulaic quality bearing the strong imprint of their clergymen editors and, in many London cases, that of the Ordinary of Newgate Gaol.[33]

But in this case the moralising was even more emphatic. The account of Matthew Henderson by the Rev. Thomas Boughton (1712–77), a London clergyman, Methodist convert and long-serving secretary of the SPCK, was much longer than normal in such cases and was indeed a substantial tract rather than simply a pamphlet. The material relating to Henderson himself – though it formed the centrepiece and gave the work its title – occupied only a few pages and did not begin until p. 39. The rest was generalised moralising about the respective duties of servants and masters and, in the light of crimes like Henderson's, about the paramount need for domestic order and the regular practice of household religion to counteract the corrupting influences of town life, especially those abounding in London. As general advice to servants on how to conduct themselves, and a stark warning of the possible consequences of straying from the narrow path, Broughton's tract had a long shelf life. A fifth edition of it appeared as late as 1787, long after Henderson's death and a decade after Boughton's own demise; an old case could still be made to serve a useful purpose. It was marketed at a special discounted price for large quantities. Clearly, it was felt that no one should be left in any doubt about the likely fate which would befall transgressing servants.[34]

Unavoidably in a society in which servants formed so large a part, the law covered, weighed down on and reached out to them in a huge number of ways. Legal experts like Blackstone were obliged to take account of servants. By the later decades of the eighteenth century taxes were raised on servant-keeping. Household servants, especially those whose condition brought them under the provisions of the Poor Law, often felt the heavy hand of the legal system, and servants of all kinds were periodically brought before magistrates and the courts for a variety of offences, many of them involving deviations from their contracts and for petty theft. There were correlations – such was the sexual vulnerability of maidservants – between those in household employment and bastardy cases and, indeed, with infanticide, though this was much less common. There were relatively few cases of servants in the dock charged with arson or murder. But as well as being many times on the receiving end of the law household servants were commonly *used by* the law – since they were notable or even notorious as the eyes and ears of private households and rural and urban communities – to provide testimony in many kinds of court case, fornication, adultery and divorce among them. Additionally, as we have seen, with increasing frequency and confidence servants, with surprisingly large numbers of women among them, *made use of the law* on their own account to seek redress, often against their employers. Before things changed in the early nineteenth century there were many instances of the courts finding in their favour, elite-dominated though the legal system undoubtedly was. That they could find themselves on the wrong side of the law was, unquestionably, one of the reasons why eighteenth-century employers perceived, and bitterly complained of, a widespread 'servant problem' which threatened not only the stability of individual households, especially those in the capital, but that of society at large. It often seemed to these pessimists that their comfortable world was being turned upside down. 'By a prodigious reverse of nature,' lamented a Leicester magistrate in 1721, 'we are vilely and contemptibly become the slaves of our servants and the equals of our slaves'.[35]

NOTES

1 See pp. 208–13. M. Dalton, *The Countrey Justice* (London, 1677), pp. 336–7.

2 Blackstone, *Commentaries on the Laws of England* (Oxford, 1765–69).

3 Bird, *The Laws Respecting Masters and Servants* (London, 1795). See also J. Huntingford, *The Laws of Masters and Servants Considered* (London, 1790).

4 *The State and Case of the Native Servants* [*of Ireland*] (Dublin, 1750) had proposed a £5 annual tax on all foreign servants, while a correspondent in the *London Chronicle* in 1765 suggested that black servants should be taxed at the annual rate of 40s each, the proceeds to be used to help offset the national debt (cited in Gretchen Gerzina, *Black England. Life before Emancipation* London, 1995), pp. 41–2; Trusler, *London Adviser*, pp. 51–3; Bird, *Laws Respecting Masters and Servants*, p. 12; Hecht, *Domestic Servant Class*, p. 33. On under-recording of servants in the tax returns see P. Langford, 'The uses of eighteenth-century politeness', *TRHS*, 6th ser., 12 (2002), 324. Schwarz, 'English servants and their employers during the eighteenth and nineteenth centuries', 236–56, appears too inclined to accept the servant tax returns at face value.

5 Atkinson, *Quarter Sessions Records*, North Riding, *passim*; J. M. Rosenheim (ed.), *The Notebook of Robert Doughty, 1662–1665*, Norfolk Record Society, 54 (1989), *passim*; Bennett and Dewhurst, *Quarter Sessions Records, County Palatine of Chester, 1559–1660*, p. 68; Margaret J. Hood (ed.), *Borough Sessions Papers, 1653–1688*, Portsmouth Record Ser., 1 (1971), p. 227.

6 'A domestic servant's indenture of apprenticeship in 1732', *Devon Notes and Queries*, 1 (1900), 13–14; Gillian Clark (ed.), *Correspondence of the Foundling Hospital Inspectors in Berkshire*, Berkshire Record Society, 1 (1994), p. 179; S. Hindle, *On the Parish? The Micro-politics of Poor Relief in Rural England, c. 1550–1750* (Oxford, 2004), pp. 198, 391; K. Wrightson, *Earthly Necessities. Economic Lives in Early Modern Britain* (New Haven, CT, and London, 2000), p. 323; Dorothy George, *London Life in the Eighteenth Century* (London, 1925), pp. 253–4.

7 R. Burn, *A History of the Poor Laws* (London, 1764), pp. 211–12, quoted in Carolyn Steedman, 'Lord Mansfield's women', *Past & Present*, 176 (2002), 111–12. Rev. G. Glover, *Observations on the Present State of Pauperism in England* (London, 1817), p. 392, quoted in Snell, *Parish and Belonging. Community, Identity and Welfare in England and Wales, 1700–1950*, p. 146; Steedman, 'Lord Mansfield's women', *passim*; Sokoll (ed.), *Essex Pauper Letters, 1731–1837, passim*. There is further discussion of settlement rights and the legal and social problems surrounding them in Snell, *Parish and Belonging*, pp. 86, 99, 102, 115, 123.

8 Moore, *Wedlock*, p. 86; Gowing, *Domestic Dangers*, p. 48; Willis Bund (ed.), *Worcestershire County Records. Calendars of Quarter Sessions Papers*, 1, *1591–1643, passim*; Walker, *Crime, Gender and Social Order*, pp. 164–5, 89–90, 82–3.

9 *Deposition Book of Richard Wyatt*, p. 46.

10 These and other cases are examined in L. Stone, *The Road to Divorce in England, 1530–1987* (Oxford, 1990), pp. 226, 219, 213.

11 Gowing, *Domestic Dangers*, pp. 113, 96; Merritt, *The Social World of Early Modern Westminster*, p. 249; Amanda Flather, *The Politics of Place. A Study of Church Seating in Essex, c. 1580–1640* (Woodbridge, 2007), pp. 153–4; Hair, *Before the Bawdy Court, passim*; D. A. Postles, *Social Proprieties. Social Relations in Early Modern England, 1500–1680* (Washington, DC, 2006), pp. 97, 102; Brinkworth, *The Bawdy Court of Banbury. The Act Book of the Peculiar Court of Banbury, Oxfordshire and Northamptonshire 1525–1638*, Banbury Historical Society, 26 (1997); S. King and A. Tompkins (eds.), *The Poor in England, 1700–1850. An Economy of Makeshifts* (Manchester, 2003), p. 152; Huntingford, *Laws*, p. 99; cited in D. Jarrett, *England in the Age of Hogarth* (London, 1974, 1986), p. 109.

12 Gowing, *Domestic Dangers*, pp. 202–3; Malcolm, *Anecdotes of the Manners and Customs of London during the Eighteenth Century*, p. 102. For more on the footman lothario Jones see pp. 167, 199, 228. The Middleton case is discussed at considerable length in L. Stone, *Broken Lives. Separation and Divorce in England, 1660–1857* (Oxford, 1993).

13 A. J. Willis (ed.), *Winchester Consistory Depositions, 1561–1602* (Winchester, 1960), p. 26. Much more dramatically in a later Swedish witchcraft case a maidservant was evidently willing to face execution herself so long as she dragged her hated mistress with her to the same fate. (Fauve-Chamoux, *Domestic Service*, p. 50); *Deposition Book of Richard Wyatt, JP, 176–1776*, p. 248; *Quarter Sessions Records* (North Riding), pp. 99, 248.

14 A maidservant in Memmingen, Germany, who was accused by her master of wrongdoing in 1529 lodged counter-charges against him, saying he had promised marriage before seducing her and then, having had his way, scorned her. The court found in her favour. (Merry E. Wiesner, *Working Women in Renaissance Germany*, New Brunswick, NJ, 1986, p. 90; McIntosh, *Working Women in English Society, 1300–1620*, p. 54.) Between 8 per cent and 17 per cent of the Equity cases examined in this study relate to servants; *Worcestershire Quarter Sessions Papers*, II, p. 337; cited in Quaife, *Wanton Wenches*, p. 66; J. S. Cockburn (ed.), *Western Circuit Assize Orders, 1629–1648*, Camden Society, 4th ser., 17 (1976), pp. 84, 229; L. Fox (ed.), 'Diary of Robert Beake, Mayor of Coventry, 1656–1657', in R. Bearman (ed.), *Miscellany* I, Dugdale Soc. (1977), p. 124; cited in Holmes, 'Domestic Service in Yorkshire', pp. 254, 130; Rosenheim, *The Notebook of Robert Doughty, 1662–1665*, pp. 18, 19; Horn, *Flunkies and Scullions*, p. 268; Hitchcock and Black (eds.), *Chelsea Settlement and Bastardy Examinations*, pp. 72–3; Hecht, *Domestic Servant Class*, p. 80; *Deposition Book of Richard Wyatt*, pp. 258, 309.

15 Stokes, *The Blechley Diary of the Rev. William Cole*, pp. 253–4; *Observations and Advices Oeconomical*, p. 46; *Public Nuisance Considered*, p. 40; D. Hay, 'Master and servant in England: using the law in the eighteenth and nineteenth centuries', in W. Steinmetz (ed.), *Private Law and Social Inequality in the Industrial Age. Comparing Legal Cultures in Britain, France, Germany, and the United States* (Oxford, 2000), p. 237; D'Archenholz, *Picture of England*, p. 206.

16 Horn, *Flunkies and Scullions*, pp. 268–9.

17 Hay, 'Master and servant', pp. 231, 255.

18 Walker, *Crime, Gender and Social Order*, p. 185; North Yorkshire County Record Office, QSB Thirsk 23 April 1723, cited in Holmes, 'Domestic Service in Yorkshire', p. 267; R. Paley (ed.), *Justice in Eighteenth-Century Hackney. The Justicing Book of Henry Norris and the Hackney Petty Sessions Book*, London Record Society, 27 (1991), pp. 249, 259. Holmes, 'Domestic Service in Yorkshire', pp. 253, 252, 254.

19 Anon., *Satan's Harvest, or, The Present State of Whorecraft . . .* (London, 1749), pp. 3–5, cited in Stone, *Road to Divorce*, pp. 218–19; M. Faraday, *Ludlow, 1085–1660. A Social, Economic and Political History* (Chichester, 1991), p. 75; Hood (ed.), *Borough Sessions Papers, 1653–1688, passim*; Dennison *et al.*, *Aberdeen before 1800*, p. 57.

20 Horn, *Flunkies and Scullions*, p. 238.

21 K. Wrightson, 'The nadir of English illegitimacy in the seventeenth century', in P. Laslett, Karla Oosterveen and R. M. Smith (eds.), *Bastardy and its Comparative History* (London, 1980), p. 187; Brinkworth, *Bawdy Court of Banbury*, p. 103; Hitchcock and Black, *Chelsea Settlement*, *passim*.

22 Atkinson, *Quarter Sessions Records* (North Riding), p. 97.

23 Vaisey, *The Diary of Thomas Turner*, *passim*; Steedman, *Master and Servant*, pp. 176–7, 181–2.

24 In twenty-five of the thirty-one German infanticide cases from the period 1595 to 1712 examined by Merry E. Wiesner the death penalty was inflicted. (Wiesner, *Working Women*, p. 71.) On infanticide see the revealing studies by P. C. Hoffer and N. E. H. Hull, *Murdering Mothers. Infanticide in England and New England, 1558–1803* (New York, 1984), and M. Jackson, *Newborn Child Murder. Women, Illegitimacy and the Courts in Eighteenth-Century England* (Manchester, 1996), esp. pp. 29–60.

25 Quaife, *Wanton Wenches*, p. 118; Laura Gowing, 'Secret births and infanticide in seventeenth-century England', *Past & Present*, 156 (1997), 106; Holmes, 'Domestic Service in Yorkshire', p. 26; *Notebook of Robert Doughty*, p. 64; Jackson, *Newborn Child Murder*, p. 49; Anne Marie Kilday, 'Maternal monsters: murdering mothers in south-west Scotland, 1750–1815', in Yvonne G. Brown and Rona Ferguson (eds.), *Twisted Sisters. Women, Crime and Deviance in Scotland since 1400* (East Linton, 2002), pp. 167–8; S. Schama, *The Embarrassment of Riches. An Interpretation of Dutch Culture in the Golden Age* (London, 1987), p. 459; Horn, *Flunkies and Scullions*, p. 263.

26 This summary is based on a conflation of the two tracts mentioned above, which corroborate each other at every turn.

27 *Newes from the Dead*, pp. 6, 25, 28; Fuller, *Worthies*, p. 341.

28 *The Papists Plot of Firing Discovered* (London, 1679), pp. 22, 27, 28. The author in the Margaret Clark case may have been Nathaniel Gardiner, curate in Kingston, whose name heads the list of witnesses printed at the end of the longer of the two tracts. A maid in Nuremberg, Germany, who set fire to her master's barn in 1583 was decapitated and her head stuck on a pole. (Wiesner, *Working Women*, p. 90.)

29 Dyer and Richardson, *William Dugdale*, pp. 26, 131; Bird, *Laws Respecting Masters and Servants*, p. 6.

30 R. Franklin, *A Murderer Punished and Pardoned, or, A True Relation of the Wicked Life and Shamefull, Happy Death of Thomas Savage, imprisoned, justly condemned and twice executed at Ratcliff, for his Bloody Act in killing his Fellow Servant* (London, 1668).

31 *The Vain Prodigal Life and Tragical Penitent Death of Thomas Hellier* (London, 1678), *passim*, especially pp. 7, 20. The system of indentured service, in fact, began in Virginia, which suffered from acute labour shortages, and spread to other colonies. On post-1660 tensions in the colony see P. Linebaugh and M. Rediker, *The Many Headed Hydra. Sailors, Slaves, Commoners and the*

Hidden History of the Revolutionary Atlantic (London, 2000), p. 135. For a very different, and more positive, account of indentured service in Virginia see E. M. Riley (ed.), *The Journal of John Harrower. An Indentured Servant in the Colony of Virginia, 1773–1976* (Williamsburg, VA, 1963).

32 *A True Copy of the Paper delivered the Night before her Execution by Sarah Malcolm to the Rev. Mr Piddington, Lecturer, of St Bartholomew the Great* (London, 1733). Two sixteenth-century Frankfurt maids tried and found guilty of killing their employer were buried alive. (Wiesner, *Working Women*, p. 90.)

33 See J. A. Sharpe, ' "Last dying speeches": religion, ideology and public execution in seventeenth-century England', *Past & Present*, 107 (1985), 144–67, P. Linebaugh, 'The Ordinary of Newgate and his *Account*', in J. S. Cockburn (ed.), *Crime in England, 1550–1800* (London, 1977), pp. 246–70, and Linebaugh, *The London Hanged. Crime and Society in the Eighteenth Century* (London, 1991).

34 Thomas Broughton, *A Serious and Affectionate Warning to Servants . . . occasioned by the shameful and untimely death of Matthew Henderson* (London, 1746).

35 Quoted in Horn, *Flunkies and Scullions*, p. 190.

10

EARLY MODERN SERVANTS IN PERSPECTIVE

Foreign visitors to England, bringing with them their own cultural baggage, and fond of making comparisons with what they had left behind, were generally impressed with the standards of household service with which they were met – though encountering demands for vails for the first time was always a severe shock. De Saussure, in England in the late 1720s, certainly dwelt in hostile fashion on this particular perk, but commented favourably on the neatness of dress of English servants and the scrupulously maintained cleanliness of the households in which they worked. D'Archenholz, in the last years of the same century, was firmly of the view that 'no part of Europe abounds with better domestics'. He took note of their 'good order . . . zeal and activity', their politeness to strangers and their handsome appearance. Register offices, which he encountered for the first time in England, were 'a singular institution' in his view, worthy of imitation elsewhere. The good qualities of English household servants tended always to be praised in the following decades by comparison with domestics in the United States. The very word 'servant' was despised in that country, so many travellers in both directions observed, due to its tainted association with the indenturing system of the seventeenth and early eighteenth centuries. Indentured service was in no sense the exact American equivalent of household service in England, since it covered a much wider range of occupations, some of them unconnected with what has been discussed in these pages. Under this much practised arrangement poor migrants had travelled to the American colonies from England and elsewhere in Europe and, often 'sold' by the ship's captain who had brought them there, became bound to a master on arrival for a fixed term. Indentured servants, therefore, featured in a large number of crafts and trades in the early colonies, where labour was in scarce supply and reinforcements of all kinds were desperately needed. American attitudes to household service in Cobbett's day and later were also inevitably influenced by the survival of slavery; 'servant' in that nation was a term that often implied abject servitude. No man in the former American colonies, observed William Cobbett in 1819, will 'wear a livery any more than he will wear a halter round his neck'. Household servants, and those who supplied the needs of travellers in hotels, despised their work and were truculent towards those who demanded it.

> What a difference it would make in this country [declared Cobbett] if it could be supplied with nice, clean, dutiful English maidservants . . . As to bringing them with you, it is as wild a project as it would be to try to carry the sunbeams to England. They will begin to change before the ship gets on soundings . . .[1]

The implicit and explicit comparisons between household service in different countries made by contemporaries can be supplemented by the work of modern historians. The wide-ranging, but ultimately disappointing, collection edited by Antoinette Fauve-Chamoux, *Domestic Service and the Formation of European Identity* (2004) was referred to at the beginning of this book. (See pp. 10–11.) Historical studies of household service in eighteenth-century France – Sarah J. Maza, *Servants and Masters in Eighteenth-Century France* (Princeton, NJ, 1983), and Cissie Fairchilds, *Domestic Enemies. Servants and their Masters in Old Regime France* (Baltimore, MD, 1984) – provide the most useful findings to place alongside those offered in the present volume. Both Maza's and Fairchilds' books (both published in the United States) cover similar ground and there is necessarily some overlap between them. Maza's book has more than Fairchilds' on changing attitudes to service and servants, including those expressed by the Ancien Régime *philosophes*; Diderot despised servants for *choosing* subordination. She makes good use of French drama, with its abundant servant characters, as a source and she highlights their changing dramatic functions. Only eight of the 250 French comedies published between 1610 and 1700 had no servant presence in their *dramatis personae*, but over the course of the period the stock servant characters depicted in these plays tended to change from clumsy fools to constantly alert, all-seeing, cunning, unreliable schemers. (Beaumarchais's Figaro, of course, is the uncontestedly pre-eminent servant character in French drama.) Both books deal with recruitment and mobility. Both address the shift over the course of this period from paternalist to contractual notions of service, though Maza sees the trend starting earlier. Both see service as a relationship, not simply as an occupation. Both take note of the increasing feminisation of household service. France and England were in line on this and, as in England, life-cycle service was more commonly a part of the female than of the male experience of servanthood. Both deal with the impact of the French Revolution on service and servants – clearly far more resounding in many respects than in the case of the English upheavals in the middle of the previous century. In France so much of Ancien Régime service was tied up with an aristocracy and with a Church that were swept away. Servants were distrusted by the revolutionaries as mere appendages of noble and clergyman masters, some of whom indeed were saved through their servants' help. Many servant jobs disappeared as aristocratic *châteaux* and town houses closed or were severely downsized. The contraction of the population of Versailles, not surprisingly, was particularly spectacular. Servants were not given the vote by the Revolution and they were not a major presence in popular politics. Relatively few of them joined the army or the National Guard. The English Revolution involved servants as activists in ways in which the French Revolution did not.

Fairchilds' study has more of a quantitative edge than Maza's. Based chiefly on Paris, Toulouse and Bordeaux, Fairchilds' book is replete with statistical tables on the social distribution of servants, their parentage, marriage prospects, mobility, sexuality, literacy, and on the extent to which servants figured as legatees in their employers' wills. As in eighteenth-century England, servant-keeping in France is depicted here as being on the increase in France among the middle classes. The spatial separation of master and servant, so much a feature of the development of the architectural context of service in England, though it happened in France, had a somewhat different, later, chronology in that country. The attitudinal challenges which household servants encountered in respect of marriage and old age were essentially the same in France as in England. What is presented in Fairchilds' book about servant psychology and sexual encounters and vulnerability reveals a world similar to that depicted in the present volume. The absence of a distinct servant 'class' and well defined homogeneous servant subculture was no less notable in France than it was in England.

Studying household servants in early modern England, no less than in Ancien Régime France, clearly has not taken us into an arcane historical backwater. Servants accounted for a considerable portion of the total population, and on those grounds alone need to be properly noted. As this book has repeatedly emphasised, they were a ubiquitous presence in English society at the time. At least 40 per cent of all households included servants. Moreover, though servant-keeping was a conspicuous charac-teristic of the life style of those with wealth and social standing it was, nonetheless, a vertical feature of English society. Servants could be found (generally as pauper apprentices) in some of the poorest households. Service also, as we have seen, was often age-related. As an occupational category for young people in the fifteen to twenty-four age group this kind of employment dominated the field; 60–70 per cent of such young people worked in this sector, often as a stage in their life cycle. Most, especially the young women among them, left service when they married.

The gender dimension of service, like the age-related dimension, is also interesting, as other studies have previously observed. In the long term over the early modern period the feminisation of this sector of employment became a noticeable tendency, certainly in elite establish-ments. By the late eighteenth century to find a preponderance of male servants employed in a sizeable household was highly unlikely, a trend accentuated by new taxes on menservants and the opening up of new employment opportunities in industry and commerce. In the early sixteenth century it had been standard for feudal households to be predominantly masculine in their structure and composition; female servants, such as there were, constitituted only 'an island of womanhood' within them.[2] For households of the middling classes and below, however, more gender continuities in this feature of service were to be found. In these socio-economic settings women servants were a characteristic of Tudor no less than of Georgian households, and as the servant-keeping habit spread among the *nouveaux riches* and others in the later period, as London grew, and as a colonial empire expanded, more servants were needed. More and more of them were female. The broadening range of employers, many of them involved in the world of business, and some of not much greater wealth and higher social standing than those who worked for them, helps explain the growing shift towards a system of service that was essentially contractual in nature. A much more articulated and pervasive class con-sciousness in the nineteenth and twentith centuries had obvious implica-tions for servant-keeping and servants. (It is the subject of an article in the journal *Past & Present*, 2009.) So had the increasing separation of homes and workplaces, the changing social and domestic roles of middle-class women, and the increase in Irish immigration to England.

The importance of servants, however, in the early modern period rested on more than mere numbers. In a labour-intensive society servants were economically and socially indispensable. Without them the superstructure which rested on their often taken-for-granted efforts could not have been sustained. Without servants, for instance, two of the most eye-catching economic phenomena of the period – the exponential growth of London and the development of the American colonies – would almost certainly have been inconceivable. Adam Smith, the justly famous and usually astute eighteenth-century economist, was surely wrong to regard the labour of servants as unproductive and to dismiss servant-keeping merely as an expression of conspicuous consumption.[3]

Studying servants undoubtedly helps the historian understand the labour market in its broader sense; that labour exchanges initially arose chiefly in relation to household servants is just one index of the prevalence and importance of this occupational category. Studying servants also, as this book has repeatedly shown, assists in coming to terms with such subjects as occupational mobility – servants, without doubt, were one of the most mobile groups in society – the complex relations between London and the provinces and between town and countryside. Self-evidently, studying servants promotes our understanding of labour relations, contract law, wages, the moral economy of perks, and the coexistence of employment and by-employments. Early modern moralists might have continued to extol old ideals of service based on paternalism and loyalty but the insistent realities for those engaged in service were often starkly different.

Servants directly underpinned society and not only the economy. This study, like some of the others which have preceded it, has shown that household servants were integral to *families* in this period. The word 'family' was indeed used at this time in an inclusive way to embrace all those – servants and apprentices no less than blood relations – who lived in the same unit. Servants, said Halifax in 1688, 'are the wheels of your family . . . if these engines stop or move wrong the whole order of your house is either at a stand or discomposed'.[4] It is simply not possible to understand the family as the most basic molecular unit of early modern English society without taking account of the servants who were one of its essential constituent parts; Christopher Durston's book on *The Family in the English Revolution* (Oxford, 1989), which inexplicably left them out, in that real sense was a contradiction in terms. The Civil Wars of the mid-seventeenth century, as chapter 7 of this study demonstrated, brought about a great testing time for families – servants included – and their allegiances, as the Protestant Reformation of the previous century had done, though in different ways. As the mid-seventeenth-century crisis deepened some servants lost their jobs as employers had to trim their expenditure in the face of falling income and as some households collapsed under the impact of war. In the 1640s servants petitioned, rioted, took up arms and were conscripted for campaign and transport duties. They were to be found among the Levellers and other radical groups. Servants can be found participating in what, for a time at least, looked like a world being turned upside down.

Studying household servants clearly assists in making sense of England's social hierarchy and interlocking social relations in the early modern period. Looking at how employer–servant relations – the most common contractual bond in existence – operated at this time must tell us a great deal about how society in general functioned. Household service also offers a window on to gender relations, not just in terms of the increasing feminisation of this occupational category between the sixteenth and eighteenth centuries but in terms of gender stereotypes of work, and of sexual vulnerability in the workplace. In due course, as negro servants became more than an occasional oddity, service also provides a new window on to race relations. Chapters 6 and 7 documented some of the ways in which household service opens up investigations of social engineering and the social pathology of the time. That so much was written about servants and the perceived problems of servant-keeping, especially in London, at this time gives us access to a running commentary on a wider range of social priorities, ideals and perceptions of the social order.

This study has also made clear that servants were important as cultural bridges or, cultural amphibians, between the world of the workplace and their own social setting.[5] Service entailed frequent social encounters and social mingling or first-hand observing and a carrying back to their own *milieu* of the differences and novelties which had been experienced and learned in their masters' households. The high level of mobility associated with service and the life-cycle character of this form of employment for many lent further weight to these amphibian tendencies. Fads and fashions in diet and dress disseminated more widely in society through servant channels. The plethora of criticism of maidservants dressing above their station shows how fashion consciousness had permeated society. Without servants, tea-drinking and the tobacco (and snuff-taking) habit, even though encouraged by falling prices, are unlikely to have spread so quickly and widely in the eighteenth century. The wider diffusion of improved personal cleanliness also, it seems likely, owed something to servants as well as to cheap soap, cotton fabrics and John Wesley.

Servants and their employers lived in close physical proximity. At the beginning of the period studied in this book separate living accommodation for servants was unknown, even in elite households; they found a place to sleep as best they could in passageways, closets, cellars, attics and stable lofts and counted themselves lucky if they had any kind of bed as their own. Sometimes they slept vulnerably close to lustful masters, even in the same room. By the end of this period, though shared accommodation for many servants was still commonplace – only high-ranking upper servants in the best households could expect separate rooms or even a suite of rooms – increasingly they had some kind of place of their own. Newly built or enlarged and refashioned country houses and town houses in London, Bath and elsewhere had designated servants' quarters and bedrooms with back-stairs entrances, concealed doors and internal corridors. A spatial separation of spheres within the household – even in better-off farmhouses – was being established to begin to satisfy the growing demand for domestic privacy and for keeping most servants out of sight, except those like footmen and butlers who were deliberately foregrounded for display purposes. Bell systems in the new elite houses designed by Vanbrugh, Roger North and Roger Pratt brought servants into contact with their employers only when required. Privacy, of course, unachievable in an absolute sense, given the pampered life style of the elite, heavily reliant on underlings to assist with the most intimate of daily routines, was an upper-class luxury (and illusion).

> Many of our acquaintances [declared a sharp-eyed late eighteenth-century commentator] seem absolutely incapable of motion till they have been wound up by their valets. They have no more use of their hands for any office about their own persons than if they were paralytic. At night they must wait for their servants before they can undress themselves and go to bed. In the morning, [they lie] helpless and sprawling in bed, like a turtle upon its back upon the kitchen table of an alderman.[6]

Hardly any menial servants could expect a room of their own or a key to a shared room to exclude others; for most their own lockable box was their only partially defensible last bastion. (That this was portable, however, demonstrated the severe limits of servant defensibility.) In the largest households, at least, a nominal 'upstairs/downstairs' segregation was being established by the Georgian period in a way which was to become more standardised across a broader social range of households in the following much more overtly class-conscious century. There was no distinct servant 'class' in the eighteenth century; that word was wisely omitted from the title of the reprint of J. Jean Hecht's classic book in 1981. Since servants were a vertical feature of English society, that obviously made them an exceedingly plural occupational group, multi-layered and varied, with those at the top of the servant hierarchy having little in common with those at its base. Except in London, with its enormous concentration of servants of all kinds, and to a lesser extent for part of each year in Bath and other fashionable gathering places, horizontal bonding of servants across, and not simply within, households was scarcely feasible. Proto-trade unions among footmen, for instance, were rumoured to exist in the eighteenth-century capital with collective ambitions to protect the interests of members and keep up wage levels and preserve prized perks, especially vails, but there is little firm evidence to suggest that they had a tangible, regular existence outside the fears of employers and hostile commentators. Even in the twentieth century trade unionism among household servants followed a slow, difficult and ultimately unsuccessful course.[7]

The 'servant problem' of the eighteenth century, discussed here in chapter 8, was largely a construction made by employers, moralising commentators and those in authority, and was defined chiefly by contrasting admittedly imperfect and disappointing contemporary realities against lofty, and perhaps unattainable, ideals and against a largely imagined Golden Age which had supposedly existed in the past. And it was overwhelmingly a London phenomenon. Similarly, as discussed in chapter 6, the great outpouring of publications chiefly in the seventeenth century on godly households above all expressed a striving for an ideal rather than documented a widespread reality. Despite what Defoe and others argued with deafening shrillness in the early eighteenth century, the 'servant problem' of their own age was not something which was intrinsically new; laments about all kinds of servant shortcomings had been heard from at least the sixteenth century. But new sensibilities, new refinements, new tastes, new heights and forms of conspicuous consumption in the increasingly prosperous eighteenth century certainly imposed new standards by which servants might be judged and found wanting. New organisations sprang up for encouraging and rewarding good and faithfully long-serving household servants; they were a prized species.

The largely unspoken subtext of the explosion of publications about the 'servant problem' was that servants had become too powerful. An inverted world had been allowed to come into existence while masters and the law both slumbered, thundered Defoe, with servants now holding their betters to ransom. Servant 'power' of a kind – it is one of this book's main findings – had indeed consolidated itself by the eighteenth century, especially in London where the largest number of those employed in that sector could be found. As demand for their services increased from a broader section of a prospering society household servants could, and did, exploit the labour market to their advantage. Masters were in competition with each other for good servants, even not-so-good ones. Servants' pay, particularly in the capital, where demand was greatest, went up considerably. On top of this their much prized perks – especially vails – gave servants lucrative sources of independent income. They laid claim to household left-overs which could be sold for a profit. Some servants who were directly involved with provisioning claimed 'poundage' on household goods purchased from shopkeepers. They enjoyed licence to collect Christmas 'boxes' – that is how the now familiar term originated – from family, neighbours and visitors. They sometimes had by-employments – spinning, laundering, brewing, petty money-lending, dressmaking and so on – which brought in extra cash and reduced their dependence on their wages and on their employers. For most servants their money wages, allowed for in their contracts of employment, were an accumulating nest egg and were not needed for immediate use. (The characteristic pattern of infrequent payment underlined the point very clearly.) With lodging, food and sometimes clothes provided by their employer, and with perks and occupational sidelines offering a periodic financial boost, their day-to-day 'running costs' were covered. The live-in servant economy was not primarily based on the regular flow of cash into their pockets.

Household servants characteristically were employed on a renew-able annual contract. They were one of the most mobile groups in the work force, much more mobile than apprentices – similar in age but bound by their longer indentures. Household servants might find themselves placed under employers they resented, but if so they could, and did, move on, especially in London. Numerous instances were given in chapter 4 of this conspicuous feature of servant employment and of the revolving doors through which they frequently passed. Samuel Pepys's small household employed thirty-eight servants in all at different points between 1660 and 1669; thirteen of them lasted for less than six months. The fastidious, hard-to-please Elizabeth Shackleton of Alkincoats in Lancashire hired twenty-nine female domestics in 1772 alone, of whom ten stayed for less than thirty days. Some servants became adept at forging character references, just as, for a variety of largely selfish rea-sons, some employers gave them too glibly. This was, undeniably, a real problem which was wrestled with throughout the early modern period and beyond. But some servants were hired on a casual, daily basis anyway and operated outside readily enforceable regimes of labour discipline.

Some servants, this study has shown, found it easy to take advantage of their employers. Since it was much complained of, we may be fairly sure that many servants became skilful at practising 'eye service', especially in larger households, working hard only when their master or mistress was watching. Some expediently exploited the advantage, though it is also true that some suffered as a result, of dysfunctional households in which master and mistress did not agree or were openly estranged. Earlier in this study the case was instanced of an early seventeenth-century Somerset small farmer who entrusted his servant maid, and not his wife, with the keys of the house – a doubly extraordinary thing to do. And then there was the notorious case in 1715 of the London footman/ sexual athlete Thomas Jones who exploited to the full his mistress's infatuation with him. (See pp. 167, 199.) For better or worse, servants could gain influence over their employers' children, if only because in larger households they probably saw more of them than their parents did. John Locke was well aware of the problem. Religious writers warned employers of the defiling consequences for their children's upbringing of contact with ungodly servants. By virtue of their household roles some servants – footmen, for example – were well placed to function as 'gatekeepers' controlling access to the establishment where they worked, both officially when acting under orders and unofficially when being deliberately remiss or when exacting revenge on those discredited guests who on an earlier occasion had defaulted on the vails expected of them. Some jealously defended their own specialist territory in the household against all intruders. Well paid cooks with high self-esteem in larger establishments were notorious for this; even their employers sometimes held them in awe. Widows and spinsters when heads of household in their own right could sometimes experience great tribulations from ungovernable servants. Chapter 8 recounted the sad case histories of Lady Sarah Cowper (1644–1720) and Gertrude Savile (1697–1758) and the domestic battlegrounds over which they nominally presided. Bachelors and widowers sometimes found themselves out of their depth in the field of domestic management.

Privacy was slow to establish itself in early modern households, and then only incompletely even in elite establishments which boasted the new architectural features of attics, back or side staircases, concealed doors, and corridors. Servants, we have seen, easily gained access to imperfectly guarded family secrets as well as to open disagreements and abuse and to the existence of sexual irregularities and adulterous relationships. And once in possession of such knowledge they were prone to gossip both within the household and, more dangerously, outside it, threatening the public reputation, the much prized honour, of their employers. Character assassination of their masters and mistresses was servants' ultimate weapon and, when activated, became the principal plank in their power base. For this reason, as we have seen, some masters preferred not to employ servants drawn from the immediate locality where they would have had existing gossip-hungry networks. Servants were well placed to act as witnesses in matrimonial disputes and other cases grounded in dysfunctional households, since they routinely saw and heard so much of what went on around them. Hobbes advised masters to allow servants to speak freely in their presence rather than unwittingly encourage them to utter poisonous, damaging remarks about them behind their backs. 'A gentleman may get an honest, a careful, or a diligent servant without much difficulty,' Robert Dodsley observed in the following century, 'but a discreet one is seldom to be found.'[9]

Another part of the 'power base' of some servants by the eighteenth century at least was that an increasing number of them could read and write. A world wider than that of the immediate household was open to them, news filtered through, and they could be targeted directly, and not simply through the mediation of their employers, by writers seeking to engage their attention. Mandeville and others in the eighteenth century deplored the fact that too many servants had been educated above their station and were convinced that their generation was paying a heavy price. Conservative employers, even in the early twentieth century, still agreed. Education made servants too 'uppish' and argumentative; deference was fading away. It was rumoured in the early eighteenth century that servants of MPs in London were not only claiming special privileges but were also flexing their political muscles by setting themselves up as a kind of third chamber of parliament.[10]

A modicum of education certainly encouraged household servants to resort to the law when they saw the need, challenging their masters' instinctive and long-practised reliance on it as the preserve only of the elite. The frequency of such cases increased in the eighteenth century and more women became adept at appealing to the law for help. That some, at least, of these servant litigants were successful and had damages or some other form of redress awarded them is indicative of the fact that servanthood in this period was far from being a uniformly depressed, downtrodden, helpless and exploited condition, though partly it undoubtedly was. Servant appropriation of wit (as fictional characters in drama) and of satire (in their own authentic verse and prose) was another challenge, very different in nature but similar in intention and effect, to the class pre-rogatives of the elite of their day.

Household service, as this book has repeatedly emphasised, covered a broad spectrum and in a number of respects changed over time. It was surely one of the most multi-layered occupational categories of the early modern period, its recruits came from a wide social range, and they fulfilled a considerable variety of functions. Some servants in large households were chiefly there for display and drew attention to the status of the master who could afford to employ them; unremitting toil was the lot of large numbers of less fortunate others. Service was an occupational category which involved complex relationships between servants themselves as well as between employers and employed; Shakespeare's plays provide endless reminders of those fundamental facts. Static representations of service do scant justice to situations and relationships that were always in flux. The varying size of a household brought into play different condi-tions of service, different roles, different perspectives and different kinds of bonds between masters, mistresses and their men and women. The experience of service was also deeply gendered. In addition it was also partly, at least, age-specific. Local variations in service and servant-keeping were enormous. A book on servants like Hecht's or Meldrum's which centred on London, uniquely different in so many ways, can hardly serve as an accurate guide to the rest of the country. And an exclusively top-level view of this subject makes us blind to insistent realities at the bottom. The fast-changing drama of the early modern period from Shakespeare and Jonson to Congreve and Goldsmith, as chapter 2 showed, provides one way of accessing the multivocal pluralism of both servants and employers at this time. But the surprisingly large number of authentic autobiographical traces, from women no less than from men, opened up at some length in chapter 3, takes us very close to the different lived realities of servants' own experiences from the sixteenth century to the eighteenth. Whereas Hecht's classic study of 1956 offered a view of the subject that was pro-vided largely by the employing classes, and much constrained by it in consequence, it is now absolutely clear that today we are no longer obliged to follow this unavoidably narrow path. Using a wider range of sources, pursuing different lines of enquiry, reinterrogating evidence which has long been known to historians, makes servants themselves more audible and visible. Studying their life stories and relationships undoubtedly gives us a clearer and more rounded understanding not only of their own imme-diate worlds but, more generally, of the society whose workings they con-stantly facilitated and indeed, in the last analysis, made possible.

NOTES

1 De Saussure, *Foreign View of England*, pp. 120–1, 127, 98; D'Archenholz, *Picture of England*, pp. 206, 207–8; Cobbett, *Journal of a Year's Residence in the United States of America* (1819, repr. Stroud, 1983), pp. 187–8. See Jane Louise Mesick, *The English Traveller in America, 1785–1835* (New York, 1922, repr. Westport, CT, 1970). The later comments of Frances Wright (1821), Frances Trollope (1832) and Catherine Beecher (1841) all echoed those made by Cobbett.

2 Kari Boyd McBride (ed.), *Domestic Arrangements in Early Modern England* (Pittsburgh, PA, 2002), p. 8.

3 Smith, *An Inquiry into the Nature and Causes of the Wealth of Nations* (London, 1776), I, p. 400. 'The labour of a menial servant adds to the value of nothing . . . The maintenance of a menial servant is never restored;' Selina Todd, 'Domestic service and class relations in Britain, 1900–1950', *Past & Present*, 203 (2009), 181–204.

4 Halifax, *The Ladies New Year Gift, or, Advice to a Daughter* (London, 1688), p. 66.

5 The phrase 'cultural amphibian' seems to have been first coined by P. Burke, *Popular Culture in Early Modern Europe* (New York, 1978), pp. 28, 63. Burke did not, however, explore in any depth the specific question of servant involvement in cultural mediation.

6 John Moore, *A View of Society and Manners in France, Switzerland and Germany* (6th edn., London, 1786), I, p. 15, quoted in Hecht, *Domestic Servant Class*, p. 45.

7 Horn, *Life below Stairs in the Twentieth Century*, pp. 184–90.

8 Locke, *Some Thoughts on Education* (London, 1693), p. 58.

9 Hobbes, 'Of masters and servants', p. 153; Dodsley, *Servitude. A Poem* (London, 1729), p. 13.

10 Turner, *What the Butler Saw*, p. 41.

ℰ

BIBLIOGRAPHY

PRIMARY SOURCES

Manuscripts

British Library

Egerton Mss 3054. Account book of Joyce Jefferies, 1638–47.

Hampshire County Record Office, Winchester

202/M85/5/12/1, concerning seating at Hursley church, 14 November 1689.
44/M69/E8/4/22. Small account book relating to Britford compiled by Thomas Jervoise, 1692–1709.
19/M61/1441. Robert Kingsmill. Receipt book for servants' wages, 1774–81.

Huntington Library, San Marino, California

Ellesmere. EL 1180. Orders for the household of Sir Thomas Egerton, *c.* 1603.
HAP 26/22. Orders to be observed in the lord's family (Earl of Huntington), *c.* 1604–1606/07.
Ellesmere. EL 6833. Memorial inscription to a servant, appended to that of James, Lord Egerton, Viscount Brackley, died 30 December 1620, aged four.
Temple. HM 66348. Orders and duties for the better ordering and direction of the house of Lionel Cranfield, Earl of Middlesex, 1621–22.
Ellesemere. EL 6487. Letter from the Countess of Derby to her son-in-law, Lord Bridgewater, 1631, concerning William Salisbury, servant.
Temple Family Addenda, Box 1. HM 46389. From William Harte to Hester, Lady Temple, concerning the taking of his daughter into service, 24 December 1631.
HM 46390. Further letter on the same subject (Box 2), 14 January 1632.
Temple Family Addenda Box 2. HM 46363. Letter from William Chaplyn to Hester, Lady Temple, 20 December 1632, concerning his kinswoman, her ladyship's maidservant.
Ellesmere. EL 6682. Accounts, 15 September 1634.

Ellesmere. EL 6553. Draft letter from Lord and Lady Bridgewater to the Lord Keeper, Lord Coventry, recommending a servant, 3 October 1635.

Temple Family Addenda, Box 2. HM 46489. Joan Swaine to Hester, Lady Temple, on behalf of a kinswoman seeking employment in service, February 1650.

Ellesmere. EL 8139. Rules for the household of the Earl of Bridgewater at Ashridge, Herts, during his absence, 17 November 1673.

Stowe. ST 175. Sir Richard Temple, third Baronet, servants' contracts, 11 October 1680.

Ellesmere. EL 8656. A checklist of servants' names and wages for the quarter ending 29 September 1690.

Stowe. ST 26(1). James Brydges, Journal of my Daily Actions, 1697–1701.

Stowe. ST 44. James Brydges, first Duke of Chandos, instructions to his servants, 1721.

Stowe. ST 82. James Brydges, first Duke of Chandos, payments to tradesmen and servants, 1722–32.

Stowe. ST 87. James Brydges, first Duke of Chandos, wages receipt book, 1718–20.

Professor Godfrey Davies, research notes, boxes 61 and 70.

Printed

Adams, Samuel and Sarah, *The Complete Servant* (London, 1825), ed. Ann Haly, with an introduction by Pamela Horn (Lewes, 1989).

'A domestic servant's indenture of apprenticeship in 1732', *Devon Notes and Queries*, I (1900).

Alsop, George, *A Character of the Province of Maryland* (London, 1666).

Anon., *Advice to Servants* (Bath, no date, *c.* 1800).

— *The Courte of Good Counsell* (London, 1607).

— *Cyvile and Uncyvile Life* (London, 1579).

— *A Declaration of the Maids of the City of London* (London, 1659).

— *Domestic Management, or, The Art of Conducting a Family* (London, 1800).

— *The Duties of Servants. A Practical Guide to the Routine of Domestic Service* (London, 1894, repr. East Grinstead, 1993).

— *An Earnest Exhortation to Housekeepers to set up the Worship of God in their Families* (5th edn., London, 1719).

— *Family Religion Revived, or, An Attempt to promote Religion and Virtue in Families* (New Haven, CT, 1755).

— *The Footman's Looking Glass* (London, 1747).

— *A Health to the Gentleman's Profession of Servingmen* (London, 1598).

— *Hell upon Earth, or, The Town in an Uproar* (London, 1729).

— *The Ladies Cabinet Enlarged and Opened* (4th edn., London, 1654).

— 'A letter sent by the Maydens of London' (1567) ed. R. J. Fehrenbach, in Kirby Farrell *et al.* (eds.), *Women in the Renaissance* (Amherst, MA, 1988).

— *The Maids Petition . . . presented Tuesday 9 August 1647*.

— *Newes from the Dead* (Oxford, 1651).

— *Observations and Advices Oeconomical* (London, 1669).

— *Public Nusance Considered* (London, 1754).

— *The Servants' Friend* (London, 1780).

— *A Short Prayer for Children and Servants* (London, 1700).

— *The State and Case of the Native Servants* [of Ireland] (Dublin, 1750).

— *The Vain Prodigal Life and Tragical Penitent Death of Thomas Hellier* (London, 1678).

— *A Warning for Servants and a Caution to Protestants, or, The Case of Margaret Clark, lately executed for firing her Master's House in Southwark* (London, 1680).

— *A Wonder of Wonders, being a Faithful Narrative and True Relation of one Anne Green, Servant to Sir Thomas Read, in Oxfordshire* (Oxford, 1651).

Anselment, R. A. (ed.), *Remembrances of Elizabeth Freke, 1671–1714*, Camden Soc., 5th ser., 18 (2001).

Ashford, Mary, *Life of a Licensed Victualler's Daughter, written by Herself* (London, 1844).

Atkinson, J. C. (ed.), *Quarter Sessions Records*, North Riding Record Soc., I (1884).

Austin, F. (ed.), *The Clift Family Correspondence, 1792–1846* (Sheffield, 1991).

Baker, D. (ed.), *The Inhabitants of Cardington in 1782*, Bedfordshire Historical Record Soc., 52 (1973).

Barker, Anne, *The Complete Servant Maid* (London, c. 1770).

Basse, William, *Sword and Buckler, or, The Servingman's Defence* (London, 1602).

Baxter, Richard, *The Poor Man's Family Book* (London, 1675).

Bayly, Lewis, *The Practice of Pietie* (London, 1613).

Becon, Thomas, *Catechism* (London, 1560).

Beeton, Isabella, *The Book of Household Management* (London, 1861, repr. 1986).

Behn, Aphra, *The Rover*, ed. F. M. Link (Lincoln, NB, 1967).

Bennett, J. H. E., and J. C. Dewhurst (eds.), *Quarter Sessions Records. County Palatine of Chester, 1559–1760*, Record Soc. of Lancashire and Cheshire, 94 (1940).

Berland, K., *et al.* (eds.), *The Commonplace Book of William Byrd II of Westover, Virginia* (Chapel Hill, NC, 2001).

Bernard, Richard, *Joshua's Godly Resolution in Conference with Caleb touching Household Government for well Ordering a Family* (London, 1612).

Bird, J. B., *The Laws respecting Masters and Servants* (London, 1795).

Blackstone, William, *Commentaries on the Laws of England* (Oxford, 1765–69).

Braithwaite, Richard, *The Turtles Triumph* (London, 1641).

Brinkworth, E. R. C. (ed.) *The Bawdy Court of Banbury. The Act Book of the Peculiar Court of Banbury, Oxfordshire and Northamptonshire, 1525–1638*, Banbury Historical Soc., 26 (1997).

— *Shakespeare and the Bawdy Court of Stratford* (Chichester, 1972).

Broughton, Thomas, *A Serious and Affectionate Warning to Servants . . . occasioned by the Shameful and Untimely Death of Matthew Henderson . . .* (London, 1746).

Bunyan, John, *Christian Behaviour* (London, 1663).

Burn, Richard, *History of the Poor Laws* (London, 1764).

Burnett, J. (ed.), *Useful Toil. Autobiographies of Working People from the 1820s to the 1920s* (London, 1974).

Butler, C. V., *Domestic Service. An Enquiry by the Women's Industrial Council* (London, 1916).

Carter, Thomas, *Christian Commonwealth* (London, 1627).

Chamberlain, C., *The Servant Girl of the Period, or, The Greatest Plague of Life* (New York, 1873).

Chapone, Hester, *Letters on the Improvement of the Mind, addressed to a Young Lady* (Dublin, 1773).

Clark, Gillian (ed.), *Correspondence of the Foundling Hospital Inspectors in Berkshire*, Berkshire Record Soc., I (1994).

Cleaver, Robert, *Godly Forme of Household Government* (London, 1598).

Clemit, P. (ed.), *Political and Philosophical Writings of William Godwin*, V, *Educational and Literary Writings* (London, 1993).

Clemsell, Richard, *A Pleasant New Dialogue, or, The Discourse between the Servingman and the Husbandman* (London, c. 1635).

Cobbett, William, *Journal of a Year's Residence in the United States of America* (London, 1819, repr. Stroud, 1983).

Cockburn, J. S. (ed.), *Western Circuit Assize Orders, 1629–1648*, Camden Soc., 4th ser., 17 (1976).

Collier, Mary, *Poems on Several Occasions* (Winchester, 1762).

— *The Woman's Labour* (London, 1739). See Thompson, E. P.

Colvin, H., and J. Newman (eds.), *Of Building. Roger North's Writings on Architecture* (Oxford, 1981).

Cooper, J. P. (ed.), *Wentworth Papers, 1597–1628*, Camden Soc., 4th ser., 12 (1973).

Cullwick, Hannah, *Diaries of Hannah Cullwick, Victorian Maidservant*, ed. Liz Stanley (London, 1984).

Cust, R. (ed.), *The Papers of Sir Richard Grosvenor, first Baronet, 1585–1645*, Record Soc. of Lancashire and Cheshire, 134 (1996).

Dalton, M., *The Countrey Justice* (London, 1677).

D'Archenholz, M. D., *A Picture of England* (Dublin, 1791).

Dare, Josiah, *Counsellor Manners his last Legacy to his Son* (London, 1710).

Defoe, Daniel, *Everybody's Business is Nobody's Business* (4th edn., London, 1725).

— *The Family Instructor* (15th edn., London, 1761).

— *The Great Law of Subordination Considered* (London, 1724).

— *Religious Courtship* (London, 1722, 10th edn., 1796).

Dent, Arthur, *The Plain Mans Pathway to Heaven* (London, 1612).

de Saussure, César, *A Foreign View of England in 1725–1729. Letters of César de Saussure*, ed. Mme van Muyden (London, 1992, 1995).

Ditchfield, G. M. and B. Keith-Lucas (eds.), *A Kentish Parson. Selections from the Private Papers of the Rev. Joseph Price, Vicar of Brabourne, 1776–1786* (Stroud, 1991).

Dodsley, Robert, *The Economy of Human Life* (London, 1750).

— *The Muse in Livery, or, The Footman's Miscellany* (London, 1732).

— *Servitude: a Poem* (London, 1729).

— *The Toy Shop* (London, 1735).

Downame, John, *A Guide to Godlynesse* (London, 1629).

Duck, Stephen, *The Thresher's Labour* (London, 1730). See Thompson, E. P.

Edelen, G. (ed.), *The Description of England, by William Harrison* (Washington, DC, and New York, 1994).

Evelyn, John, *Memoirs for my Grandson* (London, 1926).

Etherege, George, *Dramatic Works*, ed. H. F. B. Brett-Smith (2 vols., Oxford, 1927).

Farquar, George, *Plays* ed. W. Archer (London, 1949).

Fielding, Henry, *Enquiry into the late Increase of Robbers* (London, 1751).

— *The Intriguing Chambermaid* (London, 1734).

— *A Plan of the Universal Register Office* (London, 1751, repr. Middletown, CT, 1988).

Fielding, John, *Extracts from such of the Penal Laws as particularly relate to the Peace and good Order of this Metropolis* (new edn., London, 1768).

Firth, C. H. (ed.), *The Life of William Cavendish, Duke of Newcastle* (London, 1886).

Fleetwood, William, *Relative Duties of Parents, Children, Husbands, Wives, Masters, Servants* (London, 1705).

Fletcher, John, *The Elder Brother* (London, 1637), ed. W. H. Draper (Cambridge, 1915).

Floyd, Thomas, *The Picture of a Perfit Commonwealth* (London, 1600).

Fosset, Thomas, *The Servants Dutie, or, The Calling and Condition of Servants* (London, 1613).

Fox, L. (ed.), 'Diary of Robert Beake, Mayor of Coventry, 1656–1657', in R. Bearman (ed.), Dugdale Soc., *Miscellany*, I (1977).

Franklin, R., *A Murderer Punished and Pardoned, or, A True Relation of the Wicked Life and Shamefull, Happy Death of Thomas Savage* . . . (London, 1668).

Fuller, Thomas, *History of the Worthies of England* (London, 1662).

Garrick, David, *Bon Ton, or, High Life above Stairs* (London, 1776).

— *The Lying Valet* (London, 1741).

Gataker, T., *Marriage Duties* (London, 1620).

Gibson, D. (ed.), *A Parson in the Vale of White Horse. George Woodward's Letters from East Hendred, 1753–1756* (Stroud, 1982).

Gibson, Edmund, *Family Devotion* (London, 1726).

Gibson, J. S. W., and E. R. C. Brinkworth (eds.), *Banbury Corporation Records*, Banbury Historical Soc., 15 (1977).

Glass, D. V. (ed.), *London Inhabitants within the Walls, 1695*, London Record Soc., 2 (1966).

Goodwin, Philip, *Family Religion Revived* (London, 1655).

Gosse, E. (ed.), *Restoration Plays, from Dryden to Farquar* (London, 1912, 1925).

Grey, Oliver (pseud. James Townley), *An Apology for the Servants* (London, 1760).

Griffith, Matthew, *Bethel or a Forme for Families* (London, 1633).

Groseley, M., *A Tour to London* (3 vols., London, 1772).

Hair, P. (ed.) *Before the Bawdy Court* (London, 1972).

Hallen, A. W. C. (ed.), *The Account Book of Sir John Foulis of Ravelston, 1671–1707*, Scottish Historical Soc., 16 (Edinburgh, 1894).

Hands, Elizabeth, *'The Death of Amnon. A Poem', with an Appendix containing Pastorals and other Poetical Pieces* (Coventry, 1789).

Hanway, Jonas, *Eight Letters to his Grace the Duke of — — on the Custom of Vails giving in England* (London, 1760).

— *The Sentiments and Advice of Thomas Trueman, a Virtuous and Understanding Footman* (London, 1760).

Harrington, H., *Nugae Antiguae* (London, 1775).

Harrison, G. B. (ed.), *Advice to his Son, by Henry Percy, ninth Earl of Northumberland* (1609, repr. London, 1930).

Haywood, Eliza, *A Present for a Serving Maid* (London, 1744).

Heasel, Anthony, *The Servants' Book of Knowledge* (London, 1773).

Heltzel, V. B. (ed.), *'Richard of Carbery's advice to his son'*, *Huntington Library Bulletin*, 11 (1937).

Hendley, W., *A Defence of the Charity Schools* (London, 1725).

Herbert, George, *The Elixir* (1633), in C. L. Martz (ed.), *George Herbert/Henry Vaughan*, Oxford Authors (Oxford, 1986).

Hilder, T., *Conjugall Counsell* (London, 1653).

Hinde, William, *A Faithfull Remonstrance of the Holy Life and Happy Death of John Bruen, of Bruen Stapleford, in the County of Chester, Esq.* (London, 1641).

Hitchcock, T., and J. Black (eds.), *Chelsea Settlement and Bastardy Examinations, 1733–1766*, London Record Soc., 33 (1999).

Hobbes, Thomas, *'Of masters and servants'*, in F. O. Wolf (ed.), *Die neue Wissenschaft des Thomas Hobbes* (Stuttgart, 1969).

Hood, Margaret J., *Borough Sessions Papers, 1653–1688*, Portsmouth Record ser., I (1971).

Hughes, Anne, *Diary of a Farmer's Wife, 1796–1797* (Harmondsworth, 1964, 1980, 1981).

Huntingford, John, *The Laws of Masters and Servants considered . . . to which is added an Account of a Society for the Increase and Encouragement of good Servants* (London, 1790).

Irons, W. J., *The Christian Servants' Book* (London, 1849).

Jackson, Abraham, *The Pious Prentice* (London, 1640).

Janeway, James, *Duties of Masters and Servants* (London, 1676, 2nd edn. 1726).

Jessopp, A. (ed.), *The Lives of the Norths* (3 vols., London, 1890).

Jones, Charles, *The History of Charles Jones, Footman, written by Himself* (London, 1797).

Jones, Erasmus, *The Man of Manners, or, The Plebeian Polished* (London, 1737).

Kitchiner, W., *The Housekeeper's Oracle* (London, 1829).

Leapor, Mary, *The Works of Mary Leapor*, ed. R. Greene and Ann Messenger (Oxford, 2003).

Locke, John, *Some Thoughts concerning Education* (London, 1693).

Lucas, J. (ed.), *Kalm's Account of his Visit to England on his Way to America* (London, 1892).

Lucas, Richard, *The Duty of Servants* (London, 1685).

McCormick, I. (ed.), *Secret Sexualities. A Sourcebook of Seventeenth and Eighteenth-Century Writing* (London, 1997).

MacDonald, John, *Travels in Various Parts of Europe, Asia and Africa* (London, 1790).

Malcolm, J. P., *Anecdotes of the Manners and Customs of London during the Eighteenth Century* (2nd edn., 2 vols., London, 1810).

Mandeville, Bernard, *The Fable of the Bees* (London, 1729), ed. P. Harth (Harmondsworth, 1970).

Marshall, J. D. (ed.), *The Autobiography of William Stout of Lancaster, 1665–1752*, Chetham Soc., 3rd ser., 14 (1967).

Martineau, Harriet, 'Modern domestic service', *Edinburgh Review*, 115 (1862).

Mather, Cotton, *A Good Master well Served* (Boston, MA, 1696).

Matthews, W. (ed.), *The Diary of Dudley Ryder, 1715–1716* (London, 1939).

Mayhew, Augustus, *The Greatest Plague of Life, or, The Adventures of a Lady in Search of a Servant* (London, 1847).

Mayo, Richard, *A Present for Servants* (London, 1693).

Mitchell, L. G. (ed.), *The Purefoy Letters, 1735–1753* (London, 1973).

Munby, A. J. (ed.), *Faithful Servants, being Epitaphs and Obituaries recording their Names and Services* (London, 1891).

Paley, R. (ed.), *Justice in Eighteenth-Century Hackney. The Justicing Book of Henry Norris and the Hackney Petty Sessions Book*, London Record Soc., 27 (1991).

Parkinson, R. (ed.), *The Life of Adam Martindale*, Chetham Soc., 4 (1845).

Peel, Mrs C. S., *Waiting at Table. A Practical Guide* (London, 1929).

Pennington, Lady Sarah, *An Unfortunate Mother's Advice to her absent Daughters* (London, 1761).

Perkins, William, *Christian Oeconomie* (London, 1590).

Reynolds, E. E. (ed.), *The Mawhood Diary. Selections from the Diary Notebooks of William Mawhood, Woollen Draper, of London, 1764–1790*, Catholic Record Soc., 50 (1956).

Richardson, Samuel, *The Apprentice's Vade Mecum* (London, 1734), Augustan Soc. repr. 169/70 (London, 1975).

— *Pamela* (London, 1740), ed. P. Sabor, with an introduction by Margaret A. Doody (Harmondsworth, 1980, 1985).

Riley, E. M. (ed.), *The Journal of John Harrower, an Indentured Servant in the Colony of Virginia, 1773–1776* (Williamsburg, VA, 1963).

Rosenheim, J. M. (ed.), *The Notebook of Robert Doughty, 1662–1665*, Norfolk Record Soc., 54 (1989).

Rushworth, John, *Historical Collections* (London, 1659).

Savile, George, Marquess of Halifax, *The Ladies New Year Gift, or, Advice to a Daughter* (London, 1688).

Saville, A. (ed.), *Secret Comment. The Diaries of Gertrude Savile, 1721–1757*, Thoroton Soc., 41 (1997).

Scott, John, *Observations on the Present State of the Parochial and Vagrant Poor* (London, 1773).

Scott-Moncrieff, R. (ed.), *The Household Book of Lady Grisell Baillie, 1692–1733*, Scottish History Soc., new ser., 1 (1911).

Seaton, Thomas, *The Conduct of Servants in Great Families* (London, 1700).

Shakespeare, William, *As you like it.*

— *King Lear.*

— *The Taming of the Shrew.*

— *Twelfth Night.*

Silverthorne, Elizabeth (ed.), *Deposition Book of Richard Wyatt, JP, 1767–1776*, Surrey Record Soc., 30 (1978).

Smith, Adam, *An Inquiry into the Nature and Causes of the Wealth of Nations* (London, 1776).

Smith, W. J. (ed.), *Herbert Correspondence . . .* , Board of Celtic Studies, University of Wales History and Law series, 21 (Cardiff, 1968, 1998).

Sokoll, F. (ed.), *Essex Pauper Letters, 1731–1837*, British Academy Records of Social and Economic History, new ser., 20 (Cambridge, 2001).

Southey, Robert, *Lives and Works of the Uneducated Poets* (London, 1925).

The Spectator, ed. G. G. Smith (4 vols., London, 1907).

Stokes, F. G. (ed.), *The Blechley Diary of the Rev William Cole, 1765–1767* (London, 1931).

Storey, M. (ed.), *Two East Anglian Diaries, 1641–1729. Isaac Archer and William Coe*, Suffolk Record Soc., 36 (1994).

Streeten, J. W. (ed.), *Epitaphia, or, A Collection of Memorials inscribed to the Memory of Good and Faithful Servants* (London, 1826).

Strutt, E., *Practical Wisdom, or, The Manual of Life. The Counsels of Eminent Men to their Children* (London, 1824).

Stubb, Henry, trans. G. della Casa, *The Arts of Grandeur and Submission* (London, 1665).

Swift, Jonathan, *Directions to Servants* (Dublin, 1745).

Swinnock, George, *The Christian Man's Calling* (London, 1668).

Tancred, Christopher, *A Scheme for an Act of Parliament for the better Regulating of Servants* (London, 1724).

Tawney, R. H., and Eileen Power (eds.), *Tudor Economic Documents*, I (London, 1924).

Tayler, William, *Diary of William Tayler, Footman, 1837*, ed. Dorothy Wise (London, 1962, 1998).

Taylor, Ann, *The Present of a Mistress to a Young Servant* (10th ed., 1832).

Thompson, E. P., and Marian Sugden (eds.), *The Thresher's Labour, by Stephen Duck, and The Woman's Labour, by Mary Collier. Two Eighteenth-Century Poems* (London, 1989).

Thompson, S. (ed.), *The Journal of John Gabriel Stedman* (London, 1962).

Tierney, J. E. (ed.), *The Correspondence of Robert Dodsley, 1733–1764* (Cambridge, 1988).

Tilley, M. P. (ed.), *A Dictionary of the Proverbs in England in the Sixteenth and Seventeenth Centuries* (Ann Arbor, MI, 1950).

Townley, James, *High Life below Stairs* (London, 1759).

Trenchfield, Caleb, *A Cap of Gray Hairs* (London, 1671).

Trimmer, Sarah, *Reflections upon the Education of Children in Charity Schools* (London, 1792).

True Confession of Margaret Clark, who consented to the Burning of her Master's House in Southwark (London, 1680).

A True Copy of the Paper delivered the Night before her Execution by Sarah Malcolm . . . (London, 1733).

Trusler, John, *London Adviser and Guide* (London, 1786).

Tyndale, William, *The Obedience of a Christian Man* (London, 1528).

Tyrer, F. (ed.), *The Great Diurnal of Nicholas Blundell, 1702–1728*, Record Soc. of Lancashire and Cheshire (3 vols., 1968–72).

Vaisey, D. (ed.), *The Diary of Thomas Turner, 1754–1765* (Oxford, 1984, repr. East Hoathly, 1994).

Vanbrugh, John, *The Complete Works*, ed. B. Dobrée and G. Webb (London, 1927).

— *The Relapse*, ed. C. A. Zimansky (London, 1970).

Verney, Frances P. (ed.), *Memoirs of the Verney Family during the Civil War* (4 vols., London, 1892).

Von Kielmansegge, Count Friedrich, *Diary of a Journey to England in the years 1761–1762* (London, 1902).

Wake, Joan, and Deborah C. Webster (eds.), *The Letters of Daniel Eaton to the third Earl of Cardigan, 1725–1732*, Northamptonshire Record Soc., 24 (1971).

Watkins, H. G., *Hints and Observations seriously addressed to Heads of Families in reference chiefly to female Domestic Servants* (London, 1816).

Whately, William, *Prototypes* (London, 1640).

Whitford, R., *A Work for Householders* (London, 1531).

Whitney, Isabella, *A Sweet Nosegay* (London, 1573).

Willis, A. J. (ed.), *Winchester Consistory Depositions, 1561–1602* (Winchester, 1960).

Willis Bund, J. W. (ed.), *Worcestershire County Records. Calendar of Quarter Sessions Papers, 1591–1643* (Worcester, 1900).

Woodforde, James, *Diary of a Country Parson*, ed. J. Beresford (5 vols., London, 1931, repr. 1981).

Woodward, D. (ed.), *The Farming and Account Books of Henry Best, of Elmswell*, British Academy Records of Social and Economic History, new ser., 8 (Cambridge, 1984).

Woolley, Hannah, *The Gentlewoman's Companion, or, A Guide to the Female Sex* (London, 1673).

Yearsley, Ann, *Poems on Various Subjects, 1787*, ed. J. Wordsworth (Oxford, 1994).

Yorke, P. C. (ed.), *The Diary of John Baker* (London, 1931).

Yorke, Philip, *Crude Ditties* (Wrexham, 1802).

SECONDARY SOURCES

Addison, W., *Essex Heyday* (London, 1949).

Anderson, Linda, *A Place in the Story. Servants and Service in Shakespeare's Plays* (Newark, DE, 2005).

Bailey, Joanne, *Unquiet Lives. Marriage and Marriage Breakdown in England, 1660–1800* (Cambridge, 2003).

Belasco, P., 'Notes on the labour exchange idea in the seventeenth century', *Economic History Supplement to the Economic Journal*, I (1926–29).

Ben-Amos, Ilana K., *Adolescence and Youth in Early Modern England* (New Haven, CT, and London, 1994).

Berkowitz, G. M., *Sir John Vanbrugh and the End of Restoration Comedy* (Amsterdam, 1981).

Berry, Helen, and Elizabeth Foyster (eds.), *The Family in Early Modern England* (Cambridge, 2007).

Burke, P., *Popular Culture in Early Modern Europe* (New York, 1978).

Borsay, P., *The English Urban Renaissance. Culture and Society in the Provincial Town, 1660–1770* (Oxford, 1989).

Botelho, Lynn, and Pat Thane (eds.), *Women and Ageing in British Society since 1500* (Harlow, 2001).

Bowen, Dorothy, 'Thomas Mort of Dam House', *Huntington Library Quarterly*, 8 (1944–45).

Braddick, M., *God's Fury England's Fire. A New History of the English Civil Wars* (London, 2008).

Brown, Kathleen M., *Good Wives, Nasty Wenches and Anxious Patriarchs. Gender, Race and Power in Colonial Virginia* (Chapel Hill, NC, 1996).

Burnett, M. T., *Masters and Servants in English Renaissance Drama and Culture* (London, 1997).

Capp, B., *When Gossips Meet. Women, Family and Neighbourhood in Early Modern England* (Oxford, 2003).

Carlton, C., *Going to the Wars. The Experience of the British Civil Wars, 1638–1651* (London, 1992).

Christmas, W. J., *The Lab'ring Muses. Work, Writing and the Social Order in English Plebeian Poetry, 1730–1830* (Newark, DE, 2001).

Clark, Alice, *Working Life of Women in the Seventeenth Century* (London, 1919).

Clark, P., *The English Alehouse. A Social History, 1200–1830* (Harlow, 1983).

Cliffe, J. T., *The World of the Country House in Seventeenth-Century England* (London, 1999).

Coates, B., *The Impact of the English Civil War on the Economy of London, 1642–1650* (Aldershot, 2004).

Cobb, R., *The French and their Revolution*, ed. D. Gilmour (London, 1998).

Cockayne, Emily, *Hubbub. Filth, Noise and Stench in England, 1600–1770* (New Haven, CT, and London, 2007).

Cressy, D., *England on Edge. Crisis and Revolution, 1640–1642* (Oxford, 2006).

— *Travesties and Transgressions in Tudor and Stuart England* (Oxford, 2000).

Dabydeen, D., *Hogarth's Blacks. Images of Blacks in Eighteenth-Century English Art* (Manchester, 1987).

Dawson, M. S., *Gentility and the Comic Theatre of late Stuart London* (Cambridge, 2005).

Dennison, E. Patricia, *et al.* (eds.), *Aberdeen before 1800. A New History* (East Linton, 2002).

Dingwall, Helen, *Late Seventeenth-Century Edinburgh. A Demographic Study* (Aldershot, 1994).

Downes, K., *Sir John Vanbrugh. A Biography* (London, 1987).

Duffy, E., *The Voices of Morebath. Reformation and Rebellion in an English Village* (New Haven, CT, and London, 2001, 2003).

Durston, C., *The Family in the English Revolution* (Oxford, 1989).

Dutton, R., *A Hampshire Manor. Hinton Ampner* (London, 1968, 1988).

Dyer, C., and Catherine Richardson (eds.), *William Dugdale, Historian, 1605–1686. His Life, his Writings, and his County* (Woodbridge, 2009).

Eales, Jacqueline, *Puritans and Roundheads. The Harleys of Brampton Bryan and the Outbreak of the English Civil War* (Cambridge, 1990).

Earle, P., *The Making of the English Middle Class. Business, Society and Family Life in London, 1660–1730* (London, 1989).

Elwin, M., *The Noels and the Milbankes. Letters for Twenty-five Years, 1767–1792* (London, 1967).

Ewan, Elizabeth, 'Mistresses of themselves? Female domestic servants and by-employments in sixteenth-century Scottish towns', in Fauve-Chamoux, *Domestic Service*, q.v.

Fairchilds, Cissie, *Domestic Enemies. Servants and their Masters in Old Regime France* (Baltimore, MD, 1984).

Fairfax-Lucy, Alice, *Charlecote and the Lucys* (Oxford, 1958).

Faraday, M., *Ludlow, 1085–1660. A Social, Economic and Political History* (Chichester, 1991).

Fauve-Chamoux, Antoinette (ed.), *Domestic Service and the Formation of European Identity. Understanding the Globalization of Domestic Work, Sixteenth to Twenty-first Centuries* (Berne, 2004).

Ferguson, Moira, *Eighteenth-Century Women Poets. Nation, Class and Gender* (New York, 1993).

Flather, Amanda, *Gender and Space in Early Modern England* (Woodbridge, 2007).

— *The Politics of Place. A Study of Church Seating in Essex, c. 1580–1640*, Friends of the Department of English Local History, University of Leicester, Papers, 3 (Leicester, 1999).

Fletcher, A., *Gender, Sex and Subordination in England, 1500–1800* (New Haven, CT, and London, 1995).

Foyster, Elizabeth, *Marital Violence. An English Family History* (Cambridge, 2005).

Froide, Amy M., *Never Married. Single Women in Early Modern England* (Oxford, 2005).

Galenson, D., *White Servitude in Colonial America. An Economic Analysis* (Cambridge, 1981).

George, M. Dorothy, 'The early history of registry offices', *Economic History Supplement to the Economic Journal*, I (1929).

— *London Life in the Eighteenth Century* (London, 1925).

Gerzina, Gretchen, *Black England. Life before Emancipation* (London, 1995).

Gilboy, Elizabeth W., *Wages in Eighteenth-Century England* (Cambridge, MA, 1934).

Gowing, Laura, *Common Bodies. Women, Touch and Power in Seventeenth-Century England* (New Haven, CT, and London, 2003).

— *Domestic Dangers. Women, Words and Sex in Early Modern London* (Oxford, 1996).

— 'Secret births and infanticide in seventeenth-century England', *Past & Present*, 156 (1997).

Green, I. A., *The Christian's ABC. Catechisms and Catechising in England, 1530–1740* (Oxford, 1996).

Greene, R., *Mary Leapor. A Study in Eighteenth-Century Women's Poetry* (Oxford, 1993).

Griffiths, P., *Youth and Authority. Formative Experiences in England, 1560–1640* (Oxford, 1996).

— Fox, A., and S. Hindle (eds.), *The Experience of Authority in Early Modern England* (London, 1996).

Gunter, R. T. (ed.), *The Architecture of Sir Roger Pratt* (Oxford, 1928).

Habib, I., *Black Lives in the English Archives, 1500–1677. Imprints of the Invisible* (London, 2008).

Hay, D., 'Master and servant in England: using the law in the eighteenth and nineteenth centuries', in W. Steinmetz (ed.), *Private Law and Social*

Inequality in the Industrial Age. Legal Cultures in Britain, France, Germany, and the United States (Oxford, 2000).

Gurr, A., *Playgoing in Shakespeare's London* (3rd edn., Cambridge, 2004).

Hackel, Heidi Brayman, *Reading Material in Early Modern England. Print, Gender and Literacy* (Cambridge, 2005).

Harris, T. (ed.), *Popular Culture in England, c. 1500–1800* (London, 1995).

Harrison, B., 'The servants of William Gossip', *Georgian Group Journal*, 6 (1996).

Hecht, J. J., 'Continental and colonial servants in eighteenth-century England', *Smith College Studies in History*, 40 (Northampton, MA, 1954).

— *The Domestic Servant Class in Eighteenth-Century England* (London, 1956, repr. Westport, CT, 1981).

Herrup, Cynthia, *A House in Gross Disorder. Sex, Law and the Second Earl of Castlehaven* (Oxford, 1999).

Hill, Bridget, *Servants. English Domestics of the Eighteenth Century* (Oxford, 1996).

— *Women Alone. Spinsters in England, 1660–1850* (New Haven, CT, and London, 2001).

Hill, C., *Society and Puritanism in Pre-revolutionary England* (London, 1964).

Hindle, S., *On the Parish? The Micro-politics of Poor Relief in Rural England, c. 1550–1750* (Oxford, 2004).

Hitchcock, T., *et al.* (eds), *Chronicling Poverty. The Voices and Strategies of the English Poor, 1640–1840* (London, 1997).

— *Down and Out in Eighteenth-Century London* (London, 2004).

Hoffer, P. C., and N. E. H. Hull, *Murdering Mothers. Infanticide in England and New England, 1558–1803* (New York, 1984).

Holmes, Jane, 'Domestic Service in Yorkshire, 1650–1780', D.Phil. thesis, University of York, 1989.

Horn, Pamela, *Flunkies and Scullions. Life below Stairs in Georgian England* (Stroud, 2004).

— *Life below Stairs in the Twentieth Century* (Stroud, 2001).

— *The Rise and Fall of the Victorian Servant* (London, 1975).

Houlbrooke, R., *The English Family, 1450–1700* (London, 1984).

Houston, R. A., *Social Change in the Age of the Enlightenment. Edinburgh, 1660–1760* (Oxford, 1994).

Hudson, D., *Munby, Man of two Worlds* (London, 1972).

Hufton, Olwen, *The Prospect before Her. A History of Women in Western Europe, 1500–1800* (London, 1995).

Hughes, Ann, *Gangraena and the Struggle for the English Revolution* (Oxford, 2004).

Ingram, M., *Church Courts, Sex and Marriage in England, 1570–1640* (Cambridge, 1987).

— 'The reform of popular culture: sex and marriage in early modern England', in B. Reay (ed.), *Popular Culture in Seventeenth-Century England* (London, 1985).

Jackson, M., *Newborn Child Murder. Women, Illegitimacy and the Courts in Eighteenth-Century England* (Manchester, 1996).

Jardine, Lisa, *On a Grander Scale. The Outstanding Career of Sir Christopher Wren* (London, 2002).

Jarrett, D., *England in the Age of Hogarth* (London, 1974, 1986).

Kachur, Barbara A., *Etherege and Wycherley* (Basingstoke, 2004).

Ketton-Cremer, R. W., *Felbrigg. The Story of a House* (1962, London, 1986).

Kilday, Anne Marie, 'Maternal monsters: murdering mothers in south-west Scotland, 1750–1815', in Yvonne G. Brown and Rona Ferguson (eds.), *Twisted Sisters. Women, Crime and Deviance in Scotland since 1400* (East Linton, 2002).

King, S., and A. Tompkins (eds.), *The Poor in England, 1700–1850. An Economy of Makeshifts* (Manchester, 2003).

Klaus, H. Gustav, *The Literature of Labour. Two Hundred Years of Working Class Writing* (Brighton, 1985).

Kugler, Anne, *Errant Plagiary. The Life and Writing of Lady Sarah Cowper, 1644–1720* (Stanford, CA, 2002).

Kussmaul, Ann, *Servants in Husbandry in Early Modern England* (Oxford, 1981).

Landry, Donna, *The Muses of Resistance. Laboring Class Women's Poetry in Britain, 1739–1796* (Cambridge, 1990).

Langford, P., 'The uses of eighteenth-century politeness', *TRHS*, 6th ser., 12 (2002).

Laslett, P., *The World we have Lost* (London, 1965, 1983).

Laurence, Anne, *Women in England, 1500–1760* (New York, 1994).

Light, Alison, *Mrs Woolf and the Servants. The Hidden Heart of Domestic Service* (London, 2007).

Lindley, K., *Popular Politics and Religion in Civil War London* (Aldershot, 1997).

Linebaugh, P., *The London Hanged. Crime and Society in the Eighteenth Century* (London, 1991).

— 'The Ordinary of Newgate and his *Account*', in J. S. Cockburn (ed.), *Crime in England, 1550–1800* (London, 1977).

Loftis, J., *et al.* (eds.), *The Revels History of Drama in English*, V, *1660–1750* (London, 1976).

Macfarlane, A., *The Family Life of Ralph Josselin, a Seventeenth-Century Clergyman* (Cambridge, 1970).

Maître et serviteur dans le monde anglo-americain aux XVII et XVIII siècles (Rouen, 1986).

Marcombe, D., *English Small Town life. Retford, 1520–1642* (Nottingham, 1993).

Marshall, Dorothy, *The English Domestic Servant in History*, Historical Association pamphlet G13 (London, 1949).

— 'The domestic servants of the eighteenth century', *Economica* 9 (1929).

— *The English Poor in the Eighteenth Century* (London, 1926, repr. 1969).

Maza, Sarah, *Servants and Masters in Old Regime France* (Princeton, NJ, 1983).

McBride, Kari Boyd (ed.), *Domestic Arrangements in Early Modern England* (Pittsburgh, PA, 2002).

McCormick, F., *Sir John Vanbrugh. The Playwright as Architect* (University Park, PA, 1991).

McIntosh, Marjorie K., *Working Women in English Society, 1300–1620* (Cambridge, 2005).

Meldrum, T., *Domestic Service and Gender, 1660–1750* (Harlow, 2000).

Mendelson, Sara, and Patricia Crawford, *Women in Early Modern England, 1550–1720* (Oxford, 1998).

Merritt, J. F., *The Social World of Early Modern Westminster. Abbey, Court and Community, 1525–1640* (Manchester, 2005).

Mesick, Jane Louise, *The English Traveller in America, 1785–1835* (New York, 1922, repr. Westport, CT, 1970).

Moore, Wendy, *Wedlock* (London, 2009).

Morgan, E. S., *The Puritan Family* (Boston, MA, 1944, new edn. New York, 1966).

Mortlock, D. P., *Aristocratic Splendour. Money and the World of Thomas Coke, Earl of Leicester* (Stroud, 2007).

Neil, M. (ed.), Special section, 'Shakespeare and the Bonds of Service', in *The Shakespearean International Yearbook* (Aldershot, 2005).

Neile, R. S., *Bath. A Social History, 1680–1850* (London, 1981).

Norman, F. A., and L. G. Lee, 'A further note on labour exchanges in the seventeenth century', *Economic History Supplement to Economic Journal*, I (1928).

Norton, Mary Beth, *Founding Mothers and Fathers. Gendered Power and the Forming of American Society* (New York, 1996).

Owen, Susan J. (ed.), *A Companion to Restoration Drama* (Oxford, 2001).

— *Perspectives on Restoration Drama* (Manchester, 2002).

Platt, C., *The Great Rebuilding of Tudor and Stuart England* (London, 1994).

Porter, S., *Destruction in the English Civil Wars* (Stroud, 1994).

— (ed.), *London and the Civil War* (London, 1996).

Postles, D. A., *Social Proprieties. Social Relations in Early Modern England, 1500–1680* (Washington, DC, 2006).

Priestley, U., and Penelope Corfield, 'Rooms and room use in Norwich housing, 1580–1730', *Post-medieval Archaeology*, 16 (1982).

Purkiss, Diane, *The English Civil War. A People's History* (London, 2006).

Quaife, G. R., *Wanton Wenches and Wayward Wives. Peasants and illicit Sex in early Seventeenth-Century England* (London, 1979).

Reay, B. (ed.), *Popular Culture in Seventeenth-Century England* (London, 1985).

— *The Quakers and the English Revolution* (London, 1985).

Richardson, R. C., *Puritanism in North-west England. A Regional Study of the Diocese of Chester to 1642* (Manchester, 1972).

— 'The generation gap: parental advice in early modern England', *Clio*, 32:1 (2002).

— 'Social engineering in early modern England: masters, servants and the godly discipline', *Clio*, 33:2 (2004).

Rinebaugh, P., and M. Rediker, *The Many-headed Hydra. Sailors, Slaves, Commoners and the hidden History of the Revolutionary Atlantic* (London, 2000).

Sackville-West, Vita, *Knole and the Sackvilles* (London, 1931).

Salinger, Sharon V., *'To serve well and faithfully'. Labor and Indentured Servants in Pennsylvania, 1682–1800* (Cambridge, 1987).

Sambrook, Pamela, *A Country House at Work. Three Centuries of Dunham Massey* (London, 2003).

— *The Country House Servant* (Stroud, 1999).

— *Keeping their Place. Domestic Service in the Country House* (Stroud, 2005).

Schama, S., *The Embarrassment of Riches. An Interpretation of Dutch Culture in the Golden Age* (New York and London, 1987).

Schochet, G. J., *Patriarchalism in Political Thought . . . in Seventeenth-Century England* (Oxford, 1975).

Schucking, L. L., *The Puritan Family* (1929, English trans. London, 1969).

Schwarz, L., 'English servants and their employers during the eighteenth and nineteenth centuries', *Economic History Review*, 52 (1999).

Seaver, P. S., *Wallington's World. A Puritan Artisan in Seventeenth-Century London* (London, 1985).

Seleski, Patty, 'Women, work and cultural change in eighteenth and early nineteenth-century London', in T. Harris (ed.), *Popular Culture in England, c. 1500–1850* (Basingstoke, 1995).

Sharpe, J. A., '"Last dying speeches": religion, ideology and public execution in seventeenth-century England', *Past & Present*, 107 (1985).

Sharpe, Pamela, *Population and Society in an East Devon Parish. Reproducing Colyton, 1540–1840* (Exeter, 2002).

— (ed.), *Women's Work. The English Experience, 1650–1914* (London, 1998).

Slater, Miriam, *Family Life in the Seventeenth Century. The Verneys of Claydon House* (London, 1984).

Snape, M., *The Church in an Industrial Society. The Lancashire Parish of Whalley in the Eighteenth Century* (Woodbridge, 2003).

Snell, K. D., *Parish and Belonging. Community, Identity and Welfare in England and Wales, 1700–1950* (Cambridge, 2006).

Somerville, Margaret R., *Sex and Subjection. Attitudes to Women in Early Modern Society* (London, 1995).

Souden, D., 'Migrants and the population structure of later seventeenth-century English provincial cities and market towns', in P. Clark (ed.), *The Transformation of English Provincial Towns* (London, 1984).

Spacks, Patricia Meyer, *Privacy. Concealing the Eighteenth Century Self* (Chicago, 2003).

Spufford, Margaret, *Small Books and Pleasant Histories. Popular Fiction and its Readership in Seventeenth-Century England* (London, 1981).

Staves, Susan, *A Literary History of Women's Writing in Britain, 1660–1789* (Cambridge, 2006).

Steedman, Carolyn, 'Lord Mansfield's Women', *Past & Present*, 176 (2002).

— *Master and Servant. Love and Labour in the English Industrial Age* (Cambridge, 2007).

Stone, L., *Broken Lives. Separation and Divorce in England, 1660–1837* (Oxford, 1993).

— *The Family, Sex and Marriage in England 1500–1800* (London, 1977).

— *The Road to Divorce. England, 1530–1987* (Oxford, 1990).

— *Uncertain Unions. Marriage in England, 1660–1753* (Oxford, 1992).

— and Stone, Jeanne C. Fawtier, *An Open Elite? England, 1540–1880* (Oxford, 1984).

Stuart, Dorothy Margaret, *The English Abigail* (London, 1946).

Styles, J., 'Involuntary consumers? Servants and their clothes in eighteenth-century England', *Textile History*, 33 (2002).

Tadmor, Naiomi, *Family and Friends in Eighteenth-Century England* (Cambridge, 2001).

Thirsk, Joan, *Food in Early Modern England. Phases, Fads and Fashions, 1500–1760* (London, 2007).

Thomas, D., *William Congreve* (London, 1992).

Thomson, Gladys Scott, *Life in a Noble Household, 1641–1700* (London, 1937).

— *The Russells in Bloomsbury, 1669–1771* (London, 1940).

Todd, Selina, 'Domestic service and class relations in Britain, 1900–1950', *Past & Present*, 203 (2009), 181–204.

Turner, D. M., *Fashioning Adultery. Gender, Sex and Civility in England, 1660–1740* (Cambridge, 2002).

Turner, E., 'On the domestic habits and mode of life of a Sussex gentleman', *Sussex Archaeological Collections*, 23 (1871).

Turner, E. S., *What the Butler saw. Two Hundred and Fifty Years of the Servant Problem* (London, 1962, repr. Harmondsworth, 2001).

Turner, L. W., 'A good master well served.' Masters and Servants in Colonial Massachusetts* (New York, 1998).

Underdown, D., *Fire from Heaven. Life in an English Town in the Seventeenth-Century* (London, 1992).

Vickery, Amanda, 'An Englishman's home is his castle? Thresholds, boundaries and privacies in the eighteenth-century London house', *Past & Present*, 199 (2008).

— *The Gentleman's Daughter. Women's Lives in Georgian England* (New Haven, CT, and London, 1998).

Walker, Garthine, *Crime, Gender and Social Order in Early Modern England* (Cambridge, 2003).

Waterfield, G. *et al.*, *Below Stairs. Four Hundred Years of Servants' Portraits* (London, 2003).

Waterson, M., *The Servants' Hall. A Domestic History of Erdigg* (London, 1980).

Weil, Judith, *Service and Dependency in Shakespeare's Plays* (Cambridge, 2005).

Whyman, Susan E., *Sociability and Power. The Cultural Worlds of the Verneys* (Oxford, 1999).

Wiesner, Merry E., *Working Women in Renaissance Germany* (New Brunswick, NJ, 1986).

Wright, L. B., *Middle Class Culture in Elizabethan England* (1935, 2nd edn., London, 1958).

Wrightson, K., *Earthly Necessities. Economic Lives in Early Modern Britain* (New Haven, CT, and London, 2000).

— 'The nadir of English illegitimacy in the seventeenth century', in P. Laslett *et al.* (eds.), *Bastardy and its Comparative History* (London, 1980).

INDEX

Publications are generally listed under the name of the author

Beale, Mary 13
Beatson, Phoebe (Yorkshire
    maidservant) 11, 86, 205
Beckford, William 169
Becon, Thomas 133–4
Beeton, Mrs Isabella 73, 150
Behn, Aphra
    The Rover 29
bell systems, novelty of 225
bequests, by or to servants 39–40, 79
Bernard, Richard 162
Best, Henry 80, 106, 160
black servants 67–9, 224
Blundell, Nicholas 4, 73, 81, 151, 162
board wages 84–5
Booth, George 80
Bowes, Mary Eleanor, Countess of
    Strathmore 163
boxes, servants' 98
Braithwait, Richard 150
Bristol, servant population in 65
Broughton, Thomas 105, 129,
    191, 213
Bruen, John 78, 109, 135–7, 138
Buckingham, Duchess of 153
Bunyan, John
    Christian Behaviour 132
Burn, Richard
    History of the Poor Laws 197
Burnett, Mark Thompson 7, 24, 27
butler, duties of 187–8
by-employments, servants' 85–6, 112
Byrd, William II 166

Cadogan divorce case 198
calling, servants' 131, 145
Calvert divorce case 198
Cappe, Mrs 197
career servants, 57, 58
Carter, Elizabeth (bluestocking) 82
Carter, Thomas 132, 134
    Christian Commonwealth 125, 129
cast-off clothes to servants 87

catechisms 113, 134, 135, 143n56
certificates of service 73, 202
Chamberlain, C.
    The Servant Girl of the Period 192
chambermaids, duties of 189
Chandos household 83–4, 101, 103
The Changeling (play by John
    Middleton and William
    Rowley) 24
chapbooks, servant characters in 115
Chapone, Hester 149
charity schools 74, 184–5, 193n19
Charlecote, Warwickshire 100
Charles I, King 154
Charles II, King 155
charwomen 117–18
Cheap Repository Tracts 56
children, servant influence over 160,
    228
Christian Servants Book (1849) 141n12
Christmas boxes 87, 227
church attendance by servants 112–14
church, disturbances by servants in
    113, 199
Civil Wars, impact of 43, 153–5, 223–4
Clark, Alice 1
Clark, Margaret 208–9
Clarke, Timothy 109
cleanliness, moral and personal 129
Cleaver, Robert 126–7, 129
    *Godly Forme of Household
    Government* 125
Clifford, Lady Anne 115
Clift, William 106
Cobbett, William 220
Coke, Thomas, Earl of Leicester
    83–4, 103
Cole, Rev William 77–8, 85, 159, 201
Collier, Mary (servant poet) 47–50,
    116
comfort, standards of 101
communion at church, non-receipt
    of by servants 113

Jones, John (servant poet) 61n34
Jones, Thomas (footman) 167,
    199, 228

Kingsmill, Robert 81
kitchen scraps and left-overs as
    servants' perks 87
Knole, household size 66
Kyd, Thomas
    Spanish Tragedy, The 24
Kussmaul, Ann 7

labour shortages in American
    colonies 10, 11, 130, 218n31
Landry, Donna 51
Laud, Archbishop William 134, 169
law cases involving servants 191, 198,
    199, 200
law relating to servants 62n52,
    194–5, 210
law, servants' own resort to 200–1, 214
Leapor, Mary (servant poet) 50–3
letters from servants 39
Letter sent by the Maydens of London
    42
Lilburne, John 154
literacy, servant 115–16
liveries 107–8
London, servant-keeping in 64–5,
    81–2, 100, 156, 226
London Foundling Hospital 74, 204
London Society for the
    Encouragement of Honest and
    Industrious Servants 147
long service 75–6, 92n30, 147
Lucas, Richard 124, 127, 131,
    141n14
    Duty of Servants, The 79, 126
Lucy, Sir Thomas 135

MacDonald, John (valet) 56, 75,
    161, 167
Machiavelli, Niccolo 145

Maids' Petition (1647) 43
Malcolm, Sarah (maidservant) 212
Malvolio (*Twelfth Night*) 25
Mandeville, Bernard 82, 96, 116,
    184–5, 229
    Fable of the Bees, The 184–5
Mansfield, Lord Chief Justice 69,
    197
marriage portions 77–8, 136
marriages, employer/servant 167–8,
    174n43
marriages, servant 76–8
Marshall, Dorothy 1–2
Martindale, Adam 104–5, 109
Martineau, Harriet 74, 192
masterless men, fear of 25, 131, 194
master/mistress relations 162–4
master/servant relations 118,
    chapter 6 *passim*
Mather, Cotton 126, 130, 131
    Good Master well served, A 126,
    128
Mawhood, William 109
Mayhew, Augustus
    Greatest Plague of Life, The 191
Mayo, Richard 97, 126, 132, 158
    Present for Servants, A 126
Maza, Sarah J.
    *Servants and Masters in Eighteenth-
    Century France* 220–1
Meldrum, Tim 5–6, 100, 230
Methodist servants 71
Middleton v Middleton divorce case
    167, 199
mobility, servant 74–5
model employers 78, 109, 115, 135–7,
    138, 147–8
Moll Flanders (Defoe) 117
Montague, Elizabeth 52, 53
More, Hannah 52, 53, 161
mourning dress for servants 108
multi-tasking required of servants 7,
    112